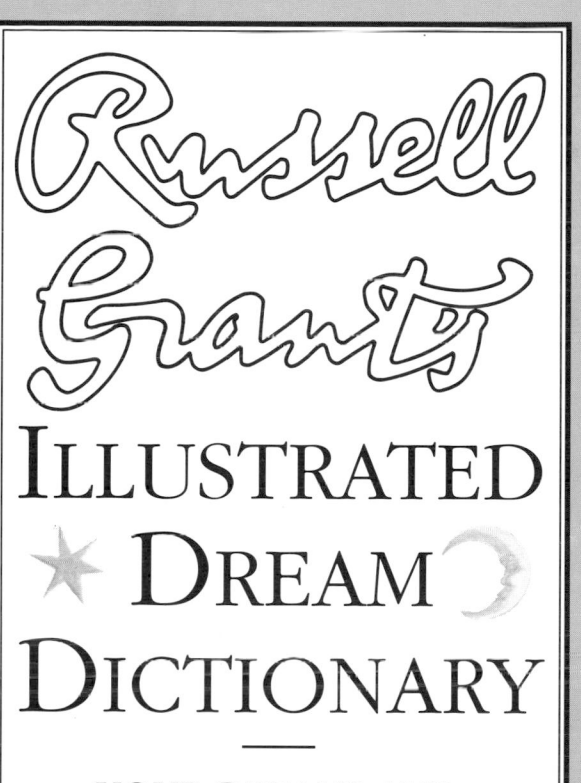

Russell Grant's

ILLUSTRATED ★ DREAM ☾ DICTIONARY

YOUR DREAMS AND
WHAT THEY MEAN

ILLUSTRATED BY VICKY EMPTAGE

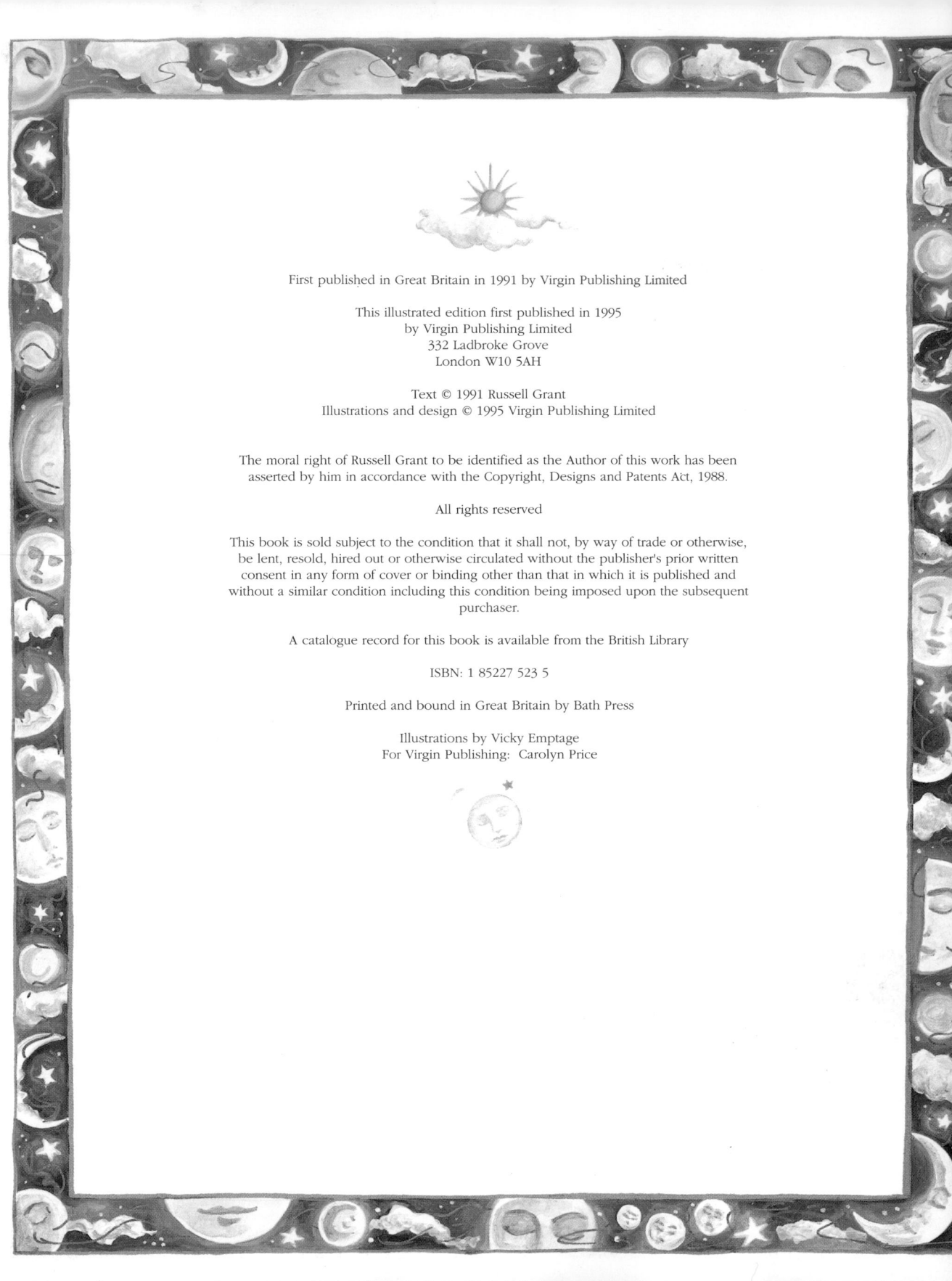

First published in Great Britain in 1991 by Virgin Publishing Limited

This illustrated edition first published in 1995
by Virgin Publishing Limited
332 Ladbroke Grove
London W10 5AH

ISBN: 1 85227 523 5

Printed and bound in Great Britain by Bath Press

Illustrations by Vicky Emptage
For Virgin Publishing: Carolyn Price

INTRODUCTION

Dreaming is one of our most intimate experiences. We all dream every night and every dream is unique. Our dream world, however confusing, frightening, wonderful, or saucily sexy, reveals all our secrets.

Every human emotion and experience can be reflected in our delicious dreams: they mirror our deepest desires, hopes, fears, and fantasies. Our hidden self, the one we often try to keep from the outside world, emerges from our subconscious in our sleep. There's no holds barred in a dream; we see ourselves in the raw, sometimes quite literally! It's this complete exposure that makes our dreams so important.

Because dreams reveal so much about us, interpreting them can help us to understand ourselves. A dream can warn us of potential danger, and decoding our dreams often helps to solve problems. Frequently, things that trouble us crystalise in a dream. Some dreams even predict the future.

Studying and interpreting dreams isn't new, as they have fascinated man since the dawn of time. Dreams have been carved on cave walls, set in stone, and every Roman Legion had a soothsayer to try and make sense of 'nocturnal visions'. In ancient times, priests consulted oracles and shrines for guidance to try and make sense of dreams. Our ancestors believed that dreams were messages from the gods, and in days gone by, interpreters of dreams were visited much as doctors are today.

Times may have changed, but the fascination of dreams remains. Many now-famous people have put forward theories of dream interpretation. Sigmund Freud thought that much of what we dream is in some way sexual. Another psychoanalyst, Carl Jung, recognised that man has other deep desires to drive him. In his fascinating book *An Experiment with Time*, Professor Dunne put forward the idea that all time is like a river, and that it can be navigated backwards or forwards in the vessel of dreams.

Sleep is the road to dreamland. And these days, thanks to advances in medical science, we certainly know more about that than our predecessors.

On average, we sleep for a third of each day; by the time we're 75, we have slept for 25 years – and dreamt for 10 of them. That's a lot of sleeping, and a lot of dreaming! Recent studies show that what occurs in dreams takes place in a real-life time-span,

so, for instance, simple things like shopping or eating take just as long in a dream as they do in reality. In more complicated dreams, however, where you're, say, in far-flung places, you're simply seeing the 'edited highlights'.

Studies also have shown that it's possible to dream with your eyes open, which happens when the brain becomes overloaded with the toxins created by fatigue. In extreme exhaustion, the person will succumb to the need for sleep—but the dream will be cut short by an inbuilt desire to survive, for example, if they have started dreaming at the wheel.

It's long been accepted that the ideal position for a good night's sleep is to lie on the right-hand side. The bed should be facing north–south, so the body can make maximum use of the lines of magnetism running from the Poles. Try running your hands in cold water before retiring as well: it can get rid of surplus static. If you find it hard to sleep, try breathing very deeply in through your nose and out through your mouth. This is a very helpful technique for becoming calm.

When we fall asleep each night, a complex series of changes in our consciousness takes place. Deepest sleep comes upon us almost immediately. This is followed by a shorter period of lighter sleep in which our eyeballs dart about beneath our closed lids. This period of Rapid Eye Movement or REM is when we dream. It happens about five times in an eight-hour period. We usually wake up after the last one, and naturally these are the dreams we remember best. There is some evidence that women dream for longer periods than men. Perhaps they simply enjoy their dreams more!

Any kind of drugs – whether stimulants or sedatives diminish the amount of dream time. So if you're ill or taking medication, you're less likely to dream. Dreams that you have while ill can be discounted as you're reacting to the illness rather than to a normal course of events.

Some people claim they never dream, but this is simply because they don't remember their dreams as well as others. Clinical tests have proved that when so-called non-dreamers are woken during REM sleep, they give vivid accounts of the images they have just seen, which are, like real-life events, in colour. Even our pets dream. If you watch a sleeping dog or cat, you can detect their Rapid Eye Movement.

Many people claim they can't remember the content of a dream on waking. Because dreams are an expression of our true selves – including desires we can't admit even to ourselves, let alone others, – dreaming is the only way we have of expressing them. We sometimes find it hard to accept the messages that are being given in a dream, and so we censor them. Dreams are heavily loaded with emotion, and that can distort our memory.

To help remember your dreams, try keeping a dream diary. On waking, don't get out of bed or even change position. Keep a notepad and pen by the bed, or even a tape recorder, and note down or record everything you can remember. Try and recall, too, what you were preoccupied with before going to sleep as this can provide vital clues in interpretation. Try to recapture the mood of the dream, which is important. If you still can't remember, but an event later in the day triggers your memory, write it down. It could be helpful in working out the meaning of the dream. Train yourself to do this regularly, and gradually memories of your dreams should follow.

Dreams are a proven creative artistic source: some of our greatest writers and poets, like Robert Louis Stevenson and William Wordsworth, regularly recorded their dreams and were inspired by them.

In dreamland, many wonderful things can happen: we can travel to distant places, meet loved ones, even take tea with Princess Diana! Some dreams, however, can be simply scary, and a particularly frightening dream is called a nightmare. These severe anxiety dreams – where you wake up in a cold sweat feeling very afraid, – occur because what is happening in the dream is too overwhelming to be contained while asleep, so you wake up. True nightmares occur in the non-dream phase of sleep, and have little remembered content.

I vividly remember a nightmare of my own. I woke up in a terrible state. In my dream I was walking around carrying my own dead body in a big wicker basket. A few weeks later, I landed my job with Breakfast Time, in the days of Frank Bough and Selina Scott, at the BBC. What I had really seen in my dream was the casting off of my old self, getting ready to go on to new things. Death isn't always bad in a dream. For me it meant new beginnings, the end of an era. With the help of this book, you will see that even the scariest dreams aren't necessarily bad omens.

Sex plays a major part in our dream world. That's because it has an important role in our everyday lives. It's a powerful driving force, like hunger and ambition. While we're awake, sex is ruled by social restrictions and conventions, but in our dreams, even the most timid of us can have explicit and excitingly sexy dreams once our repressed selves are asleep. That's why the prissiest of spinsters often uses filthy language when waking from an anaesthetic.

Sex is a significant bodily need, and any unusual or enforced period without it might result in a sexual dream. Frank sexual dreams can occur frequently in adolescence, and often result in actual orgasm. In adults, everyday sexual needs and preoccupations are dealt with indirectly in dreams. Sexy images often express feelings of closeness or intimacy in the dream. Feelings of control, loss of control, issues of superiority or inferiority, can all be expressed in a sexual dream. So if you dream of a passionate encounter with your boss, it doesn't necessarily mean you're going to have one!

If you have a sexual dream, you must ask yourself: is it due to unfulfilled sexual tension? Or is it an expression of problems in your sex life? Many sexually based dreams use symbols for the male and female organs. Long pointed objects represent the penis, and hollow receptacles the vagina.

But can dreams come true? Can we really predict the future in our sleep? These are questions I'm asked all the time. The answer is 'Yes'. Such dreams – known as precognitive dreams – can occur, but many apparently precognitive dreams really are triggered by things that have happened in real life. For example, if you dream that your car has broken down, and the next day it does just that, it could well be that you had noticed a minor change in the engine noise but forgotten to do anything about it. However, if your dream involved a hire car you had never driven before, then it truly was a precognitive dream.

Once I dreamt I had gone to Euston Station. I looked at the clock and it was ten past four. Then the clock suddenly read twenty-five past seven, which even in my dream I thought was odd. I kept looking at that clock and it kept changing. About a week later, a friend was going to Blackpool from Euston on the ten-past-four train. I warned him, 'Don't get on that train. Get on the next one.' The ten-past-four train was derailed. If he had been on it he could have been injured or even killed. Instead he took my advice and got on the next train. It left Euston at twenty-five past seven.

Precognitive dreams tap directly into our psychic source through our sub-conscious. Not only can they produce information about real-life events, they can also tell us important things about our general state of mind.

Sometimes the same dream recurs time and time again. These dreams are important because they show us the weak and strong parts of our personality. The recurring dream deals with some aspect of life that hasn't been sorted out, or hasn't been laid to rest. Or a problem that hasn't been solved. These dreams often reflect a loss – perhaps a relationship, or other form of pleasure or excitement. Once the issue is resolved, the repetitive dream stops. Dreams are repeated time and time again because their message hasn't been received or understood. This book can help to stop that same old record being played over and over again.

Familiar people often crop up in our dreams, particularly parents and grandparents. Nine times out of ten they shouldn't be interpreted as themselves, but as the image they represent. Our mothers, for example, represent the feminine principles of comfort and compassion, while our fathers often stand for authority. Brothers and sisters can be seen in terms of platonic love. The dustman, the doctor, the plumber all have symbolic counterparts – so when a policeman turns up in your dreams, you can bet it relates to the law and order in your life. That kind of symbolism is very important when interpreting a dream.

People who are dead sometimes manifest in our dreams too. This is because important relationships don't end when someone dies. Something about the dead person may be relevant to the current situation you're in, or relate to a problem you're wrestling with. The same applies to famous people who appear in dreams. Although we have never met them, a part of their personality may have touched us in a very personal way, and we express this affinity in a dream.

Events in dreams frequently seem illogical and bizarre. That's because our emotional time-bomb ticks away unheard during the day and finally explodes only at night as we dream. The point is we're not concerned with the natural order of things as we sleep, but with reordering it to represent our feelings in a visual way.

Just as some people are seen symbolically, so symbols represent ideas. Often things must be taken at much more than just their face value. A key, for example, unless you have recently lost one and it's playing on your mind – often means a door is about to open with new opportunities for you. A ladder can be showing you the way to the top. That's why it's important when you're recalling your dreams or keeping your dream diary to include everything. Nothing is trivial in a dream, it *all* must be evaluated.

Our lives are full of predicaments, some bigger than others. The anxieties we face over these appear in our dreams, creating what are called 'contrary dreams', which sum up the opposing pulls we're facing in everyday life. For example, dream of asserting yourself and the fact is that in reality you're worried about being put upon. Dream of independence, and you fear you're beginning to rely on someone or something too much.

There are certain dreams we all seem to have at one time or another, which seem to be the easiest to remember: flying or floating through the air; being naked and unable to do anything about it; falling; teeth; water; being unable to cry for help; rooted to the spot in the face of danger; helplessly pushed or drawn into danger. The reason these are common dreams is that they deal with the sort of emotions we all feel at one time or another.

Before trying to interpret your dreams with the help of this guide, remember that outside influences on our sleep can make significant differences to the importance of a dream. The following checklist is to help you discount dreams that are of no importance: dreams that occur when you have overeaten or gone to bed a bit the worse for drink; outside noises like traffic, music, or hammering also influence a dream; how many times have you dreamt of ringing bells and woken to find you need to answer the telephone? or dreamt you were freezing and found the bedclothes on the floor? or even dreamt you were surrounded by water, and woken desperate to go to the loo?

Other external influences need to be taken into account before you can successfully interpret your dreams. If you have just had a major shock, are bereaved or have just watched a scary TV show, then disregard the dream: that's simply your imagination working overtime. Obviously, dreams that are directly connected with things you have seen or done during the day can be discounted.

Before you try to interpret specific items or events in your dreams with the help of this book – and have used the checklist to eliminate those of no consequence – the following guidelines may help: going up indicates success or improvement; going down signifies the reverse. Clean or shiny objects or conditions are usually good omens, but dirty ones mean obstacles or difficulties. If you're ill in a dream, it's best to have a medical check-up. Successful efforts in a dream are good, failure means difficulties.

Although dreams are made up of all sorts of things, one main feature will probably stand out. This is the head word to look up first. Next, look up all the other elements, and add them to get a complete picture. Sometimes you will find a *'See also'* reference next to a head word. If you look up this heading, you will find many associated subjects listed in addition. If you can't find your dream subject in the main part of the book, you can also check the Index of Related Dream Subjects at the back, see pages 133–143. Remember, too, the feel of the dream: was it happy or gloomy? This will also help you to work things out.

Our mysterious, inexplicable dreams can reveal all. When we dream we free ourselves from the tension of everyday life. We express our anxieties, problems, and complete state of mind in our sleep. We reveal that part of our personality we barely understand and seldom show in public. By using this guide to interpret your sleep images, perhaps you will understand your inner self more completely.

Sweet dreams!

ABANDONMENT *See also:* Childhood. Being abandoned is a dream of contrary and means you will get back together with a lover or quickly recover from trouble. Abandoning someone close spells trouble. But by heeding the warning dream you can overcome it. Abandoning something nasty means good news, money-wise. Witness an abandonment and important news is on the way.

ABDICATION *See also:* Arriving/Leaving. A king, queen or a president abdicating signifies disorder in business. Try to be more methodical.

ABDUCTION See yourself abducted and you will triumph against the odds. If someone else is abducted, unexpected news is coming.

ABNORMALITY Dream of anything abnormal, for example a dog covered in feathers or a man who hops like a kangaroo, and a happy solution to your troubles is on its way.

ABORTION If you're a man, abortion means failure in either love or money. For a woman, it's a warning to look after your health.

ABROAD *See also:* Foreign Places/People. Going abroad by ship signifies a new influential friend. Dreaming of being abroad means things are unsettled and a possible move is on the cards.

ABSCONDING *See also:* Arriving/Leaving. For a man this is a sign of treachery among his colleagues. For a woman it's a warning she must be careful where she places her affections.

ABSENCE *See also:* Arriving/Leaving; Death. If a loved one is absent, danger is afoot in your love life. Dream of other people being absent and you will be able to master things. The death of an absent friend predicts a wedding.

ABSTINENCE *See also:* Drink. Abstain from drink, cigarettes, or any other temptation and it's a dream of contrary: don't get over-confident. But abstaining out of necessity rather than choice spells success and prosperity.

ABUNDANCE An abundance of something is a warning to conserve your resources. An abundance of lots of things is a very good omen.

ABYSS *See also:* Falling. This is an obstacle dream. If you don't fall you will overcome difficulties, but plunge in and you must be extremely careful in business dealings.

ACCIDENT The meaning of this dream depends on the circumstances surrounding the accident but in general it's a warning. A car accident and you should try not to travel more than necessary for a while. Accidents at sea relate to love affairs, whilst those on land relate to business matters. In general, whatever the accident involves, for example, electricity, knives, fires, etc, try to avoid them.

ACCOSTING Being accosted by a man shows a false friend is trying to frame you. But money could arrive in the shape of a legacy or profit if it's a woman, someone you know or a beggar.

ACCOUNTS/ACCOUNTANTS *See also:* Money. This is a very straightforward dream. Adding up accounts means don't lend money. You could lose it. But if they balance perfectly, a profitable proposition is coming your way. Work out your boss's accounts and you must beware of your enemies.

ACID This is a warning. Handling acids means danger looms via a promise. If others handle acid it predicts the death of an enemy.

ACQUAINTANCE *See also:* Relationships. Meet a new acquaintance or renewing an old one, and you will find something you thought you had lost, or recover money. Meeting a slight acquaintance spells a boost for your social life, but quarrel with one and you should see a doctor over a minor ailment.

ACROBAT *See also:* Performing. Watch them perform and it's a warning not to take any trips for at least a week. See yourself as an acrobat and you will beat your enemies. A friend or relative performing acrobatics means look out for deception from the person involved. See an acrobatic fall or have an accident and it's a dream of contrary: you will have a lucky escape from danger.

ADAM AND EVE See either of these in your dream and it's a good omen for one of your deepest desires. Speaking to them means a delay in a cherished plan, though only a temporary one. Adam and Eve together is a tremendously lucky sign. If you're a woman and dream of Adam, you will have a baby. A man dreaming of Eve will give a family dinner.

ADDRESSES *See also:* Places/Settings. Writing one is a warning not to gamble if it's a personal address. A business address, however, means a flutter could be fortunate. Hearing or talking about an address means be discreet about your personal life.

ADMINISTRATION *See also:* Work. If it's your own affairs, an inheritance is coming your way. The affairs of others and your business relations will improve.

ADOPTING Adopt someone and relatives will ask for help. If you're adopted, watch out for your enemies. Adopting children forecasts difficulties in love.

Plate 1 · The Animal Kingdom

ADORATION Adoration of a person or object means a period of deep peace and contentment is about to begin.

ADULTERY *See also*: Relationships; Sexuality. Any dream involving adultery predicts problems in your love life. You are undergoing traumas and probably, if the truth be known, at your wit's end. If your wife is committing adultery, then quarrels with the neighbours are coming. If it's your husband, then you could receive an inheritance. If you commit it, guard against telling your friends your secrets. Resist temptation and some disappointing set-backs will be short-lived.

ADVANTAGE A good omen whether you take the advantage or someone takes advantage of you. Your family will prosper.

ADVENTURE An exciting adventure means big changes in the future. See yourself as an adventurer and torment could be heading your way. Going on an adventure with a man signals new surroundings and interests. With a woman, someone is watching you.

ADVERSARY *See also*: Anger/Confrontation. A dream of contrary. If it's a business opponent or a social rival, you may have some momentary difficulties but try hard and you can conquer them.

ADVERSITY This relates to money matters. If you undergo the adversity it's a good, prosperous omen. Adversity in business means you will achieve high ambitions. But adversity in love is a warning to guard against those wagging tongues!

ADVERTISEMENT Seeing a TV or radio advertisement in your dreams does not augur well. It shows nerves and worries are overcoming your ability to reason, and that could affect your judgement and lead to silly mistakes. If you see an advertisement hoarding, unexpected changes in your way of life are coming.

ADVERTISING Advertising something warns against some speculative plan. But read an advertisement and your plans will materialise. It's a very good sign if the advertisement has illustrations.

AEROPLANE *See also*: Death; Flying. An airplane taking off signals success. If it lands, then beware of jealous friends. An airplane crashing suggests a major failure, probably in business. Pilot the plane yourself and you're about to achieve something unusual. But simply travelling in it suggests you have a few ups and downs to face soon. Being in a plane disaster but not being killed signals financial gains. But seeing yourself killed in an airplane disaster is a warning to control those passions of yours!

AFFLICTION *See also*: Ill-health. This is a true dream of contrary. The greater the affliction, the bigger the success. If a husband or wife are afflicted, business success is approaching rapidly. If you are afflicted by others, a change for the better is coming soon.

AFFLUENCE *See also*: Money. A straightforward dream of improvement. The greater the affluence, the quicker your financial problems will be solved.

AGE Worrying about your age is a warning to see a doctor as illness could be approaching. If you worry about your partner's age, then you're being deceived. Fretting over a relative's age indicates a death in the family. But see old people in your dream and it's an omen of great good luck. Reach retirement age and, sorry, but a lot of hard work is on the way.

AGENT Negotiating with or via an agent of any kind indicates a pleasant change in surroundings.

AGREEMENT (WRITTEN) *See also*: Reading/Writing. If you do not go through with an agreement, then you have a lot of hard work to do.

AGRICULTURE Success due to hard work is the message here. See yourself in the agriculture business and you will prosper. Dream you are new to it, and you will have security.

AIR *See also*: Weather. The interpretation of this dream depends on exactly what you see. Clean air and blue skies signify success. Cold air foretells unhappiness in family relationships; misty air and you are being deceived. Foggy air is a warning to reconsider your present plans. If the air is damp, a misfortune will end your high hopes; and stormy air is a warning that an illness or danger is coming.

AISLE *See also:* Religion. The aisle of a church suggests you're due to be beset by difficulties and misfortune. If it's the aisle of a theatre, it's an omen of the death of a friend. Walking down a theatre aisle means you will be guilty of something naughty!

ALIEN Meeting aliens predicts important changes. See yourself as an alien and valuable new friends are about to enter your life.

ALIMONY *See also*: Money. Careless pleasures have to be paid for, and this is what this warning dream tells you if you're the one paying alimony. Receive it, and a cherished wish will come true.

ALLERGY *See also:* Ill-health. Having an allergy yourself means you can expect some pleasant social news. If the allergy is someone else's, then your current plans will turn out well.

ALLEY A dark alley signifies that neighbours are gossiping. If it's clear, then you have an easy road ahead. But an alley with a dead-end is a warning for you to think carefully before acting.

ALLOWANCE *See also*: Money. Receive the allowance and happy times are ahead. If you give it, then beware of family rows.

ALLOY *See also*: Metals. If you are single and dream of combining metals, then you will have a happy marriage. If you are married it signifies an increase in family responsibilities.

ALMANAC *See also*: Time. If you are a woman, an almanac is a warning not to sacrifice your personal obligations for the sake of a bit of social climbing. For a man, it's a sign of a good business deal.

ALMS *See also*: Money. A contrary dream to a certain extent. Plead for or receive alms and your financial status will improve. If you give alms, you will also be lucky, but if you refuse to give you will have to face an unexpected hardship. An almshouse says your efforts will be rewarded with security.

ALPHABET *See also*: Reading/Writing. See letters of the alphabet and an absent friend will return. If you are writing out the alphabet, then unexpected good news is on its way. If the letters of the alphabet are foreign, a mystery will soon be solved.

ALPINE Alpine scenery means unexpected gains. See an alpine climber and it's a warning to guard against spiteful gossip.

ALTITUDE *See also*: Flying. This is a warning to avoid involvement with inferiors, which could cause you embarrassment.

ALUMINIUM *See also*: Metals. If the metal is dull you may experience frustrations. If it is shiny there are happy days ahead.

AMAZEMENT *See also*: Confusion. You are about to get an unusually exciting experience, if this emotion features in your dream.

AMBASSADOR *See also*: Uniforms. An ambassador is a sign that faithful and even influential friends are at hand. See yourself as an ambassador and you could lose your present position. Being in conference with an ambassador means you will achieve high ambitions.

AMBITION *See also*: Success. This is a dream of contrary: if you achieved it, you will face set-backs. If

you are thwarted, persevere; you will get there in the end.

AMBULANCE *See also*: Doctors/Hospitals. In general this is a warning against indiscretion with the opposite sex. If you see an empty ambulance it means you will lose a friend. If you call for one for yourself you will soon recover from illness. Call one for a relative and you could have money troubles soon.

AMMONIA This is a warning not to take any unnecessary risks. Bad luck in love is likely.

AMOROUS *See also*: Sexuality. If you feel amorous, then a friendship is about to explode into an exciting romance. But if you receive amorous advances from someone of the opposite sex, then take care. One relationship could involve you in scandal.

AMPUTATION *See also*: Doctors/Hospitals. This is a dream of risk, danger and personal loss. You could lose something precious, a friend may suddenly go out of your life, or a job you're enjoying may be suddenly taken away from you.

AMUSEMENT The greater the amusement, the greater the satisfaction is coming your way.

ANAGRAMS *See also*: Confusion. This word game signals a happy solution to current problems.

ANARCHIST This is a warning to be extremely cautious in any business dealings. Dream of being an anarchist and you could be losing your freedom in some way.

ANCESTORS Your own dead ancestors mean happiness is yours. Other people's ancestors signifies good money prospects. But the dream can also be a warning not to trust people who say they're in love!

ANECDOTE Hearing an anecdote means a big social event in the offing. Telling one means you're likely to have unusual social success soon.

ANGER/CONFRONTATION This dream can be the opposite of what you might at first think.

Just as in reality, anger in a dream can be expressed in many different ways. See yourself verbally **abused** and bad business is forecast. Abusing others in this way means someone will take advantage of you. Abusing your children verbally means success in your love life.

Sometimes we **accuse** people in anger, and if you find yourself accused it's a warning to guard against unscrupulous people. Defend yourself against it and you will overcome trouble. See yourself as the accuser and your personal relationships could be riding for a fall. If you are accused by a woman, some upsetting news could be on the way; by a man, and you will have success in business beyond your wildest dreams.

If the anger in your dream results in an **argument**, this can be a lucky sign. Having an argument is an omen for a good and long life.

But if it spills over into a full pitched **battle**, then some serious quarrels are forecast. Win the battle and your love life will go well. Lose, and the unwise business deals of others will hurt you in some way.

Unlike being abused, **beating** in anger can be a good sign. If you are beating or being beaten by friends or loved ones, it's a good sign for personal affairs. But if strangers are involved, it's a sign not to put things off. Beating animals or carpets is a warning to concentrate and try to get yourself organised otherwise things will go wrong. If you suffer blows rather than an actual beating, you will make it up after the quarrel. Dish them out, and you will find something you thought you had lost.

An old-fashioned **duel** is a sure sign someone is making mischief. Sort them out before it causes trouble with family or friends. A more modern-day fight and there are a few people against you at the moment, aren't there? If you win they won't be able to do you any harm. See others fighting and it's a sign you're squandering your time and money on pleasures. Try and knuckle down to some hard work.

Direct anger at a **friend** and you will gain materially through a friend. But if the object of your anger is unknown, you will soon be celebrating some good news.

Scream in anger and it's a good sign for your closest concerns. Hear someone else scream, and distressing news will follow.

Really fly into a rage and a **temper tantrum** could lose you an influential friend. If someone else is in a rage, calming them down suggests you could do with a change of pace or even a move.

ANIMALS The interpretation here depends on the animal in question, but in general stroking animals suggests a fortune is ahead for you. Feeding them is another pointer to wealth. Push them away, and you could be heading for divorce.

An **alligator** is a sign you're surrounded by enemies. See several of them, and you should take care in new ventures. They might not be all they're cracked up to be.

Bankruptcy could be on the cards if you see an **anteater**. So be careful with business arrangements and don't take any financial risks.

Someone close is bound to have confided in you if you dream of an **antelope**. It can also be a sign of sudden improvement money-wise.

Apes in a cage means you will have to face some opposition in your love life. They are also a warning to guard against a mischief-maker in your circle of friends, and a hint that it's time to buckle down and pay more attention at work.

Baboons, on the other hand, are a good sign for the single. Marriage could be just around the corner. If you're married, a baboon spells a rise in status and suggests a lucky time ahead for business deals.

Business skills will win you prosperity if you dream of a **badger**. Kill one and you're about to fall in love.

Bats flying around in daylight are a symbol of reassurance and calm, but if you see one at night a problem is just around the – corner, and it's either a family or financial one. If a bat brushes against you as it flies past, it's to remind you that bad luck will soon pass.

There certainly won't be any bad luck in your life if you see a caged **bear**. Future success is assured. A dancing bear means have a little flutter. Gambling could be lucky for you. Fighting off or killing a bear suggests you will beat your enemies. But if he attacks you then look out. Someone looks set to persecute you.

Dangerous wild animals usually signify bad luck, and chasing or running from a wild **boar** suggests you're in for a big disappointment. But kill it or see it being killed and promotion at work could be just round the corner.

Buffalos suggest you'll shortly be making a quick profit. But see one killed or injured and you should think carefully about a new business venture.

You're facing some tough competition in your love life if you see a **bull**, although a white one indicates a real stroke of luck. Being chased by one means a gift is on its way to you.

Plate 2 · The Black Cat

You're about to make some new and interesting friends if it's a **bullfrog**. Catch one and beware, there is a cuckoo in your nest!

A cherished hope is about to be realised if you dream of a **calf**. Buy one, and you're about to fall madly in love. But see one slaughtered and you are in for a bitter disappointment.

The noble, long-suffering **camel** means you will have to pull out all the stops work-wise to overcome difficulties. Ride on one and the future is bright.

Cats are generally not a good omen. They spell deceit and are often a sign your lover is being unfaithful. Kill one and you will soon fall into bad company. A **black cat** is a sign of illness to come, but chase one away and you may get a surprise stroke of good luck. For a woman, a **kitten** is a sign of a pleasant flirtation. For a man, a disappointment in love.

A contented grazing **cow** is a sign of good luck. But if it's thin or chasing you, a cherished plan is under threat. Milking a cow means you will soon be in the money.

Don't trust your colleagues if a **crocodile** crops up. If you are chased or threatened by him, you're in for some good luck. If you are caught or injured, business will be bad for a while. Kill a crocodile and success beyond your wildest dreams will be yours.

Some nice times are ahead if your dream features **deer**. But if captive or hunted they spell disappointment; someone you trust will let you down. Kill a deer or see a dead one, and take a close look at your friends; one is bitching about you behind your back.

Dogs symbolise friends. A **friendly** pooch means happy times ahead in good company. A **snarling** one means don't trust one of your chums. If the dog actually **bites**, then a so-called friend is up to some trickery which can harm you. See a dog **barking** and you could be in some legal trouble, so don't park on any double yellow lines or try avoiding your bus fare! Dogs **fighting** suggests you'll be asked to intervene in a row between friends. A **white dog** is a sign of good luck. A **black one** means treacherous friends. A **watch dog** predicts an argument with your lover. A **police dog** is a sign of a business row, and a **guide dog** means lean times ahead. A **stray**, and bad news is on the way. If you are married, a dog means you're in for a spat with the other half. If you are single, watch out, you're about to be seduced!

Dolphins are lovely creatures, but sadly not a good sign in a dream. They mean worries, dangerous journeys, the failure of a pet project, or illness of a friend.

Donkeys are a sign that although you have problems you will see them through with a bit of patience. For a single girl, a donkey means her future husband will be a determined sort, although not very rich. Braying donkeys and it's time to end that illicit affair; you're about to be found out, and it will cause a lot of embarrassment. See a white donkey and your sex life will sizzle.

Mythical **dragons** suggest a powerful person will push you towards success and it will mean mountains of money.

Elephants show you are in good health. You are also about to meet someone important who will influence your career.

Don't listen to spiteful gossip if you see a furry **ferret**. And a few emotional dramas are on the horizon if you see a ferret hunting.

Dream of the sly old **fox** and it represents someone you dislike, or even a love rival. It's a warning to watch them. Kill the fox, and you will be able to outwit them.

A long-necked **giraffe** is a warning to stop meddling in other people's affairs.

Goats are a pointer that only patience will help you overcome your problems. See one perched on a rock or high mountain and money is coming. If you are butted or chased by a goat, don't bet you simply can't win.

A **hare** is a good luck sign. See it running towards you and a friend is about to pay you a visit. If you are a single girl, then your future husband is about to enter your life. But see a hare being coursed and you will soon face serious risks.

A difficult choice is about to present itself if a **hedgehog** features. To make money or get that promotion you are going to have to lose a friend; think carefully before you decide.

A wallowing **hog**, and you are about to be offered a profitable new business opportunity. See it clean and you're in for some unusual success. A wild hog is a warning that someone is jealous of you and could start spreading malicious gossip.

A **hippo** in the wild represents a rival who could be dangerous. See him in the zoo, and the future is full of frustrations.

A **horse** is a good sign unless it is black; then it predicts grief. Riding a horse indicates happiness through independence.

An unusual social event or interesting new friends are on the cards if you see an **iguana**.

Jackals indicate someone is trying to find your weak spot and use it against you. Go carefully and you can outwit them.

A **kangaroo** predicts an exciting, unexpected trip.

Lambs are a sign of an uplifting experience. See them gambolling and happy family times are ahead. Hear them bleating and you will be faced with new responsibilities. An old friend will reappear on your scene if you find a lost lamb. Eat or cook lamb and you will come into money.

Leopards are a symbol of enemies or rivals. Simply see one and you will win in the end. Kill one and you will have to fight hard to get what you want. A running leopard is a sign of serious illness.

Social success can be yours if you see a **lion** in your dream. Hear him roar and you will have to cope with a bit of jealousy. A lion cub predicts a valuable new friend.

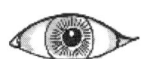

Success is also on the cards in current projects if you see a **llama** or anything made from its wool.

Hidden hostility is the message from a **lynx**. You could be persecuted if you don't watch out.

Minks spell hard work and not much play. The fur is a warning you're being too greedy over something.

Someone you trust is in danger of undermining you when **moles** crop up in a dream. Catch or kill one and you will be promoted.

Monkeys warn that you are surrounded by lies and deceit. Feed them and a friend is about to betray you.

The main theme with **mice** is rows with family or friends. Scare them away and all will be resolved. If you are frightened by a mouse, you are about to be embarrassed in a social situation. Kill one and you will make money. Catch one in a trap and unwelcome news is on the way. See mice chased or killed by a cat and it's a warning not to take advice from others. Trust your own judgement.

That rainy day could be closer than you think if you see an **otter.** Try saving your money for it.

For lovers, **oxen** are a sign of marriage. Grazing in a field means business will boom.

Lovable black-eyed **pandas** are a sure sign you are worrying too much. Some of your problems are simply in your mind.

Pigs are good news for the family but bad news for business. The fatter the pig, the better at home and the worse at work.

You're a nice enough type if you dream of a **porcupine**, but often hurt others without knowing it. Try and put yourself in their shoes.

Rabbits spell good luck and also fertility. For a married woman they predict a pregnancy. A group of rabbits spells a pleasant new responsibility. Rabbit fur means you will eventually be able to afford mink.

Some new talent or hobby is going to make you money as well as give you a lot of pleasure if you spot a **raccoon**.

Don't be a doormat! That's the message a **ram** is giving you. People are walking all over you and it's time to stand up for yourself.

Rats predicts lots of problems on the horizon but they will all be little ones. If you are in love, someone is determined to steal your heart's desire from you. If you're married, so-called friends are about to upset you.

Someone you trust is going to let you down if you see a **rattlesnake**. Avoid it and you can outwit your rivals. If it bites you then you are in for a fight.

A surprise gain is on the cards if you dream of **reindeer**. You will find something you thought you'd lost, or discover that some piece of junk is in fact extremely valuable.

Rhinos are a warning to make sure you meet your obligations. In a zoo they suggest your sexual magnetism is at its height. You'll be fighting off the opposite sex for quite a while.

Seals predict prosperity. But kill them and business will be bad.

Sheep grazing are a sign of good fortune. See them shorn and marriage is on the horizon. In a pen, and you will be offered a good opportunity. But an empty sheep pen shows your life lacks direction.

A **snail** is not a good omen. You are being a bit unreliable and moody.

A **snake** coiled around you is an indication you are a slave to your sexual passions! If you are bitten you are in for a struggle. More than one snake means you are about to be seriously let down by someone you trust. Kill a snake and you will succeed despite opposition. See a snake charmer and gossip is going round about you.

Feed **squirrels** and life will be comfortable thanks to hard work. See them running about and your love life is on the skids. Squirrels running up a tree are a warning you're about to be financially embarrassed. Try and tighten your belt.

See a **stable** full of cows and it means a major success. See donkeys instead and there are work problems ahead. But horses in a stable predict prosperity.

A business rival is about to make a major challenge if **toads** feature. If you have partners they could be about to sell you down the river, I'm afraid. But kill a toad and professional success is assured.

A **unicorn** isn't a good sign. You're facing problems caused by people who aren't as trustworthy as you first thought.

Weasels are a warning someone of the opposite sex has a devious nature. Watch them!

Protective influences are working around you, and your worries will soon be over if you dream of **whales**.

Wolves are a bad omen. Hunt one and danger is just around the corner. See yourself chased by one, and it's a sign you're over-anxious about something. But kill one, and a small success is on the cards.

A herd of **zebra** are warning you against putting all your eggs in one basket. Just one and you will make a gain from a surprise source.

ANIMOSITY *See also*: Anger/Confrontation. This is a warning to rethink a moral question in your life.

ANNOY *See also*: Anger/Confrontation. A contrary dream: if you are annoyed all your plans will go smoothly. Annoying others means your earnings will go up.

ANTENNA *See also*: Communicating. A bonus is on its way. Putting up antennae or an aerial means you will recover something you thought was lost and gone forever.

ANTHEM *See also*: Music. If it's tuneful, all music is a favourable sign. Hearing an anthem means you will get news from a distance. Singing the anthem is a warning not to waste so much time!

ANTIQUES You will have a long life. Buy antiques and an inheritance is coming. Selling them, however, means a large loss of money. Simply looking at them indicates your home life will be happy.

ANTLERS A smashing omen of happiness for the future.

ANVIL Some really spectacular luck is heading your way. If it's being banged loudly, an unexpected change of location is likely. Buy an anvil and happiness is assured.

APARTMENT *See also*: Home. Seeing yourself in an apartment in your dream is a warning to avoid revels. Owning one means family quarrels. Someone else's apartment spells trouble ahead. If the apartment is small and uncomfortable, you will have to try hard to avoid family squabbles. But large and lavish and you can expect a steady increase in prosperity.

APOLOGY *See also*: Communicating; Speaking. This refers to friends. If you receive an apology, you will be happy with your lover. If you do the apologising, an old friend will come back on the scene.

APPARITION *See also*: Supernatural. This means good news, unless the apparition frightened you, in which case it's a warning to have a medical check-up. Seeing the apparition of a dead relative signifies prosperity.

APPETITE *See also*: Food. Having a small appetite is an omen of poor health to come. A big appetite refers to money and is a warning to handle it carefully or your finances will become chaotic. Losing your appetite spells danger.

APPLAUSE *See also*: Performing. Receiving applause is a sign you are a bit of a vain one. Beware of jealousy. You can overcome it but you'll need to use some tact. If you hear others applauding, friends may do the dirty on you!

APPRECIATION A contrary dream. If you receive appreciation, then unexpected criticism is about to be hurled at you. But if you show it, then you are in for some luck, unless you are approving something you normally would not: in that case, a friend is deceiving you.

APPRENTICE *See also*: School. Learning a trade is good news for your love life and business plans. If you're teaching an apprentice, a windfall is coming to you.

APPROACHING This basically means mind your own business! If someone approaches you or you approach someone, then don't get involved in family spats.

APRIL/APRIL FOOL *See also*: Time. Dream of being an April Fool and you will have power over someone in a new situation. Playing an April Fool trick on others means the loss of a friend.

AQUEDUCT *See also*: Bridges. If the aqueduct is dry, you will face some small sorrow, but see water running through it and contentment and good health are forecast. An aqueduct being built means success will be postponed, and if you see it being repaired you will achieve high ambitions.

ARCH An arch signifies wealth and promotion. Passing under one means people are going to ask you for favours. A damaged arch is a signal to mend your ways!

ARCHER If you are single you will soon find Mr or even Ms Right. If married, don't be tempted to stray or it could cost more than you think.

ARCHITECT If an architect is involved, a difficult plan will be successful. See yourself as an architect and it's a suitable time to pursue your chosen love. So go for it!

ARCHIVES A bad sign for unexpected legal matters.

ARK *See also*: Sea/Water/Travel. Important events are on their way.

ARMCHAIR *See also*: Furniture. Sitting in a comfy armchair means whatever favour you are after will be yours. If someone else or a cat or dog is in the armchair, unwelcome visitors are coming soon. An empty armchair signifies a mystery that will take a long time to solve.

ARMISTICE A dream of opposites. You could lose a friend because of wagging tongues.

ARMOURY *See also*: Weapons. This building means there's a rival to be reckoned with, but if you're inside it then a venture that involves lots of activity will be a success.

ARMY A marching army and you will have to travel to get what you want. If they are fighting be warned, treason is afoot!

ARRANGING *See also*: Tidiness. Arranging books on a shelf means renewal of a project you thought had been abandoned. Arranging things in a drawer means you are worried about your problems. Arranging a table for a meal means good health and strength and is a sign that you are being decisive and confident and deserve praise from the boss. Arranging tea or coffee cups is a warning to try not to be so enthusiastic about something in life. Arranging a meeting means you need help from others to sort out your problems.

ARREST *See also*: Police/Prisons. If you are arrested, you will have sadness followed by joy. If you see others being arrested a surprise gift is coming to you. If you are released from an arrest, sudden success will be yours.

ARRIVING/LEAVING Arrive yourself and it's a sure sign your efforts will be rewarded. Others arriving is a warning not to gamble. The arrival of a friend means a pleasant surprise.

If you're forced to leave somewhere and are **banished** from your home or even your country, then great wealth is on its way to you.

See yourself arrive at an entrance to a **building** and you're feeling insecure. Try and mug up on things and you will feel more confident.

Leave by a **fire escape** and you're in too much debt. Try and pay off those credit cards.

The arrival of a **letter** means work will go well.

A **parcel** arriving is a sign one of your relationships is on a strange footing. Perhaps the other person wants to be more than just good friends?

Leaving or arriving at a **railway station** suggests you're waiting for the results of something probably to do with work.

If someone leaves you, enforcing a period of **separation,** you will soon reach a better understanding with your partner.

A **telegram** arriving is a warning to watch those purse strings.

Simply see a **train** arrive and you're about to make a key friend at work. See it leave and only rational thinking will solve your problems.

ARROGANCE Any sign of arrogance means success socially.

ARROWS *See also*: Weapons. A broken arrow spells failure at work, and breaking an arrow yourself means you will fail in love; but take heart, the attachment is best severed anyway.

ARSON *See also*: Fire. An offer of a change for the better is on the way.

ART *See also*: Pictures/Painting. Seeing works of art signifies promotion. Dream of being an art dealer and your hard work will be rewarded.

ARTILLERY This signifies that you should stop showing off. No one can be loved by everyone! Just try and be yourself.

ARTIST *See also*: Pictures/Painting. Seeing an artist painting or drawing means you're wasting your time on some frivolous bit of fun. If you're the artist, you may have to revise plans to achieve your aims.

ASCENDING *See also*: Success. Any progress upwards forecasts eventual success. How easy or hard it is relates to how smooth or difficult it will be to achieve your ambitions in life.

ASHES *See also*: Death. To be covered in ashes means you must expect some irritating, though temporary, reverses. Emptying them means you may suffer financial embarrassment, but it will be your own fault for being careless. Sifting through ashes means prosperity.

ASHTRAY If it's made of glass, it means you're unhappy with the way your partner is behaving. If it's onyx, you're being too shy over something, and if it's a metal one, you could be in for a row with your boss. A clean ashtray signifies you must make a decision soon or you will make a mistake. If it's dirty, your fortunes will take a turn for the worse.

ASPIRIN *See also*: Doctors/Hospitals; Ill-health; Pain. Do try and keep that secret if you see this drug. It's especially important. So shut that mouth!

ASSASSINATION *See also*: Death. This is a bad sign, whether it's you or someone else who carries out the assassination. It suggests bad luck in many aspects of life. A loss of money, a fire, an argument with loved ones: any of these could be coming your way. It signifies a black period on the horizon.

ASSAULT See yourself assaulted and you will receive good information. Assaulting others in your dream signifies money on the way. But it also means you may have to defend an attack on your good name.

ASSISTING Receiving assistance means you will soon need help and shouldn't be shy about asking for it. But if you give assistance in your dream, you may well succeed without it.

ASTROLOGY This ancient science signifies happiness. Studying astrology predicts an important and very beneficial event is due to happen.

ASTRONOMER An astronomer means you will achieve high ambitions. But see yourself as an astronomer and it signifies illness in the family.

ASYLUM *See also*: Hiding. Dream of being in an asylum and serious trouble is ahead. You must discuss your worries with a friend or professional adviser. Avoid being put into an asylum: watch your health. Stay outside the asylum and you will be asked for help. It may involve hard work for you but you must agree to it.

ATHLETICS If this is something you do in life it's probably of no importance. However if you're not athletic and dream of being an athlete, you will have to face money worries. Becoming an athlete is a warning to take care not to overdo things. Being with an athlete means you must avoid rivals.

ATLAS You could be moving house. Consult one and you can forget your money worries. Buying an atlas means you are going to go on a long trip abroad.

ATMOSPHERE *See also*: Weather. A clear, sunny atmosphere is a very good omen of domestic bliss, faithful friends, and prosperity. But cloudy skies mean storms are brewing in your love life.

ATOMS Seeing these in a dream means a break in a long-standing relationship. But it will be for the best. If the atoms were just talked about and not seen, then it's a cue to tighten your belt!

AUDIENCE *See also*: Performing. If you ask for an audience with the Pope or Royalty, you may be getting yourself into difficulties you will find hard to overcome.

AUTOMATION If things are working automatically in your dream, you must try and be more positive and determined in life. Go on, stop being a mouse!

AUTUMN *See also*: Time. Dreaming of autumn during another season means you will find friends and friendly gestures where you least expect them.

AVALANCHE You are confronted by serious

obstacles and are nervous of them. Try and change your plans. If you're buried in the avalanche you will have a stroke of good luck. If others are buried, a change of surroundings is in the air.

AWNING A raised awning, and new strange experiences are coming to you. A lowered one means you will change your job.

AXE A sharp, shiny axe means you will be rewarded for a good job well done. A dull one and you will face a loss of prestige that could have been avoided if you'd been a bit more conscientious. Swinging an axe spells a business promotion. A broken axe signifies a loss of money.

AXLE *See also*: Driving. A broken or damaged axle means opposition from an unexpected source. But if the axle is repaired or new, you will overcome your difficulties.

ABIES *See also*: Childhood/Children. This is a very auspicious dream symbolising happiness and success in everything you do. But if you're a single girl, be warned. Someone is trying to seduce you! If the baby is newborn it suggests you have a child-like dependence on someone close to you. It also suggests you're exhausted with constant failure at something, probably work. A crying baby is a sign to take heart. Help and advice are coming to you from someone close. Beautiful babies signify fortune via friends. Ugly babies are a warning to beware of treachery on the part of someone you trust. See a baby walking and sudden independence will be yours.

BACK DOOR *See also*: Places/Settings. Use this and good changes are on their way in your life soon. See friends using the back door and you must take care when considering any new venture. Strangers or burglars at the back door are a contrary dream. It means you're in for a windfall.

BADGE *See also*: Uniforms. Any type of badge, whether you are wearing it or see it pinned on someone else, relates to your security. Whatever kind concerns you most: job, family, money will be yours.

BAG This dream depends on the type of bag. A paper one warns of financial embarrassment. A cloth one signifies business success, and a leather bag spells an unexpected journey. Heavy bags are a good omen for your wishes coming true. Carrying one bag means you will soon be in debt. Carry several and you should look out for treachery from a friend.

BAGGAGE See luggage and a long trip, probably abroad, is ahead. Having your luggage carried for you signifies happy times ahead. Losing it means an inheritance coming. But baggage seen out in the street is a warning that you may be robbed. Get those locks fixed!

BAIL *See also*: Legal matters. Needing or offering to pay bail means you're thinking of committing yourself to an unwise partnership. Try and sidestep it for your own sake.

BAILIFF *See also*: Legal matters. See yourself as a bailiff and good news is coming. Talking to one indicates unexpected money. Having trouble with a bailiff signifies misfortune.

BAIT *See also*: Fish/Fishing; Trap. Putting bait on a fishing line means wonderful things are about to happen to you. But if you see others doing it you could be in for a disappointment.

BAIZE This material is a warning not to be lazy. Someone else will get rich at your expense! Buck up before it's too late.

BAKER *See also*: Food. A good omen. If he's kneading dough, there's important news on its way. See him putting bread in the oven and you can expect a nice surprise. But if he's taking something out of the oven, an unpredictable occurrence is about to happen.

BAKERY *See also*: Food. This is a sign of riches. You will have a prosperous year.

BAKING *See also*: Food. See yourself baking and your status will soar.

BALDNESS *See also*: Hair. This is a sign of loss though not necessarily of hair! For a man it can spell illness. For a woman it suggests emotional complications that may well lead to a complete break with someone or something.

BALE Bales of anything are a sign that your greatest problems are about to be solved.

BALL *See also*: Games. Dancing at a ball means you will uncover a secret. But if it's a masked ball, beware some of your friends are false!

BALLET For a woman, this a warning to take care. Your love is being unfaithful! For a man it means failure in business. Watching a ballet being performed is a signal to look after your health.

BALLOON Seeing a balloon floating off into the sky

means you will be involved in projects that take time to come to fruition. Landing, it spells changes in your business affairs. Getting into the basket of a hot-air balloon means pleasant times are on their way. The more it ascends, the better things will be.

BALLOT A desire you had given up hope with will be yours if you cast an election ballot. Watching others doing it or simply seeing ballot boxes signifies a change of surroundings and friends that will not turn out well for you.

BALUSTRADE If you see a broken balustrade, a current plan will face serious obstacles.

BANDAGE *See also*: Doctors/Hospitals. A contrary dream. Wearing one means you can expect some good news.

BANDIT If you fall victim to one, you must watch out or you will have an accident. If you attack back, then it's a sign to trust your own judgement. See others being robbed and you're about to embark on something you suspect will embarrass you. You're right, don't do it!

BANK *See also*: Money. An empty one suggests you will suffer losses. But if you see yourself depositing money in or receiving money from a bank, you can expect financial improvement.

BANKRUPTCY *See also*: Money. This is a contrary dream. Your own bankruptcy means you will prosper. See others bankrupt and it warns you not to get involved in any shady deals—and avoid those who do.

BANNISTER Slide down this and lots of petty irritations are on their way. Going up means you will have to work hard to achieve your aim.

BANQUET *See also*: Food. A successful banquet signals lots of love and happiness in the family. But if there were empty places at the table, you must guard against a tendency to pick fights.

BAR *See also*: Drink. If you were behind it, you will be tempted to do something you know is really wrong. Drinking at the bar, do try to control those passions. Watching others at a bar means you are more highly thought of than you realise. But don't let it go to your head!

BARMAID *See also*: Sexuality. She relates to your sex life. She's telling you to be a bit more choosy with your partners!

BARNACLES *See also*: Sea/Water/Travel. These are a sign you will have a comfortable old age.

BARRACKS You will soon be safe from serious difficulties. However, if it's full of soldiers, there may be trouble on the horizon.

BARREL If it's full and upright, your finances are secure. But an empty or rolling barrel means you must take steps to safeguard your position.

BARBECUE *See also*: Food. A sure sign friends or relatives are about to impose on your good nature.

BARBER *See also*: Hair. For a woman this means you won't be as rich as you'd hoped. For a man it spells success but you'll have to work hard for it.

BAREFOOT *See also*: Clothes; Nakedness. A barefoot man signifies that success will have to be postponed. A barefoot woman means that you will never know true, lasting love. Nakedness in a dream is a very lucky omen, but if only the feet are bare, it signifies difficulties ahead.

BARGAIN If you're cheated out of a bargain, take care. Your home may be robbed. Make a good bargain and you're in for promotion. And if others manage to snap one up, have faith. You have some very loyal friends.

BARK *See also*: Trees/Plants. Tree bark is a warning to take it steady with the opposite sex. Coming on too strong is a real turn-off, you know!

BARLEY This is health-related. If the grain was poor, have a medical check-up.

BASIN *See also*: Washing. A full basin of water means you will soon find happiness. If it's empty your success is also assured. Drinking from a basin means a love affair is just round the corner. But tread carefully, the first person you meet isn't necessarily the right one!

BASKET A full one predicts new opportunities are coming. An empty or damaged basket suggests you're going to lose money and it will be your own fault. Look after it!

BASTARD A contrary dream. Dream of being one and an unusual honour is coming your way. See someone else as one, and your social standing is about to improve. Have one and you will live to regret something.

BATHING *See also*: Sea/Water/Travel. Bathing in the sea forecasts a fortune beyond your wildest dreams. In a lake, and your difficulties will pass. In a river, there's a happy surprise coming. Bathing with others is a sign a friend needs your help.

BAZAAR This indicates you're currently making decisions without thinking them through properly. But it's a good omen. You will soon have something to celebrate.

BEADS *See also*: Colours/Gems; Jewellery. These spell social success. If they're being strung or counted, you will get money unexpectedly. Lose or drop them, and you will have to cope with small disappointments.

BEAM You will have to bear some kind of burden if it's a heavy beam of wood. A light one predicts a past favour reaping rewards. A steel beam suggests money you have forgotten about.

BEARD *See also*: Hair. Basically the fuller the beard the better your luck. But if you see a bearded lady don't gamble! A false beard could mean trouble with your health.

BEAUTY A super omen for success in business and love life.

BECKONING If a friend or relative beckons you, the future will be full of pleasure. If it's a stranger, there will be a few minor reverses.

BEEHIVE *See also*: Insects. This is a symbol of honour, dignity and wealth. But see it empty, and money troubles are ahead.

BEGGAR A beggar symbolises a period of happiness with few worries. In your love life you could meet the person of your dreams. And if you give the beggar money, that love will be reciprocated.

BEHEADING *See also*: Death. A contrary dream. If you are beheaded, success will be yours. If you see others beheaded, it still signals success, but only after a few delays.

BELL *See also*: Sounds. A distant bell is a sign of good news. If it's struck with a hammer you're going to have a few worries. But if you see a bell tolling for the dead, don't panic, someone highly placed is looking after your interests. For lovers, seeing a bell means a wedding.

BELLOWS *See also*: Fire. There will be difficulties to face—but they will all be of your own making if you use these. If you simply see bellows, it's a signal to stop wasting your time on trivial things!

BENCH Watch your work or you could lose your job. A wooden bench denotes a small but pleasing gain. A stone bench means an even bigger profit. Seeing others sitting on a bench could mean the death of an enemy.

BEREAVEMENT *See also*: Death. A contrary dream.

See this, and news of a birth, engagement or wedding is likely.

BIBLE *See also*: Religion. Some good deeds you have done will reap rewards. But if you see a Bible open on a lectern, it's a sign your mind is in turmoil. Swearing an oath on one means you must assert yourself more.

BICYCLE Any dream involving a bicycle shows there is an important decision to be made. Think carefully before coming to any conclusions. If you see a cyclist going uphill in your dream or speeding down it, you will make progress and favourable changes.

BILLS *See also*: Money. A contrary dream. Worrying about bills sparks off a run of good money luck. If you pay or send out the bills, you'll be needing some financial assistance.

BINDING Binding things up or being bound yourself is a sign of embarrassing personal entanglements. Are you really in the right relationship? If you see books being bound, you will find something that was lost.

BINOCULARS If you are being watched through them, then think very carefully before you act. And if they're used for spying, you may soon have to defend your reputation. If you have the binoculars, it spells future happiness.

BIRDS Birds are generally a good omen, especially if they're singing or flying. Dead birds mean worries are on the way—unless they are birds of prey; then the worries will be shortlived. If the birds are in the nest, family happiness is coming. Birds hatching are a sign of delayed profit. A flock of birds predicts a family reunion. A bird cage signals a happy marriage, but if it's empty with an open door, it's a sign of betrayal. Individual types of birds have their own meanings:

An **albatross** is a good luck sign and means you will receive some good news and a stroke of good fortune.

A **buzzard** is an old bird warning you not to repeat gossip. It will only bounce back!

Hear a **cock** crow and some wonderful news is on the way. But fighting cocks predict family feuds.

Don't listen to gossip if you dream of a **cockatoo.** See it in a cage, and you will soon realise how indiscreet you've been.

One white **dove** says there will be a peaceful solution to your problems. See a flock of them, and you'll meet up with an old friend again soon. Cooing doves predict a lasting love affair.

Ducks are a lucky sign unless they attack you, then you will lose something. Flying ducks mean money coming soon. Swimming, they're a sign family life will be happy.

A flying **eagle** is a very good sign for business. If it perches up high, you will get fame as well as fortune. But if the eagle attacks, there are problems ahead.

The funny old **emu** indicates a well-meaning friend is feeding you duff advice. Don't listen!

See small **feathers** and an exceptional stroke of luck will bring you mountains of money. Ornamental feathers or things made from feathers, such as a boa, are a sign of social success. A white feather is a sign of a long-lasting friendship.

An exotic **flamingo** predicts new experiences in exciting places.

Geese are a sign of improvement if they're flying, swimming, or walking around. But hear them cackling, and someone is trying to con you.

See a **hawk** flying and the future is bright. If not, life is bound to be boring for a while.

A **black hen** predicts sad news. A white one good news, and a brown one money luck. A clucking one and you're about to hear some really exciting gossip. Prosperity is on the way if the hen is laying. Kill one and a few ups and downs will have to be faced. Pluck one and an unexpected bill is about to come through the letter box.

It's time to give up on something if you see a **magpie**. You are wasting energy and it's probably being directed at someone of the opposite sex who's simply not interested.

Spot an **ostrich** and your social life is about to become hectic and you'll have the money to enjoy it. The champagne's going to be on you!

An **owl** in a dream heralds disappointment; drive it away and things will improve. See an owl in the house and family troubles are inevitable.

Don't gossip is the message from a colourful, talking **parrot.**

A **stork** isn't a good sign. It's an omen of changes that will leave you worse off than before. Seen in a nest, it predicts family problems. Flying is a sign you could be about to commit a crime. Watch that speed limit!

A **black swan** means you will shortly face business problems. White ones and your love life will blossom. On a pond, a swan predicts wealth.

Strutting around, a gobbling **turkey** predicts confusion. Kill one, and a stroke of good luck is coming your way. Cook it and it's a sign of prosperity. But eat the meat and you could be about to make a serious error of judgement.

Vultures flying suggest you have a love rival. If they're eating, fortune is about to smile on you. Kill a vulture and you will soon be in complete control of your life.

BIRTH Good news is on the way, but if you're a single woman and dream of giving birth, your lover will leave you. For a married woman, a birth predicts great joy. An easy birth means you have considerable resistance to pain. A difficult one predicts problems and difficulties, but they will all be resolved thanks to your rational thinking. If you see the birth of an animal, then someone working against your interests will come a cropper.

BIRTHDAY A lucky omen whether it's your own or someone else's. Good health and peace will be yours.

BITING Dream of being bitten, and you may uncover a secret you'd rather not have known. That will teach you not to pry! Bite someone and your relationship with your lover is based on lies, I'm afraid.

BITTERNESS Experience this taste or feeling and you must think before you speak. Open that mouth of yours, and someone could thwart your ambitions.

BLACKMAIL For a man this shows a need to be loved and understood. A woman and she has money worries. A friend being blackmailed is a sign you lack self-confidence and tend to be pessimistic. See yourself as the blackmailer, and you're being excessively vain and over-ambitious at the moment!

BLACK MARIA *See also*: Police/Prisons. Locked in it, your status will improve. If you see others being taken away in one, you must expect temporary set-backs.

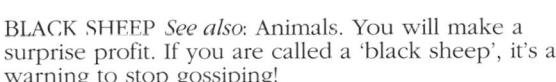

BLACK SHEEP *See also*: Animals. You will make a surprise profit. If you are called a 'black sheep', it's a warning to stop gossiping!

BLACKSMITH Dreaming of being a blacksmith indicates you will soon lose faith in yourself. Seeing a blacksmith shoeing a horse means you will have to face obstacles; simply seeing a blacksmith is an omen of misfortune and even agony in the future.

BLADE *See also*: Weapons. A clean, shiny blade denotes new friends. A rusty one is a sign of ill-health.

BLANKET If you're comfortably off, buying new blankets suggests you will lose money. If you're on an average wage, it predicts things will improve. See old blankets and good news is coming.

BLESSING *See also*: Religion. You will be forced into a marriage if you see yourself receiving a blessing, although if it comes from a priest it's a lucky sign. Seeing others receiving blessings indicates a happy family for you. If you yourself give the blessing, you're going to have to struggle to overcome obstacles.

BLINDFOLD *See also*: Deception. You've got something on your conscience if you see a blindfold. If you were wearing it, re-examine your plans. Your motives are a bit suspicious!

BLINDNESS *See also*: Deception. See yourself afflicted and someone close is about to double cross you. If you see others blind or blinded it spells deceit. Be on the look-out for treachery among those you trust the most.

BLOOD If your **arteries** are weak or cut, you will enjoy honour among your friends.

If you see yourself **bleeding** heavily you will fall into a trap. Others bleeding is a sign you will have to face some opposition soon.

A **haemorrhage** is a clear warning you're utterly exhausted, both mentally and physically. Relax, take time off, or book that holiday.

See your **nose bleeding** and others are about to hold you in contempt. Bleeding a little from somewhere else is a sign that a wish is about to come true.

BLOT/BLOTTER *See also*: Reading/Writing. A blot on clean white paper is a sign that a mystery that's been puzzling you will soon be solved. A blot on coloured paper signifies a journey soon, and a blot on a document means your affairs will improve. See a clean blotter and some astonishing news about one of your friends will reach your ears. If the blotter is used, spats and fights with family and friends are predicted.

BLUSHING Blush and you will soon discover you can't trust one of your friends. See others blushing and keep your mouth firmly shut. It's a warning against gossip!

BOG Don't get discouraged if you see this. Persevere and you'll get there in the end.

BOILER/BOILING *See also*: Heat. See a boiler and you might as well stop hoping. Whatever it is, it simply isn't going to happen. A steam boiler is a warning to take care in any business venture. Dream you're a boiler-maker and unhappiness on the home front is on the way. Don't let your emotions run away with you if you see boiling water. Boiling soups spell money luck, and if it's boiling coffee, there's going to be a bit of an emotional drama soon.

BOLTS *See also*: Doors. Fasten the bolts of your door and something is going to offend you. A broken bolt is a warning that you're being far too selfish these days. Opening a bolt signifies a new start in another location. If you see yourself bolted in, trouble is brewing.

BOMB If it explodes, you're in for some heated discussions, but they will turn out friendly in the end.

BONE *See also*: Human body. Animal bones suggest you are about to spend or lose money and the result will cause a few headaches. Find a bone and you could fall out with the family. A very large bone predicts problems with the opposite sex.

BONFIRE *See also*: Fire. Who's getting nostalgic, then? See a bonfire and you're thinking of past mistakes and events—you don't really like where they've led you, do you? You can't change things; try and make the best of it.

BOOMERANG If it comes back, watch out at work: your colleagues aren't being honest with you. If it doesn't, you will be moving house.

BOTTLE *See also*: Drink. A full one stands for prosperity. If it's full of alcohol, then good health is on the way. An empty bottle means a period of uncertainty is ahead. If it's dropped or spilt, watch out for family problems.

BOWLING *See also*: Games. A generally lucky omen—especially if you are playing.

BOX An empty one means your plans will go haywire. But if there's something in it, then you can overcome the obstacles. Opening a box signifies a long journey. If you open a full box, someone is about to propose to you.

BOXER You are spoiled for choice if you see him in the ring. If he's on the ropes, it means you have just been brought down to earth with a bang over something. See a boxer knocked out and you will lose something precious. Watch a boxing match and it's a warning not to gossip; you could miss out on an important opportunity.

BOY A schoolboy shows what a generous soul you are. See an altar boy and it's a warning to stop being so flighty! See boys fighting, and it's a sure sign you're not really in love with your partner.

BRACELET See also: Jewellery. A bracelet is a happy sign. See one on your arm and your love life will go well. If someone else puts it on for you, then expect to fall in love and marry soon. Find a bracelet and it's a warning that you will shortly meet someone who will cause you confusion. Lose one and you are in for a disappointment.

BRAINS Animal brains spell good news from an unexpected quarter. See human brains and you should try and be a bit more considerate to loved ones.

BRAMBLES See also: Thorn. Get pricked by a bramble and you must expect some reverses. If the brambles don't scratch you, then happy days will soon be here again.

BRAVERY A contrary dream. Acts of bravery show you may well suffer because you simply refuse to face up to present problems.

BREAKFAST See also: Food. See yourself eating it alone and you must think before you speak. Eat the meal with others and a little bit of patience will get you what you want.

BREAKING Break plates and your material success is assured. Cups or glasses and it shows just what a generous, enthusiastic soul you are. Breaking other household objects shows you're frustrated and disappointed with family life.

BREATHING If you're out of breath or having trouble breathing, you're feeling guilty about something you did a while back. Slow, calm breathing means you're confident about your future; you can achieve all sorts of things now.

BRIBE See also: Money. Not a good omen, whether you offer or accept it. Don't gamble, and steer clear of anyone you think might be out to exploit you.

BRICKS Bricks spell sudden change, leading to a few upsets. Unless they are being laid, then things will slowly improve. Bricklayers downing tools and having a tea-break means you need to put more energy into your work. Stop stagnating!

BRIDE, BRIDEGROOM, BRIDESMAID See also: Weddings. See her at the altar and it's good news in almost every aspect of your life. If she's on her own, however, your health is slightly risky. If you're with a bride at an altar, a secret desire could soon be yours. Kiss a bride and you'll be making a lot of new friends.

One of your pet projects will face delays if you see him. But don't give up, a new approach will win the day. If his bride is very young it's a warning of sickness in the family.

Dream of being a bridesmaid and you're in for a big disappointment. See several of them and happiness is coming.

BRIDGES If you see a bridge being **built** you have a fertile imagination. Cross one, and a job change is on the way.

See it in **concrete** or **stone** and big plans will soon be realised.

A **parapet** suggests patience is the only way to overcome the obstacles in your path at the moment.

A **railway bridge** is a sign of good luck in a risky business; but a road bridge suggests you're being far too ambitious, and this could lead to rows with your other half.

A **wooden** one is a hint that you lack willpower.

BRIDLE Put this on a horse and you'll be obliged to do something you'd rather not bother with. But you'll eventually just put it down to experience. A broken or worn bridle is a sure sign not to get involved in that clandestine love affair: you'll get caught out!

BRIEFCASE See also: Work. A battered briefcase means business success. A new one means don't make changes without finding out the facts first. A briefcase full of papers is a warning to pay more attention to your personal life. An empty one means current plans will go well. Lose your briefcase and you can expect a small profit. Find one, and you must watch your step in business, otherwise there'll be trouble.

BROOM A modern one is a sign that new exciting emotions will start charging through you. Be warned! A witch's broom is a warning you could be wasting your money on something. If the broom has

Plate 3 · The Bride and Groom

a wooden handle then a sudden change is going to throw your routine into a state of flux.

BROTHEL *See also*: Sexuality. A contrary dream. Visit a brothel, whether you're a man or a woman, and your domestic life will really improve!

BRUISE *See also*: Pain. Any kind of bruise and it's a warning you've been living life in the fast lane. If the bruises are on the legs, your reputation is at stake. Pull over and slow down!.

BRUSH A hairbrush, and if you want that sexy new partner you're going to have to make some major sacrifices. A paint brush says you're full of the joys of spring and optimistic about the future. Cleaning a brush predicts difficulties are ahead.

BUBBLES Your present problems will vanish. If you make the bubbles, it's a warning to keep a tight hold on those purse strings. Try and cultivate a more realistic attitude to money! Bubbles in a bath mean someone wants to protect you.

BURSTING If something bursts, something funny is going to happen to you: the amusing kind!.

BUS Travel by it and you're well on your way to your heart's desire. Waiting for a bus signifies temporary set-backs. You'll be financially embarrassed if you dream of a bus crash. A bus conductor predicts foreign travel.

BUSINESS *See also*: Work. You're in for a rough ride. You'll find yourself fighting hostile or even dishonest competition. But if business documents feature, all will be resolved in your favour.

BUTCHER You'll be catching up with an old friend you haven't seen in years. But see a butcher killing animals and it signifies the death of an old friend.

BUILDING *See also*: Places/Settings. A big building forecasts changes in your lifestyle. A small one spells problems in your affairs. A very tall building means you will shortly be very successful. Old, dilapidated buildings are a sign to start saving for the rainy days ahead.

BULLET *See also*: Weapons. If you're hit by a bullet, you'd better have a medical check-up. If you simply see or hear one, you could be exposing yourself to a real scandal. Try to be a bit more discreet!.

BULLFIGHT Watch a bullfight, and you will soon have to take some decisive action.

BUMPING This is a warning to take care in everything you do.

BUNDLE Carrying any kind of bundle predicts a

wonderful invitation is about to arrive. If you're wrapping it, then you're laying yourself wide open to criticism in all sorts of areas.

BUYING/SELLING Dream of buying or selling at an auction and one of your trusted friends could be trying to take advantage of you. Watch out for them.

Buy a **house**, and a short but pleasant love affair is on the horizon. Selling one is a sign you will be released from some responsibility.

If you get a **receipt** for your purchases, then better times are round the corner.

Go to a **sale** and you'll soon receive a valuable gift. Put your own things on sale and you're in for a rise. See yourself as a **salesman**, and it shows you're always ready to help people in trouble. If you are working in a **shop**, you are in for a stroke of money luck.

See yourself on a **spending spree** and it's a warning to tighten your belt. The more you buy the more careful you should be with your money. But if you dream of buying wisely, you can expect a stroke of money luck.

C AB *See also*: Driving. Ride alone in one and life will be comfortable. You've even got time now to take up that hobby. Ride in a cab at night with someone of the opposite sex then beware. Your own discretion will cause a scandal! Riding in a cab with friends means you will discover a secret.

CABIN Dream you're in a ship's cabin and you're in for a rough ride on the home front. There might be a legal wrangle on the horizon. If the cabin is in a wood or on the beach, some petty behaviour will have you steaming with anger soon.

CAGE A bird cage signals a happy marriage. But an empty one with an open door is an omen of betrayal. Buy or make a cage and an unsettled period in your life is about to come to an end. Dream you are put in a cage and rows loom large on your horizon.

CALENDER *See also*: Time. Write an appointment on a calendar and you're about to meet Mr or Ms Right. Tear off calender sheets and a surprise present is on its way.

CAMEO *See also*: Jewellery. Receive one of these and you will recover from an illness. Buy one and happiness is on the way, but lose it and it's an omen of death.

CAMERA This is a warning that some of your friends aren't as sincere as you think. Don't tell them any of your secrets.

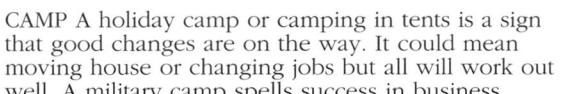

CAMP A holiday camp or camping in tents is a sign that good changes are on the way. It could mean moving house or changing jobs but all will work out well. A military camp spells success in business.

CAMPHOR *See also*: Smells. This is a warning against casual sex. Scandal or illness could result. Don't do it.

CAN Drink from a can and unexpected, wonderful things are about to happen to you. Open one and you are going to lose out in love to a rival, I'm afraid. Throwing away an empty can is a warning that a serious disaster is round the corner. Take care and you can avoid it.

CANAL *See also*: Sea/Water/Travel. A full canal is a good sign for your future security. An empty or near-empty one is a sign to stop spending so much money. See canal locks and it's a warning to look for a cuckoo in your nest of friends!

CANDLES *See also*: Darkness/Light. A burning one is a sign of unexpected events. A letter, a visit from a friend, some little surprise. Snuff a candle out and you're in for a disappointment in your love life. Dream of buying candles and you're fed up with your routine, aren't you? Go on, break out and enjoy yourself for once. See candles being carried and you can expect an increase in your social activities.

CANE If it's growing, profits will increase. See it cut and no gambling for at least a month! A school cane means success in your love life but only after a bit of a delay. Beat someone or see yourself being beaten with a cane and it's a warning not to make any major changes for the time being. A broken one is a sign you will win a victory when you least expect it.

CANNIBAL A warning not to be tempted into anything risky, no matter how promising you think it looks.

CANOE *See also*: Sea/Water/Travel. See yourself in one and it's a warning of a fire. An empty canoe is a sign of loneliness. Try and make some new friends. See one overturn and you have an enemy who is trying to ruin you.

CANOPY See yourself under this and you can look forward to a secure period in life. A canopy is a sign of protection.

CAPSULE Any kind of capsule is the green light for relationships with the opposite sex. You simply can't fail now! You're at your scintillating best.

CAPTIVE If you're held captive, your marriage is about to go through a very sticky patch. Any other form of captivity, seeing others captive or animals in captivity, is a sign you are under a lot of strain. It could be because you have been over-spending and are worrying about money.

CAR *See also*: Driving. Buy one and you're about to get an unsavoury reputation for something. Do you really have to do it? Sell a car and you could owe someone money.

CARBON Carbon copies are a warning about mischief making friends. Someone is deceiving you.

CARCASS *See also*: Death. A sign of prosperity. Rotting carcasses are a symbol of hard work. You'll get there in the end, but it will take a lot of elbow grease. See animals being slaughtered and it signifies the death of an old friend.

CARDS Playing cards or watching others playing is a warning to be careful with money. Someone could be trying to trick you out of cash. Deal them and bad news is coming.

See an **ace** and the meaning depends on the suit. If you're not aware of the suit, you will be unable to fathom out a mystery.

Clubs, success in business, but only after a few rows.

Diamonds: money luck.

Hearts: your wishes will come true and you will be lucky in love.

The **joker** in the pack is a warning to stop being lazy. Someone else is getting richer while you sit back.

Spades: sadness or work will go unrewarded.

CARNIVAL You're a bit on the melancholy side. Take part in it and you will have to overcome a few obstacles to get what you want.

CAROLS *See also*: Music; Sounds. Hear carols and a happy, contented year lies ahead.

CARPENTER This is a truly happy sign. Seeing one, being one, or even hiring one, means love, respect and happiness, and what's more, you will have time to enjoy them all!.

CARPET *See also*: Furniture. Current projects will be successful even if they seem tough at present. Beat a

carpet and important news is coming. A shabby, worn carpet is a sign you're in debt. Try to get out of it.

CART Driving or riding in one means it will be all work and no play for a while. See a hay cart and your wishes will come true.

CARTOON These are a sign that business will boom but your love life will fizzle out. Never mind, sometimes you can't have it both ways.

CASHIER *See also*: Money. Put away that credit card if you dream of a cashier. Money will soon be tight.

CASTLES *See also*: Places/Settings. That temper of yours is going to cause some arguments. An ancient castle is a signal to check your investments. Visiting one means you are about to travel a bit. A ruined castle is a warning to curb your passions. They could lead to trouble!.

CASTRATING A contrary dream. Any form of castration means you'll beat the rest no matter what the odds are.

CATTLE *See also*: Animals. Grazing, they're a sign of prosperity. Driving cattle means you will have to work hard to get what you want. Black cattle are an omen to pay attention at work or something could get lost.

CAVALRY *See also*: Uniform. For a single woman cavalry means she's going to marry a City whizz-kid! For others it's a good omen for love affairs. If a man dreams of being in the cavalry he will marry a real beauty.

CAVE/CAVERN *See also*: Places/Settings. A dark underground cave spells danger. But one on a hill or mountain and new opportunities are coming your way. See this from the outside and your lot in life will gradually improve. But dream of being in it and your ambitions are going to be frustrated. If the cavern is very deep it's a sign to completely reconsider your aims.

CEILING A cracked or damaged ceiling means a friend is going to cause trouble for you. But a nicely decorated one is a protective sign spelling happiness.

CELL *See also*: Police/Prisons. This is a warning not to be careless. If you've promised to do something, then do it—or you could lose a friend.

CELLARS *See also*: Places/Settings. A sign you're a bit depressed. But if it's full of wood or coal it's a sign you'll soon snap out of it. Bottles of wine in a cellar mean you're going to feel gloomy for a while yet, but an empty cellar is a much more cheerful sign. You will shortly feel refreshed, relaxed, and ready to take on the world.

CEMENT A happy sign. You're in for a promotion or pay rise.

CERTIFICATE Ask for one and you don't trust someone, do you? A birth certificate is an omen of new life and means good changes for you. A medical certificate is a sign of good health but a death certificate signals a family upset.

CHAINS A contrary dream. Chains are a symbol that you will soon be free of your worries. They can also spell major success.

CHALK A set-back is on the way. Hear it squeaking on a blackboard and it will be your own fault for telling tales.

CHALLENGING Dream of being challenged and it's a warning not to offend important people. If you do the challenging, someone of the opposite sex is going to give you a hard time.

CHAMPION *See also*: Success. Being a sports champ suggests your current enthusiasm for something will soon fizzle out. If someone else becomes a champion, you can expect some small successes.

CHANDELIER *See also*: Furniture. A gleaming chandelier predicts super success socially. If it's unlit, that success will take a bit longer to achieve. Hanging from a chandelier (you or someone else) is a warning against taking a mistress or a lover. Your other half is bound to find out!

CHANGING/TRANSFORMATION Find yourself **adapting** to some unusual conditions in a dream and it's a sign your financial future is secure.

Other kinds of **alterations**, to clothes, for example, mean you're being told to be strong and avoid an up-and-coming temptation.

Dream of a change of **lifestyle** by suddenly becoming famous and you're trying for something that's really out of your reach. Try and cut your cloth to suit you more.

See yourself grow **taller** and your self-confidence is increasing by the day. Someone else, and it's a sign you fear the future. A building growing taller means money is on the way.

Transform yourself into someone else by

Plate 4 · The Castle of Dreams

impersonating them and you're going through a jealous phase. This is not a very lucky omen.

CHARITY This is a contrary dream. The more generous you are, the bigger financial fix you'll be in for the next twelve months. Receive the charity and you can look forward to money luck.

CHARM Wear a charm and you will soon have an important decision to make. If you are given one, life will be full of ups and downs from now on.

CHASING A comfortable old age is forecast if you are chased or seeing a chase.

CHASTISE A contrary dream. If you are chastised, you will soon be as pleased as punch about something. See children being chastised and you should go for a medical check-up.

CHEATING See yourself cheated and you can expect a stroke of good luck. If you do the cheating, you can expect to be outwitted.

CHEERING Cheer and you're going to regret something done on impulse. Hear others cheering and it's a warning to stop spending so much!

CHESS *See also*: Games. Playing it shows you have a decisive, quick-witted personality. Losing at chess means you have been setting your sights too high. Winning means money on the way. See a lone chess piece and you must think very carefully about your image. How do others really see you?

CHEST A large one and you must be careful or you will run into debt. A small one means things will go well in your love life. An empty chest means a minor disappointment and a full one means the family will all pull together in the end but only after a few tiffs.

CHEWING *See also*: Food. Do this and you will have a disappointment, but it will be your own silly fault. See others chewing and you can expect an exciting invitation.

CHILDHOOD/CHILDREN See yourself abandoned as a child and you will quickly recover from trouble or get back together with your lover.

Happiness in the family is assured if you see yourself altering children's **clothes**.

Children's **marbles** signify the rekindling of an old flame or renewing an old friendship.

Ride on a **merry-go-round** or watch it and life is about to improve for you. But see it deserted or run-down, and things could look black for a while. But don't worry, another door is about to open up.

Seeing children at **play** is the omen of a successful romance.

See a baby's **rattle** and you will learn that life really does begin at forty—or even older! And double-trouble will be followed by twice the pleasure if you see twins. The same goes for quads, but in that case pleasure will be short-lived.

And a **rocking-horse** is a good omen for all your personal interests.

A primary **school** is a sign you will have to make a few changes. A secondary school and you will have to make a choice between a great number of options. A boarding school shows you have supportive friends. A private one and you will face something risky. Go back to school and money plans will go well. News is on the way if you see a blackboard. Chalked on, the news will affect your immediate plans. Any kind of academy predicts new friends and experiences. But be careful—it could cost you a fortune!

A **see-saw** predicts an exciting love affair. It will be short but oh so sweet.

New developments are on the horizon if you dream of other types of **toys**. But if they're broken it suggests you're being a bit childish about something. Try and grow up a bit.

CHIMNEY A factory chimney is a sign of unexpected money. On top of a house and things will be rocky for a while. See a smoking chimney and good news is on the way. A crumbling chimney spells a few troubles, but if it actually falls down, you will have something to celebrate soon. See a chimney sweep and you will be blamed for something you didn't do.

CHINA (CERAMIC) You will have happiness at home. But if you see it cracked or broken, a change is going to be forced upon you which you won't like. But it will turn out well in the end.

CHIPS *See also*: Food. Gambling chips show that now is the time for a flutter. Wood chips predict petty annoyances.

CHISEL This is telling you that you can get what you want if you really try.

CHOPPING Chopping anything or seeing a tree

chopped down is a sign that family quarrels are about to end. You will soon be kissing and making up.

CHRISTMAS Happy family times are ahead. It's a good time to make new friends and your health couldn't be better.

CHURN You will always have what you need in life. But if the churn is upset, someone you trust will disappoint you.

CIGAR *See also*: Fire. Smoking one in a dream is a symbol of success. An unlit cigar means some kind of misfortune is round the corner.

CIGARETTE *See also*: Fire. A packet of these means important business dealings are under way. Loose cigarettes mean you're about to be disillusioned about someone. Dream of lighting one and you could be in for a complete change of career. Cigarette smoke predicts a new, important friend.

CINEMA Going to the cinema is a warning not to be taken in by appearances. Particularly if the dream involves a good looking man or woman. An empty cinema means some slanderous gossip about you is doing the rounds.

CIRCLE Success beyond your wildest dreams will be yours. Draw it yourself and you're not taking advantage of all your opportunities.

CIRCUS *See also*: Performing. Dream you're there with children and it spells good luck with loot. If you're with adults, then be more careful of the impression you make on others.

CLEANING The more clean, the stronger the warning not to get involved in anything shady or unethical. It may look like fun and might promise profit but it simply isn't worth it.

CLIMBING A climbing dream indicates an increase in status and prosperity. Scaling a mountain means you think your worries are insurmountable. They're not! Climbing a ladder means promotion at work.

CLOSET An empty one is a warning not to get into debt. A full one means your business profits will soar. A linen closet is a sign of happy times ahead at home.

CLOTH The type of cloth involved is important. But as a general guide: linen means a pay-rise; wool spells security; velvet means success in your love life; silk signifies a good social life and cotton means you should try and be a bit more discreet. Nylon is a reminder that things aren't always what they seem. In satin and you're at your confident best. Cutting cloth predicts a distressing message will come from a distance.

CLOTHES *See also*: Nakedness. Basically, the fewer the better! Wear few clothes and luck is on its way. But this is a bit of a dream of opposites. Putting on clothes signifies success. Undressing forecasts some reversals. Shabby clothes are a warning not to go into business with friends, but really tatty clothes can signify an inheritance. Tight uncomfortable clothes are a sign you need to protect your reputation by cooling down your sex life!

Individual garments also have their meanings, but the more fashionable and chic the clothes, the more problems there will be. New clothes are a sign of domestic tiffs.

A crisp, clean **apron** is an omen of happiness, but if it's black or dirty it spells danger. Put one on and you could get a visit from relatives. Wash one and a new love is about to enter your life.

Get into a **bathrobe** or dressing-gown and you will need your family's help to carry out some jobs. Giving one as a present is a warning not to be so presumptuous. Back off a bit.

An old **belt** means things will start to pick up for you. A new leather belt means relationships that have been a bit tense will improve. A silk or material belt shows that some of your desires can never be fulfilled. Wear a belt and it's a sign you want to move house. Take it off, and it shows just how insecure you are feeling.

New or shiny **boots** predict promotion and financial security. Old ones mean there are difficulties ahead.

Hook yourself into a **bra** and it's a sign you're extremely adaptable. Buy one, and you've recently made the right decision—but didn't it take a long time? If it's a small bra, you're being bad-tempered and aggressive—lighten up! A big one is a sign to stop being so stubborn at work. It will lead to mistakes. A white bra is a symbol of contentment.

Fasten a **buckle** and it's a sign of a close-knit family. An unclasped one means you've got to take positive steps to avoid a row in that romance of yours. Trying to fasten or undo a buckle means you should pay more attention at work.

Anything with bright shiny new **buttons** is a sign of wealth and security. Old or broken buttons are a warning to get out of an emotional tangle you're in. Lose a button and it means you've been spending too much money lately.

Wearing a **cap** is a good omen for your love life. Buy one and you could receive an inheritance. A dirty or old cap means things may not go your way in business. A military cap is a sign you will win the day despite serious opposition.

Any **cloak or cape** forecasts a period of uncertainty. If it has a hood you're being deceived by someone you trust. Try and choose your friends more carefully. You're in for a passionate sexy love affair if you see yourself in **clogs**. But sorry, it won't last long.

Help someone on with their **coat** and you will be asked for a loan. Lend a coat and you're about to make a new friend. A shabby old coat is a symbol of money luck whereas a new one signifies business reversals. Hang a coat up and the boss is looking favourably at you.

Clean **collars** are a sign your current amour is a reliable one. But a dirty or torn collar says you are being deceived. Even perhaps deceiving yourself.

A new **dress** and you'll be a scintillating social success. An embroidered one is a sign you're red-hot sexually now, as long as you don't take it all too seriously. If you receive a dress as a present, then a man you don't know yet is going to help you.

See yourself with **ermine** and you're about to buy property. Buy it, and it's time to cling on to your cash. Sell it and someone is going to diddle you.

The sort of glossy fashion mags you're likely to see that particular **fur** in suggest you've been working too hard. Try and have some fun. Any other kind of luxurious fur is a sign you'll run into major problems thanks to others' jealousy. Put a fur coat on and you will get involved with an important relationship at work. All that sucking up to the boss could well pay off at last! Give fur as a present and you are wasting your time on risky ventures. White fur means you will lose a friend. Black says your ideas simply won't work and brown means emotional dramas. Dream of fur in a shop window and your plans will succeed because this time at least you have thought them through. Mink says you're being too greedy over something. Sable—curb your extravagance.

Different types of **gloves** all have their meanings: ski gloves are a sign of problems solved; boxing gloves mean important new contacts; white gloves symbolise VIPs you may well be about to meet; black gloves are a sign of failure; rubber ones show you have an important decision to make; leather forecast a period of melancholy, woolly gloves and some problems are about to be solved. Lose gloves and the help you were expecting simply won't materialise.

Unexpected gains are on the horizon if you put a **hat** on. Buy a new one and a silly row could lose you a friend. Try and bite your tongue. A dirty hat is a sign of a nasty emotional experience—brace yourself. A top hat means a rise in your social status. A hat-box and you are in for a pleasant surprise.

Slip into a **jacket** and you're keeping danger at bay. Take it off and it's likely to catch up with you. A new jacket is a warning of money problems. An old one and a serious suggestion is about to be made.

A highland **kilt** suggests a surprise trip is round the corner.

Keep the showers away with a **mac** and you will have a few short-term anxieties. Take one off and you must watch out for gossip. Buy one and money is coming in. Lose one and it's a sign of success.

Pants oddly enough are a very good sign. Women's pants or knickers mean change for the better. Men's are a sign of an advantageous offer. Buy a pair and life is going in your direction. Take them off and it shows what an offbeat imagination you have! Wash them and a profitable project is about to start.

Pretty **petticoats** are a warning not to be so vain. Buy one and it's time to tighten those purse strings. Lose one and someone you take for granted is going to be eyed-up by someone else. A torn petticoat is a sign you are disenchanted with life at the moment. A white petticoat predicts a beautiful gift.

Unhappiness and a tricky period health-wise are on the way if you see men's **pyjamas**. Women's pyjamas, and the family simply don't understand you at the moment. Children's pyjamas mean you are in for a long wait—and it won't be worth it in the end. Put pyjamas on and your passion for someone simply won't be returned. Take them off, and it's a sign you're feeling insecure and unloved.

A **shawl** round your shoulders shows money will be tight for a while. On your head, and it's a good sign for your love life.

Plate 5 · The Fashion Victim

A clean **shirt** is a lucky omen, but dirty it predicts a period of gloom.

Worn-out **shoes** spell success. New ones are a sign of over-confidence. Lose them and you're wasting your time on something. Shine your shoes and a new venture will go surprisingly well. Comfy sandals suggest you're in for a new romance. Tight, and there will be a row over money. White sandals show your talent is not being recognised. Children's sandals are a sign a favourable suggestion is about to be put to you.

A white **skirt** is a sign of true happiness. Any other colour and your hopes are about to come true. A short skirt says you're getting involved in something you shouldn't, and a long one predicts you're going to cheat someone. You'll score a romantic success if you see a cotton skirt.

Cosy old **slippers** suggest an emotional relationship may be in danger if they are women's. Men's indicate you have a strong and lasting relationship. Fabric ones, and you need to make some changes. Leather, and things go well. Buy slippers, and it's a good time for a flutter. If they're falling apart your career will take a step up.

Putting **stockings** on predicts profits. Take them off and changes are on their way. Laddered stockings suggest minor money problems. If they are silk a spot of money luck is on the cards. Woollen forecasts security. A garter relates to your love life. For a man it shows you have the hots for a particular lady right now. For a woman it's a sign of faithfulness. Suspenders are a warning you have fallen for the wrong man; for a man it means a surprise gain.

Torn or dirty **trousers**, and emotional problems are inevitable. But the cheaper the material the better the money luck. Cotton predicts wealth, but see silk trousers and you'll be constantly worrying about how to pay those bills.

A **veil** suggests something you're about to embark on is against your principles. Think it over carefully before committing yourself. A torn veil suggests a mystery will soon be solved. Seen on a bride it spells changes for the better. Lose one and you will soon be blushing about something. A mourning veil means something is going to make you angry.

Someone has changed their mind and it will affect

you if you see a **waistcoat**. A silk one is a sign you're hankering after the past. White, and the family will all agree on something. Black, and an unpleasant event is on the cards. But a green waistcoat and your friends are jealous of you. Put one on and you will row with a loved one.

See a broken **zip** or one that's stuck and you will soon be blushing socially. Zip something up, and all those little minor irritations will quickly be cleared up.

CLOUDS *See also*: Weather. If the sun is covered by clouds it shows you have a strong sense of duty. If it's the moon, you are patient and persevering and that will help you overcome current problems at work. Cloudy weather means you will be apt to be a bit emotional for a while. But fluffy white clouds are a sign you will soon do well at work.

CLOWN *See also*: Performing. You will soon be fuming because something you have done has been misinterpreted. If you are dressed as a clown, you will have to face a problem that could cost you a lot of money.

COAL This is a warning that financial embarrassment is forecast. But if it is burning, or you are stoking a fire, promotion at work is on the way. Shovelling coal means you are going to face a few obstacles in order to get what you want.

COBWEB *See also*: Insects. If there is no spider, then calm days and happy times are ahead. See a web being spun and you're in for some criticism.

COCAINE See this used in a medical context and business will improve, but as an addictive drug sadness will follow.

COCOA *See also*: Drink. This comfy old drink is a sign you're about to fall madly in love. See yourself drinking it and you can guarantee you've got trustworthy friends.

CODE Coded messages are a warning against deceit. Don't trust your judgement so easily. Examine things carefully first.

COFFEE *See also*: Drink. This is a sign your finances are healthy and all's well in your domestic life. Drink bitter coffee and you will break with a friend. Sweet coffee spells some surprising good news. If you spill it you're in for some disappointments.

COINS *See also*: Money; Metals. Coins mean an unexpected gain, but it is a contrary dream in that the smaller the coins, the larger the gains will be. Gold coins are an omen of misfortune. Silver spells family troubles and nickel coins mean if you work hard you can make a fortune.

COLD *See also*: Weather. Not a good omen. Being cold yourself means someone is being disloyal to you. Trying to keep out of the cold is a sign things aren't going your way. Cold hands warn of money troubles. Cold legs are a warning not to get too depressed. If you dream of actually having a cold, you will soon feel much more secure.

COLLECTING Collecting anything—stamps, coins, etc.—means you will soon make new friends. Contribute to some kind of collection and you will soon be going on a long trip.

COLLEGE *See also*: School. Despite some petty annoyances, you will soon get some sort of promotion.

COLLISION *See also*: Driving. This is a warning to make up your mind about something, double quick. If you can't, then ask for advice—but stop dithering!

COLOURS/GEMS As a general rule, bright colours signify success. Individually: blue means some outside help will solve your problems; black means bad times to come; brown signifies money luck; red is a warning to curb your temper; green means travel or news from a distance; mauve means unhappiness; orange is a sign of unusually great success; purple is an omen for a good social life; yellow warns of setbacks before things take a turn for the better, and white is a sign of success. But see black at a funeral and you will be successful—especially in your love life.

Give or receive **amber** and it relates to money. You will either get it or lose it. Simply having amber is a warning to beware of obstacles between you and your lover.

Amethyst predicts some unexpected good news which will give peace and contentment.

Aquamarine indicates happiness in your love life. But if you lose it, be careful where you place your affections.

Coral represents friends. Wear it and you'll bump into an old flame. Simply see it and your social circle will widen.

Diamonds aren't as good an omen as you'd think. If you own them in reality they signify losses. If you don't, then dreaming of them means small profits. Find a diamond and there will be unhappiness in the family.

A colour change through **dye** is a warning that you must rely on your own judgement. Hair dye is a sign you will suffer through your own silliness. Dyed clothes means success socially. If you make a mess while dying clothes you can expect a very lavish present.

There will be difficulties over an inheritance if you see **emeralds**. Selling or giving them away means a split with a lover. Simply owning them is a sign of good fortune.

Finding, stealing, or being given a **gem** when you're not aware of what type it is indicates a period of unhappiness and depression. But lose one and you will make unexpected gains. A fake gem is a sure sign some vicious gossip is going around about you.

Jade is a sign of prosperity. Some difficult task which involves a lot of careful thought will come right for you.

See **jet** and sad news is on the way. Though not necessarily a bereavement.

A colourful **kaleidoscope**, and the pattern of your life is about to change rather swiftly, but it will create new interests and successes.

Opals are an omen of good luck to come.

Pearls suggest your wealth and social status are about to go to sky-high. But you are in for a few reverses if you see a broken string of pearls.

All the colours in a **rainbow** are a sign of good luck—even if you don't find that pot of gold at the end. Pleasant changes are on the way.

Wear **sapphires** and it's a warning not to be so impulsive. See them on others, and influential friends are about to give you a lift up the social ladder.

Zircons are a sign you have misplaced your affections. Is your partner really the right one?

COLUMN Influential people are on hand to help you achieve your ambitions.

COMB *See also*: Hair. See it with all its teeth and difficult business matters must be resolved soon. If there are teeth missing, some points still need to be cleared up. A metal comb means you will win at some sport, or even a bet on the horses. A plastic one is a warning not to be so vain and over-confident. Find a comb and there will be emotional problems. Lose one and one of your friendships will be strained. Buy one and you could be moving house. Combing your own hair means you must take action now to solve a problem that's worrying you.

Combing someone else's hair means you've misplaced your trust.

COMET See this heavenly body and you'll suddenly find you face opposition—apart from in your love life. Any affair will be a sparkling success.

COMMITTEE This is a sign of some kind of upheaval. Try to be philosophical about it. It will be for the best. Hold a meeting and you will be kicking yourself over a lost appointment. Attend one and you are at your decisive best.

COMMUNICATING Make or hear an **announcement** and an acceptable change in your life is coming soon. Receive an apology and you will be happy with your lover. Do the apologising, and an old friend is about to come back on the scene. Put up antennae or an aerial and you will recover something you thought was lost and gone for ever.

Dictate something and your current plans will prove complicated. Take dictation and an important improvement in business is coming.

Simply waiting for **news** suggests you need to change direction because you're not getting the results you'd hoped for. Receiving news is a dream of contrary. The worse the news the better things will be for you.

See a **satellite** and you should try thinking for yourself a bit more. Listen to advice by all means but make up your own mind.

Use the **telephone** and a minor tiff with your partner is going to explode into a major row. Answer it and the next few days will be beset with problems.

COMPASS This signifies the start of a generally upsetting period, unless the needle points north. That's a sign to carry on with things as they are and success will follow.

CONDUCTOR *See also*: Music. An orchestra conductor and you're in for a windfall. A bus conductor predicts foreign travel.

CONE See anything in this shape and it's a sign of sexual pleasure. What a steamy time you're in for!

CONFUSION If the main theme of your dream is confusion, it's a warning to stick to your guns. Changes would not be good right now.

Total **astonishment** can be a confusing emotion, and if you feel this, you're in line for promotion. If you astonish others, good news, probably about money, is on its way.

Find yourself in a **labyrinth** and it's an obstacle dream. Find your way out and your problems will be easily solved. Get lost or be frightened and some surprise opposition may force you to change direction.

See yourself solving a **puzzle** and you're finally in control of a complicated situation. An easy puzzle shows there are things wrong in your life that must be put right. A difficult one is a sign you are worrying unnecessarily.

CONGRATULATIONS *See also*: Communicating. A contrary dream. Receive them and you're going to need help. Give congratulations and things will be more successful for you.

CONSPIRACY Take part in a conspiracy and you are deluding yourself about something. Discover one and you are being compromised to the point where you must stand up for yourself.

CONVICT *See also*: Police/Prisons. This is a contrary dream. Your worries will soon disappear, unless the convict escapes. Then you must steel yourself for some ups and downs as someone is trying to block your moves. See yourself convicted in a dream and you will prosper.

COOKING *See also*: Food. This is a very good omen. It promises many material comforts. Everything that's currently worrying you will work out all right in the end.

COPPER *See also*: Metals. An old-fashioned copper pot means someone is going to help you get a job finished. A copper coin means a long-term problem will finally be resolved. Copper wire is an indication that you've got yourself involved in a peculiar situation. Watch it!

CORD Tie one and your own efforts will get you what you want. Untying it predicts trouble in your love life. Breaking a cord is a sign that you should cut loose in a relationship. Go on, break it off!

CORK *See also*: Sounds. Pulling a cork is a sign of good news.

CORN *See also*: Food. This is a very happy dream, particularly where your wallet is concerned. Harvest it, and it's a sign of good health.

CORNER *See also*: Places/Settings. This is an obstacle dream. It's a warning not to force an issue. If the corner is outside, say in a street, a new opportunity is going to change your life. Turn a corner and you will get a nice surprise.

CORONATION/CROWN Some small successes are on their way. A paper crown, and if you give in to

Plate 6 · The Colours of the Rainbow

that temptation you will feel degraded. A gold crown means unexpected honours. A royal one means a rise up the social scale. Dream of wearing a crown yourself and you are apt to be a bit untrustworthy at the moment.

CORPSE *See also*: Death. See a stranger's and it predicts a full and happy life. But dream of someone you know as a corpse and your relationship with a lover is about to break up. A number of them spell success in areas you never dreamed possible. The corpse of a woman indicates a friend will let you down badly. A man means you have got to face life's problems even though you don't want to at the moment.

COSMETICS For a woman this is a very good dream. But if a man dreams of women's cosmetics then he should change partners. The current lady in his life could ruin his reputation!

COT Sleep in one and some good changes are coming your way. If it breaks, you will be let down by someone you rely on.

COTTON Picking cotton or seeing it growing is a symbol of prosperity—but not until later in your life. Cotton wool means you have a secret and it should stay that way. Don't tell a soul.

COUCH *See also*: Furniture. You are in danger of lulling yourself into a false sense of security. Listen to the advice of trusted friends.

COUGHING *See also*: Ill-health. Check your insurance. This is a prediction of fire, theft or even flood.

COUNTING You may be taking on too much. Try and get someone else to do their share. Counting money predicts a pay rise.

COWARD A contrary dream. You will stand any test of character that life can throw at you if you dream of cowardice.

CRASH Any kind of crash heralds a big achievement. The bigger the crash, the more you'll achieve.

CRICKET *See also*: Games. A game of complex rules and seeing it means you feel bound by other people's rules. But now is the time to escape from them! A cricket ball is a sign to stop being impatient. A bat means petty jealousies.

CRIME Hear or witness a crime and circumstances

are about to change for the better. Commit one and you will succeed in something close to your heart. Get caught and it's a warning to keep a secret.

See a **burglar** in your own house and it's a warning to beware of treachery. If you catch him redhanded, you could be in for an inheritance.

See a **robber** at a bank and you're falling headover-heels for someone who isn't really worthy of your affection. Try not to make a fool of yourself.

Organise a **robbery** yourself and some inner conflict has you so anxious you'd best resolve it as soon as possible. Take part in a robbery and you are suffering from lack of self control. If you are the victim an unexpected gain is coming.

CRIPPLE See a cripple and someone is going to ask you for help. Give it. Your assistance will end up benefiting you. Dream you are crippled yourself and you can rely on others to come to your aid.

CROSSROADS This means exactly what you would imagine. You will soon have to make an important decision. Listen to advice.

CRUTCHES An obstacle dream—unless in the dream you discard them. If not, what you want will mean such a long struggle you'll begin to wonder if it's all worth it. Why bother, try something new.

CRYSTAL This means a quick solution to something that's been puzzling you. But your emotions are a bit fragile, aren't they? Broken crystal means rows and arguments. But any household articles such as glass signify a happy social life ahead.

CUP A full one means money. An empty one means reverses, so tighten your belt. A decorated or gift cup, and you can avoid making a fool of yourself in public by listening to the advice of a trusted friend.

CUPBOARD A straightforward dream, this. If it is bare, lean times are ahead. A full cupboard and things are looking up. Put things away in a cupboard and you can make up your losses but it will take a lot of hard work.

CURB This really is a warning to curb things moneywise. Stop spending so much, particularly on credit.

CURTAINS If they are opened, you will outwit someone who is against you. Hanging new ones is a sign of increased social goings-on. White curtains mean you will have to do an irksome task, I'm afraid. Coloured ones mean your standard of living will have to be more modest for a while.

CUSHION The plumper the cushion, the more problems you will soon face. But dream of shabby old

cushions and you can expect small gains.

CYCLONE *See also*: Weather. This is a warning not to take any risks for at least six months. If you see property damaged by a cyclone, at least your social life will be happy for a while.

AGGER You can expect surprise news. Dreaming of carrying a dagger is a warning to be a bit more tactful or you could land in a sticky situation. Seeing others with daggers is a sign you will win despite stiff opposition.

DAM *See also*: Sea/Water/Travel. Water in a dam warns not to do anything impulsive—especially where money is concerned.

DANCING Generally this is a good dream. If you are dancing, there are gains on the way. Dancing in public signals a meeting that could change your life. Alone it signals sadness. You may as well stop hoping, you won't get what you want.

DANGER Face up to danger in your dream and you will overcome your problems. Simply avoid it, and it's a sign to take care of your health.

DARKNESS/LIGHT A long-standing problem will finally be solved if you see a **beam** of light. Switch a light on and you will do well at work. Turn it off and it's a sign your lover is cheating on you. A bright light is a sign of good health. A dim one signifies sickness.

Darkness suggests a major emotional upset. But if you grope your way back to the light, work will go well and your love life will flourish.

Daylight predicts renewed hope.

See an **eclipse** and it's a sign you are bored with your sex life. If you can't liven things up you had better change partners.

An **electrical** power failure suggests you're wasting your energy on something. Try a change of direction.

A **lightning** flash predicts long-lasting good fortune.

Obstacles and delays are on the horizon if you dream of **night.** A really dark night is a sign you are hiding your resentment towards someone who harmed you in the past. A starlit night suggests you're going to make an interesting discovery.

Concentration will get you what you want if you see a searchlight. Watch it lighting up the sky and you could face stiff competition.

DARNING You will patch things up with a friend with whom you have quarrelled. See someone else darning and it's a warning against idle gossip. Someone you respect simply won't want to know if you blab.

DEAFNESS Lose your hearing and you'll soon be in the money. See others who are deaf and you will soon solve your present problems. If you're trying to make yourself understood to a deaf person then you're deluding yourself in a love affair, I'm afraid.

DEATH Death is rarely a bad omen. Dreaming of being dead means the end of your worries and the start of a new era in your life. Speak to someone who is dead and you will soon get some good news. Someone else's death can mean a birth or a small warning for you to slow down as you're taking on too much. The death of an absent friend predicts a wedding. Be aware of bereavement, and news of a birth, engagement or wedding is on the way. Happiness is on the cards if you see a dead person afloat.

You've simply got to control those passions of yours if you see yourself killed in an airplane disaster.

Dreaming of a **burial** is also an indication that you will soon get news of a birth or wedding. If you see yourself buried alive, it's a warning not to get involved in something you know isn't ethical.

A **cemetery** is a contrary dream. A well-kept one is an omen of happiness and prosperity. If it's run-down, you will have to face a few troubles first. Putting flowers on a grave is a sign you're a bit indecisive and far too sensitive.

A **coffin** isn't necessarily the bad sign it seems. Simply seeing one means you will marry soon or buy property. See yourself in it, and your life is going to change in some way. But an elaborate coffin could mean the death of a partner.

Ashes from a **cremation** mean an unexpected inheritance. See your own cremation and it's a warning to stop letting others influence you. You must rely on your own judgement. If you see others cremated, it's an omen of good health and a possible inheritance. Ashes in an urn suggest you're not very enthusiastic about a current project. Others are sure to misinterpret your actions if you see an **embalming**. Why not give whatever it is a miss?

Seeing a **funeral** is a contrary dream. Watch or attend one and news of a wedding or engagement is coming. Dream of your own funeral and your worries will soon lift.

A **grave** isn't a good sign. A new one spells a broken promise. A neglected one means heartaches to come. An open grave predicts sad news from a distance. Digging a grave is an omen you're going to be beaten by someone you don't even know is trying to compete with you.

A new **gravestone** is a sign of a new opportunity; an old one means you will renew a friendship.

A **hearse** suggests your load in life is about to lighten. Drive it, and you will soon get some added responsibility.

But it's a sign you're under a lot of stress if you **kill** someone in your dream. Kill your father and you're going to have to make some sacrifices. Kill your mother and you will soon be on the wrong end of a spiteful remark. Kill your lover and a row may soon end the relationship for good. Witness a killing and a change is coming which you are not going to like.

See someone killed by a **gun**, and it's time to put an unpleasant period of life behind you and start afresh. If you fire the fatal shot then you are in for a disappointment with the opposite sex.

Read an **obituary** and you will receive some good news.

A **shroud** suggests you're about to be invited to a party. A human skull and you don't trust someone close. An animal's skull predicts an embarrassing situation.

Everything will work in your favour if you see a **tomb**. But see yourself locked in and it's time to get a medical check-up.

An **undertaker** is also a contrary sign. You will soon hear news of a wedding or birth. A mourning veil means something is going to make you angry.

See yourself make your own **will** and it's a sign you're worrying unnecessarily about your health. Someone else's will predicts family problems.

DECEPTION Deceiving someone else or being deceived yourself in a dream is a sign of anxiety, worry, and loneliness. It also suggests complications or losses in your business life.

See yourself in **disguise** and it's a warning not to be so secretive—talk things over with a friend. See others in disguise and some plan you are plotting is

a touch unethical. Think again or you could be embarrassed about the outcome.

Tell a **lie** and your own silly behaviour is going to get you into trouble. If others tell lies about you then you're about to get help from an unexpected direction.

As in real life, any kind of **mask** is an attempt to conceal the truth. Deceit is afoot and so is jealousy. Watch out for them. Put on a mask yourself and it's a sign you and your partner are having problems. Take a close look at your relationship and try to work things out.

A dream of **unfaithfulness** is an omen of contrary. See someone unfaithful to you and they will shortly display their devotion. See yourself unfaithful and temptation is coming your way. You have been warned.

DECORATING A celebration of some sort is just round the corner.

DEFENDING Defending someone means you can be sure your trust is well placed. Defending yourself means don't force an issue. You can't count on everyone you think you can.

DEFORMITY Any deformity, whether your own or someone else's, means you're too apt to trust appearances. One of your friends is simply a snake in the grass!

DELIVERY Delivery of a letter means work will go well. A parcel is a sign one of your relationships is on a strange footing. Perhaps the other person wants to be more than just good friends? A telegram is a warning to watch those purse strings.

DERELICT Anything derelict is a warning to buck up your ideas! A bit of ingenuity should see you through.

DESERTION A contrary dream. Dream of deserting someone or something and you will lose a friend, thanks to stupid tittle-tattle. But if you are deserted you can count on your friends to rally round when you need them.

DESTROYING Break or destroy something that isn't yours and things won't go well for a while. Find something destroyed and you'll have an unexpected little triumph, probably at work.

DEVIL This means danger. See him and tasty temptations are coming your way—avoid them. Talk to him and the harm's probably been done already. See yourself as the devil and troubled times are coming.

DIAL A telephone dial means someone who owes

Plate 7 · Death and Rebirth

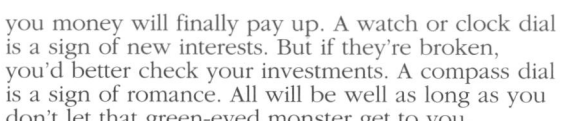

you money will finally pay up. A watch or clock dial is a sign of new interests. But if they're broken, you'd better check your investments. A compass dial is a sign of romance. All will be well as long as you don't let that green-eyed monster get to you.

DICTATION Give dictation and your current plans will prove complicated. Take it, and an important improvement in business is coming.

DICTIONARY *See also*: Reading/Writing. You're in danger of losing a friend over some silly row. Try not to be argumentative.

DIET *See also*: Food. See yourself on a diet and business will boom. A vegetarian diet and you have friends you can trust. If you're actually on a diet, the dream probably means you're hungry!

DIGGING Dig a ditch and it's a sign you're bored; try something novel and new. Digging a hole is a sign you should pay your debts as soon as possible. Digging a well signifies a row in the family. If the soil is soft and the digging easy, life will soon be the same. If the digging is slow-going, you'll have to struggle for a while.

DIPLOMA *See also*: School. For a man, this means mountains of money through his own efforts. For a woman, a diploma is a warning not to be so vain. Stop spending so much money on makeup and hair-dos. You look fine as you are!

DIPLOMAT Changes involving travel are on the way. Receive a diplomat and you should get ready for a major bit of good news.

DIRECTOR *See also*: Work. Get a place on the board and there will be good news in business or legal matters. Resign or lose your directorship and you are going to lose some status thanks to your own fool-ishness. Don't do anything you'd be ashamed of if others found out about it.

DIRECTORY *See also*: Reading/Writing. It's a good time for either a flutter or a flirtation. But don't go mad. Do nothing you will live to regret!

DIRT If you or your clothes are dirty it's a sign to get a medical check-up. Stepping or falling in dirt means a move is on the cards. Throwing dirt or having it thrown at you means someone you've confided in will try and use your secrets against you. Be ready to defend yourself.

DISASTER Disasters are contrary dreams. See one and you're in for some good luck. For those in love it spells wedding bells.

DISCOVERY Suddenly discover someone or some-thing and you could come in to an inheritance. If you're the one discovered, you'll soon be seeing new faces and places. Travel is on the cards.

DISEASE *See also*: Ill-health. This is a contrary dream and means happy times ahead. See someone you know ill, and it predicts good luck for them.

DISFIGURING A contrary dream. If you are disfig-ured, you are in for something wonderful. But if you see others disfigured, someone you trust is cheating you. Don't mix business with pleasure or do any deals with so-called friends.

DISH A silver one and an unexpected move will fol-low. A gold one shows you will achieve that ambi-tion. A full dish means good fortune. An empty one means you'll be marking time for a while. Broken or damaged dishes are a sign of family squabbles.

DISTANCES See people or action taking place a long distance away and you'll have to wait a while to get what you want. One particular obstacle from your past will have to be overcome first.
.
DIVING *See also*: Water. You'll soon be faced with a terrific temptation. If the water is clear all will be well. If it is choppy or murky, there will be some nasty results.

DIVORCE *See also*: Relationships. If you're married, this is a contrary dream. It means you can rely on your mate. If you are single, it's a warning you're misplacing your affections.

DOCKS *See also*: Sea/Water/Travel. See it from on board ship and a surprising turn of events is on the way. A dockyard means you now have enough money to start to save. Being alone on a dock signi-fies some kind of sadness.

DOCTORS/HOSPITALS *See also*: Ill-health. See a **doctor** and it's a good sign. A doctor forecasts improvement in all areas of your life.

Dream of a **hospital** and it's a sure sign you're feeling depressed. A field hospital, MASH-style, sug-gests you're missing someone who is far away. Visit a hospital or work in one and some surprise news is coming.

Take **medicine** and your troubles are trivial. Administer it and after a lot of effort you will enjoy success.

A **midwife** suggests a secret will be uncovered.

Help her and good times are coming. See yourself as a midwife and someone is out to stab you in the back. Make sure you keep it to the wall.

If you are single and see a **nurse**, then marriage is on the cards. If you are married, family unity is predicted. If the nurse is looking after you, it suggests you are feeling a bit unwanted at present. See yourself as a nurse, and some advantageous news is about to arrive.

If it's an **obstetrician**, it's a sign you are edgy over an argument with a loved one. Calm down or there will never be a reconciliation. If you see him helping with the birth of a child, you're about to make a mistake at work.

A **stethoscope** says you're about to achieve something unusual and win a large pat on the back.

A **surgeon** is a sign you could be about to change jobs.

Undergo **surgery** and your lifestyle is about to change dramatically. Watch an operation and some surprise news will arrive. A heart transplant is a sign your plans will succeed. Brain surgery means you still have to overcome a major obstacle to get what you want.

If a doctor examines the results of an **X-ray**, you are confident about your future. See yourself X-rayed and good news is coming from a distance. A chest X-ray predicts a new friendship with someone of the opposite sex.

DOLLS *See also*: Childhood/Children. A paper doll and there's a rival somewhere in your love life. A plastic one is an omen of jealousy, probably from your partner, and a rag doll is a sign that what you're experiencing now will prove useful—even if it doesn't feel that way. A walking or talking doll means don't fight with new friends. A wooden doll is a sign you are unhappy. Buy a doll and a small profit is on the way.

DOMINOES Play this and don't take any risks for a while. See them in their box and it's a sign to put off buying anything expensive—no matter how much of a bargain you think it is!

DOORS If there's a **door bell** and you push it you will meet an exciting new friend. Hear it ringing and a new pursuit will soon entrance you.

A **door knob** and you can expect an unusual stroke of luck. Now might be a very good time for a flutter.

See an **entrance** to a building and you're feeling insecure. Try and mug up on things and you'll feel more confident.

Hinges spell family problems if they're rusty. A squeaky one and some malicious gossip is about to do the rounds about you.

Hear someone **knocking** on a door and fortune is about to smile on you. Do it yourself, and you're feeling nostalgic. But don't try and recreate the past. Going back is never quite the same.

Closed or **locked** doors are a sign you are regretting missed opportunities. You can't change things so don't waste time on regrets.

An **open** door predicts your hopes will soon be realised.

A **revolving** door is a sure sign you are in a rut. Try something new. You never know, you might prefer it.

Some shock news is about to arrive if you dream of a **trap door**. Don't let it panic you into any hasty decisions.

See more than one door and you will soon have a choice of good opportunities.

DRAWERS A closed one means you're going to have to outwit a rival for something you want. An open one suggests a new opportunity, and a full drawer predicts it's the right time to start a new venture. An empty drawer is a sign of hard work on the way, and a locked one suggests a few unforeseen problems. But patience will overcome them.

DRILL An electric one means you won't be able to shake off your depression for a while. See a hand drill and you're being a bit selfish at the moment, aren't you? Buy one and it's a sign not to shirk at work. It would mean promotion in the end.

DRINK **Alcohol** in moderation is usually a sign of success, but taken in excess—then look out. You could be getting into a situation where you have to make an embarrassing apology. Give up booze and it's a dream of contrary: don't get over-confident. But if you abstain out of necessity rather than choice, then success and prosperity are round the corner.

Drink **beer** and you could be about to lose money. But if others are drinking it, the loss will only be minor. Flat beer is a warning not to get involved in gossip. It will only backfire on you.

Romance won't go well though if you dream of drinking from a bottle.

Buy **brandy** and some surprise good news is on the way. Offer it round, and it's a cue to control your passions again. Simply see it and it's a warning not to be so materialistic. You could lose valuable friends.

Unexpected wonderful things are ahead for you if you drink from a **can**. Open one and you are going to lose out in love to a rival. Throw away an empty drink can and it's a warning that a serious disaster is round the corner. Take care and you can avoid it.

As well as showing you have been left out of something, **champagne** is a bad sign for your love life. There could be a row because you're spending too much. If the champagne is at a wedding, all will be well in the end.

See **cider** and it's a warning not to spill your secrets.

See someone **drunk** in a pub and you're in poor physical shape. Get drunk yourself and a few small gains are on their way. A drunk in the street suggests you've been spending too much. A singing drunk is a sure sign you haven't got enough confidence in yourself.

Fizzy drinks—and exciting times are coming; sweet ones predict a passionate affair.

Drink **gin** and you're in for a pleasant surprise. See others swigging it and changes are going to cause confusion.

See an empty **glass** and it's likely you're being a bit too vain at the moment.

If you're single a **hangover** is a warning against casual sex. If you're married it's a sign family worries will soon lift.

Drink any kind of **juice** and someone is going to help sort out your money worries. Serve it, and you will be asked for a loan. If it's orange juice a short-but-oh-so-sweet love affair is in the air. Pineapple and you will do well at work.

Lemonade is a sign your popularity is about to take an upturn.

Milk means you will soon have success. Cow's milk is an omen of good health. Goat's and you could be in for promotion. Mother's milk is one of the luckiest omens of all. Long-lasting happiness is about to be yours. Sour milk predicts setbacks, and if you spill it

you're setting your sights too high, I'm afraid.

Drink warm or hot **water** and you'll lose money or status. But cold water is a sign you will achieve something through your own knowledge. You're in for some good luck. Spill or throw it and you're going to have to control that temper.

Red **wine** reflects your cheerful optimism, while white shows sincere friendships. Sweet wine and you're in for some romantic successes. Dry and it's a warning against excess. Pour it and an unexpected hiccup will upset you. Drink it and good health is assured.

DRIVING See yourself in the driving seat and it's a warning not to gamble for at least a few weeks. See someone else doing the driving and you will have a stroke of money luck.

Put your foot down to speed up and you will achieve your aims through your own efforts. If the **accelerator** is jammed or out of control beware of a bad habit. It could turn into a vice.

A car **accident** is a warning not to travel more than necessary for a while. But any kind of crash heralds a big achievement. The bigger the crash, the more you'll achieve.

Any dream involving a **bicycle** shows there's an important decision to be made. Think carefully before coming to any conclusions. If you see a cyclist going uphill in your dreams or speeding down it, you will make progress and favourable changes.

Put on the **brakes** in a car and you will get an offer that means more responsibility. Noisy or failed brakes mean you must think very carefully before accepting a new offer. There could well be a hidden snag.

See yourself driving a **car** for the first time in a long while and you're in control of your life.

Come to a **crossroads** and it means exactly what you would imagine. You will soon have to make an important decision. Listen to advice.

The faster an **engine** in your dream the more trials and tribulations coming your way. But if the engine stops you can count on success. A broken one means delays thanks to someone else's interference, but you will get there in the end.

See an **engine exhaust** and you will soon be wielding a bit of power.

See a **fork** in the road and you will soon have to make a decision.

Plate 8 · The Drowning Dream

Spot a **hitch-hiker** while you're driving and it's a warning to be a bit more self-reliant. If you pick a hitch-hiker up it suggests it's time to be more careful with your money. Most of all, don't lend any.

Driving a **motorbike** suggests problems at work and if you fall off your financial situation looks sticky. A motorcycle race is a sign you will get surprise help to solve a problem.

See a straight or broad **road** and good steady progress is predicted. But bumpy, narrow, or twisting and obstacles will have to be overcome. Road signs mean small but pleasant changes.

See the ultimate driving luxury, a **Rolls Royce**, and a new offer will turn out better than you think. Grab it with both hands.

See a **shunt**—more of a collision than a crash—and it's a warning to make up your mind about something double quick. If you can't, then ask for advice but stop dithering.

Change a **tyre** and you're about to get an unexpected demand on your resources. A blow-out is a warning someone is jealous of you. Buy a new tyre and your worries will soon disappear.

Drive any kind of **wagon** and it's a warning not to make any hasty purchases. If it's loaded you're about to get a surprise windfall.

DROUGHT You are in for a tough time. But it won't last long and your worries will soon be over.

DROWNING Not a good omen for business matters. But if you, or the person drowning, are saved, you will soon recoup any losses.

DRUGS Dream of being drugged and someone is so jealous of you they are trying to force you into making mistakes. Drugs used in a medical way suggest a pay rise is coming. Used for kicks they are a sign someone is trying to lead you astray. Selling or giving drugs suggests you should change your friends. They're not as honest as you.

DRUMS *See also*: Sounds. Some smashing successes will be yours. Play them yourself and they'll be simply wonderful. Drumsticks with no drum mean you must be absolutely above board in everything you do. Don't try and cheat the tax man. He'll catch up with you in the end!

DRUNK *See also*: Drink. See someone drunk in a pub and it means you're in poor physical shape. Get drunk yourself and a few small gains are on their way. A drunk in the street suggests you've been spending too much. A singing drunk is a sure sign you haven't got enough confidence in yourself.

DUNGEON *See also*: Police/Prisons. An obstacle dream. If you were stuck in the dungeon, you should try and change your plans. Escape and things will go well but only after a lot of hard work.

DUST *See also*: Tidiness. Dream of dust and you're in for a time of petty quarrels and minor embarrassments. But clean it off and these irritations will disappear. A cloud of dust is an omen of a problem on the horizon.

DWARF Dream of being or seeing a dwarf and your troubles will soon disappear as if by magic.

DYE *See also*: Colours/Gems; Hair. A colour change through dye means you must rely on your own judgement. Dyed clothes means success socially. If you make a mess while dying clothes, you can expect a very lavish present.

DYKE *See also*: Water. You're clearly worried about taking on a responsibility you think will prove too much. Discuss it with a friend or, better still, a professional.

DYNAMITE *See also*: Sounds. Unexploded dynamite suggests one of your worries either won't develop or will prove groundless. See or hear it explode and it's a warning to abandon any new plan—it won't work.

DYNAMO You've been burning the candle at both ends. Slow down or you'll break down!

ARRINGS *See also*: Jewellery. Gold earrings spell some temporary setbacks are on the way. Silver ones suggest you are being judged a bit harshly by others. Diamonds or other gems in the earrings mean you are a bit below par, or even lazy right now. Buy earrings and your ideas are a bit too extravagant. Lose them and the road is rocky, financially. Finding earrings is a warning not to have that flutter. Wear them and you're not pulling your weight at work.

EARTH Lying on it predicts sad news. Being buried in it is a sign you can afford that flutter. You're going to win! Kissing the earth is a forecast of emotional dramas and disappointments.

EARTHQUAKE You must expect a complete change of circumstances. You could move and change jobs and switch partners. Phew! But it will all be for the good.

EASEL *See also*: Pictures/Painting. See an artist with it and life will be plain sailing sooner than you think.

EASTER *See also*: Religion. An Easter parade suggests temptation is on the way. Try not to give in. Celebrate Easter and good times are coming.

EATING *See also*: Food. Eat standing up and you're being a bit slapdash. Trying to do things in too much of a hurry. Eat with your hands and it's a sign you're fed up with your mate. Secret eating means a craving for the past. Why? You can't bring it back. Eating alone means you will soon lose a friend. Eating at home is a sign of new projects round the corner; in a restaurant means all is not well in your love life. Try and sort it out before there's trouble.

ECHO *See also*: Sounds. Your own means you're in for a strange experience—probably with the opposite sex. Another kind of echo is a sign you will get a big 'yes' from a proposal you put forward; it could be marriage or a business proposition.

EDITOR *See also*: Reading/Writing. You're letting things slide too much. Buck up and pay attention to detail. See yourself as an editor and you must expect delays in projects.

ELASTIC This is a sign you will have to stretch yourself to the limit soon. But don't worry—you'll enjoy it. Snapped elastic or rubber bands mean someone is going to ask for your help.

ELECTION *See also*: Government. You will have quick success with some current plans.

ELECTRICITY *See also*: Darkness/Light. An electric shock says some surprise news is coming. Turn on the electricity and a favour you have done in the past can now be called in. Turn it off and it's a sign you need a holiday. A live wire means sudden opposition to one of your plans. Don't try and force the issue. A fuse means you're about to lose or mislay something.

ELF See an elf, goblin, or the like and your love life could soon hit a rocky patch. You also have a rival at work.

ELOPEMENT *See also*: Weddings. A contrary dream. If you elope you could soon be splitting with your partner. See others eloping and someone will try and tempt you to make a sentimental journey. Don't, it will only upset you.

EMBALMING *See also*: Death. Others are sure to misinterpret your actions. Why not give whatever it is a miss?

EMBASSY You'll soon be mixing with influential folk. If you are on official business there, you have to go all out for what you want. It won't come to you.

EMBRACE *See also*: Sexuality. Dream of being embraced and you'd better temper that impulsive streak. It will land you in trouble. Embracing others or watching others embrace means a few family rows are on the horizon.

EMBROIDERY Do this yourself and it's an omen for happiness. See others embroider and someone is out to deceive you.

EMIGRATING *See also*: Foreign Places/People. A signal to tighten your belt. Unexpected demands on your cash are coming.

EMPLOYMENT *See also*: Work. Employment is a contrary dream. If you dream of being out of a job you will shortly have a choice of opportunities. Offer jobs to others and you're getting a bit over-confident about something. It could prove expensive. See a boss you get on well with and some surprise news will soon embarrass you. See your direct boss and it's a sign you are far too impressionable. Try and make your own decisions. An angry employer means you have misplaced your trust in someone.

END *See also*: Time. The end is a symbol of new beginnings for you. But a dead end is a sign you are going nowhere in life. Try a different route for a change.

ENEMY A contrary dream. You can rely on loyal friends if you see someone you know as your enemy. Fight with your enemies and you're about to make some pretty poor decisions. Beat them and it means you're facing a problem which you still can't solve.

ENGAGEMENT *See also*: Relationships. You're in for a rough ride romantically. Try and be philosophical. Put it all down to experience. See an engagement ring and you have rivals out there somewhere.

ENGRAVING *See also*: Metals. A metal engraving and you are about to change jobs. On wood, and plenty of parties are on the horizon. In fact, any kind of engraving is a good sign.

ENTRANCE *See also*: Doors. An entrance to a building and you are feeling insecure. Try and mug up on things and you'll feel more confident.

ENVELOPE If it's empty you will soon snap out of

the doldrums. Sealed envelopes are a sign of just how busy you are. Put a letter in one and you'll find something you thought you'd lost.

ENVY Envy what someone owns and your own wealth will increase. Envy their good looks and there will be a row with your lover soon. Dream of being envied and you will soon be appreciated as never before.

EPAULETS *See also*: Uniform. For a woman, this means a sizzling love affair. For a man, promotion or a pay rise.

EPITAPH Reading one is a sign your problems aren't as bad as they seem. If the epitaph is faded, happy family news is coming.

EQUATOR *See also*: Heat. Cross this and life will change completely for you soon. See it but fail to cross it, and it's a sign you're dithering over something. Be brave, make that decision.

ERUPTION Any kind of eruption, such as a volcano, predicts things are about to change for the better.

ESCALATOR As with other dreams, up indicates success and down means reverses. But if you dream of going down on an escalator you can succeed in the end if you are determined about it.

ESCAPE An ominous dream. Watching an escape from a prison or the like means you haven't been very scrupulous lately and will lose money as a result. Take in part of one and you won't achieve those ambitions of yours. Escaping from something like fire or water means you will make a hasty decision but it will be the right one. Fail to escape and you've got a fight on your hands over something soon but you will win in the end.

ESTATE *See also*: Home. A lavish estate is a warning to stop trying to keep up with the Joneses. They can afford it, you can't!

EVACUATION Any kind of evacuation is a warning not to gamble. No risky ventures and definitely no betting or bingo.

EVENING *See also*: Darkness/Light. A moonlit evening is a sign your love life is in a tangle. A dark one and you must stop being so childish. No one thinks it's funny any more. A fine evening means a contented old age.

EVIL Evil or evil spirits suggests you should change directions. Your current plans simply won't work.

EXAM *See also:* School; Success. Fail and it's a warning your ambitions are aimed a bit too high and you should try changing course. Pass, and all your hopes will be fulfilled.

EXECUTION *See also:* Death. Whatever it is you are planning will turn out far more expensive than you thought. Dream of being condemned to execution and you will get good news over a health problem.

EXERCISE A good luck dream if you enjoyed the exercise. If it left you fagged out, then don't force an issue – you will regret it.

EXHAUST You will soon be wielding a bit of power if you see an engine exhaust.

EXPLORER A sign you're afraid of your future. If you are the explorer, it shows what a sense of adventure you have. Go on, use it!

EXPRESS See yourself on an express train and you're about to offend the boss. See one pass by and you've just missed a good opportunity. That will teach you to pay more attention.

EYEBROWS *See also:* Hair. Denis Healey-style bushy eyebrows suggest money is coming your way. Arched eyebrows mean a surprise for you. Thin ones predict a business disappointment. If your eyebrows fall out or you're worried about them, then your lover is two-timing you.

EYELASHES *See also:* Hair. Long, lustrous lashes predict a red-hot love affair. False ones mean you will discover a secret and need advice on what to do about it. See someone with no eyelashes and you must give nothing away. Keep those confidences to yourself.

 ACE Dream of your own face in a mirror and one of your secrets is about to be discovered. See a happy, smiling face and life will be the same. See a sad face and troubles are ahead. The face of someone you know signals a celebration. A stranger's face foretells upheavals and travel. See a man's face and it means you're confident about the future. See a woman's and it shows you have doubts.

FACTORY *See also*: Work. Dream of a factory and you will have a struggle on your hands but success in the end. See yourself working in a factory and some good changes are on the way.

FAIR Dream of being at a fair and your social life is about to take off. See others going and things are about to change for the better.

FAIRY Your wishes will come true when you least expect it if you dream of fairies.

Plate 9 · The Falling Dream

FALLING Dreaming of falling is very common. It is a symbol of fear in real life—perhaps of failing at work or in your love life. Falling often expresses a need to let yourself go more and enjoy life more. Dreaming of falling can often stem from isolation: however successful you are, you can still feel isolated, and this dream is common among professional men and women. Falling in the dream is an unfulfilled need for support and affection. It's a dream that often occurs when the dreamer is feeling misunderstood or not accepted in a situation.

Dream of falling a long way and you can expect quite severe reverses in life in general. Fall a short distance and things won't be so bad. Land without hurting yourself and your set-backs will only be temporary. Get hurt and you're in for a hard time, I'm afraid. If you see others falling, you can count on promotion at work.

Fall out of **bed** and it's a sign you're being over-sensitive. Fall on the **floor** and it's a warning not to trust one of your friends. Fall into **water** and you can expect money troubles.

Free-fall with a **parachute** and your love life will run smoothly. But if it fails, someone you were relying on is about to let you down.

FAME *See also:* Success. Dream of being famous and you're trying for something that's really out of your reach. Try and cut your cloth to suit you more. Dream of a famous person and it's a sign to keep trying. Help is at hand from a surprise source.

FAMILY *See also:* Relationships. If it's your own family, there's important news on the way. A large family shows you are in a comfortable state money-wise but you might soon have to make a few sacrifices. Abandon a family and there will also be money problems.

Individual family members all have their meanings:

An **aunt** on your mother's side means a family connection will benefit you. If the aunt is on your father's side, try not to be so impatient.

See an older **brother** and you're about to do something brave. A younger one heralds a family spat. If you get on well you will shortly split with a friend. If the brother behaves badly, good luck is in store.

See any kind of **cousin** and your worries will fade away.

A **daughter** is a sign of important news to come. A naughty daughter signifies an unsettled future.

Dream of your **father** and it's a sign to take advice from an older person. If he's healthy, you will benefit from someone's support. If he's ill, you must stop losing faith in yourself. If your father dies in your dreams, you're about to take on a responsibility that will gain you respect.

Grandparents are a symbol of protection and security. See yourself as a grandparent and you can achieve high ambitions.

See yourself with a **husband** when in fact you are single and a serious lovers' tiff is round the corner. Dream of your own husband and it won't be married bliss for a while. See someone else's husband and it's a sign you aren't taking things seriously enough.

See your own **mother** and it's a sign you and your mate are going through a rough patch—but it won't last, as long as you talk it through and don't allow things to fester. See your mother crying and it suggests you're over-anxious about something. See your mother-in-law and you are in for some family rows. Argue with her and an interesting new friend is on the horizon.

For a man a **sister** is a sign of emotional security. For a woman, domestic tiffs.

To have a **son** in your dreams signifies success. If he's unmarried you have problems to face. Married, and you're in for some family worries.

FAN *See also:* Heat. This dream is about your love life. Fan yourself and you are in for an embarrassing entanglement. See others fanning and you are playing the field too much. Dream of losing a fan and you will lose your mate by being too much of a flirt.

FARM *See also:* Animals. A well-kept farm in a dream is a sign of good health and money coming in. Own the farm and your bosses at work are going to help you succeed. Work on it and you'll get an advantage your colleagues don't have—a new office perhaps? A run-down farm means loss of money or property.

FASHION *See also:* Clothes. Dream of glossy fashion mags or models and you've been working too hard. Try and have some fun.

FAT *See also:* Food. The fatter you or others are in your dream, the fewer your worries will be. Eat fat and your love life will go well. Cook with it, and you will make money in business.

FEAR *See also:* Anger/Confrontation. If you are afraid in your dreams you will recognise your difficulties and find the courage to conquer them.

Any feeling of **anxiousness** is in fact a sign that your worries will soon be over.

A simple feeling of **apprehension** is telling you to stop worrying. It will never happen—so don't be tempted to change your plans.

Flee in fear and become a **fugitive** and a violent family row is looming. But keep your temper and an argument could clear the air. Dream of helping or simply seeing a fugitive and a cash shock is coming.

Hide, and one of your schemes will give you regrets later—and deep down you know it, don't you? Dream of hiding something and it's a warning not to be so secretive about your problems. Confide in someone and they may be able to help you.

FEAST *See also:* Food. Dream of having a feast and difficulties are on the horizon. Prepare one and someone else is going to get what you want.

FERRY *See also:* Sea/Water/Travel. Dream of travelling on or seeing a ferry and your efforts will be rewarded, probably at work.

FEVER *See also:* Ill-health. Dream of your own fever and you're worrying too much. It will never happen, so try and enjoy life. Fever in others signals exciting times ahead.

FIELD *See also:* Places/Settings. Dream of green healthy fields and you will be happy and make money. Dry fields predict reverses. A newly ploughed field means you can get what you want but will have to make a few sacrifices.

FIGHTING *See also:* Anger/Confrontation. Dream of fighting and there are a few people against you at the moment, aren't there? But if you win, they won't be able to do you any harm. See others fighting and it's a sign you're squandering your time and money on pleasures. Try and knuckle down to some hard work.

FILE Dream of a file and you'd better spell things out clearly to others or it could be the cause of vicious gossip. They'll get the wrong end of the stick. Filing metal means some kind of reconciliation.

FILM Dream of camera film and it's a sign you've made a spiteful remark to someone who is fond of you. Watching a film at the cinema means new opportunities are on the way. Try them, they are important job-wise. A broken film means your job is secure and if you try you could even get promotion.

FINGERNAILS Dream of long nails and you'll have trouble with the opposite sex. Short nails mean a surprise gift. Dream of varnishing your nails and it's a warning not to be impulsive: it could have scandalous results! A broken nail means you will be discontent with life for a while. Cut your nails and your prestige will soar. Bite your nails and you should get a medical check-up.

FINGERPRINTS See fingerprints and a few money troubles are on the way. Dream of being fingerprinted and you will get help from a friend.

FIRE Fire is an important element in dreams, just as it is in reality. Fire warms and purges and it can hurt if you get too close to it. So it's a powerful symbol indicating a period of renewal, but also a certain amount of painful reflection. Build or stoke a fire and an amorous adventure is on the cards. Put out a fire and you will overcome your problems. Dream of setting fire to something and you must learn to control that temper.

See fire **burn** you and it spells trouble. But there's good news on the way if it didn't. A house or building on fire means a close friend or relation is going to need your help.

If you are burned on your hands or feet it's a lucky sign. You can risk a flutter. But don't let it break the bank.

Any kind of burning is a positive sign, although it depends on what is actually burning. If it's wood, it shows what a lively mind you've got. Incense means you will get sympathy from an unexpected source.

You'll be in the money if you see smoke coming from a **chimney**. But if you don't know the source, you're heading for a disappointment.

See a **fire engine** and you will have an important stroke of money luck. Dream of driving one and you will have a lucky escape from something embarrassing.

A **fire escape** says you are in too much debt. Try and pay off those credit cards.

Peace and contentment are coming if you see a **fireplace.**

A flickering **flame** shows you are about to be disappointed. A red flame is a signal to control your temper. A bright flame is a sign of happiness.

The fires of **hell** are a bad omen. Bad luck, illness, and money losses are predicted. But escape from hell and the future looks brighter.

Strike a **match** and a pay rise is on the cards.

FIREWORKS The more spectacular the display, the longer it will take you to achieve some cherished dream.

FISH/FISHING Dream of fish swimming in clear water and you will get money and power. If the fish are biting, a useful bit of knowledge is coming to you. Eating or cooking fish means any current projects will turn out well. Bait a fish hook and a sizzling, sexy affair is predicted. Dead or rotting fish mean a bumper pay rise.

Anchovies spell luck in love, at bingo, on the horses, or anything you try your hand at.

You are wasting your talents if you dream of **angling**. And you must resist the temptation to compromise your ethics. Catch a fish and good news will follow. If you don't make a catch, beware of evil.

Watch out for business rivals or even rivals in love if you see a **crab**. Cooking one is a good sign if you want to place a few bets—but don't put your shirt on it.

Eels are a sign you're about to change jobs. But take care, you might not get on with your new boss. A dead eel is a sign you are getting the upper hand over someone who's trying to stir things up for you.

If you are single, a **goldfish** is a sign you'll marry money. If you are a married woman, it spells divorce. Goldfish in a bowl are an omen of money on the way.

A fish **hook** shows you have a secret passion for someone you have known for a long time.

Put on an act and problems will arise if you dream of **jellyfish**. Be yourself. You can't pretend for ever.

A live **lobster**, and some irritating little difficulties are about to thwart you. Serve, eat, or cook it and someone is about to repay a loan, or you will find something you had lost.

A half-fish, half-woman **mermaid** relates to your love life and the exact meaning depends on the atmosphere of the dream. Pleasant, and things will go well. But a feeling of confusion and you're in for a disappointment.

Mussels, if you eat them, show your popularity is about to increase. Collect them and a period of contentment is just around the corner.

See a big trawling **net** and it's a sign you're squandering money. A small one suggests a bumpy period in day-to-day life. See a net laid out to dry and your health is excellent. Throw one into the water and you're being unfairly suspicious of a new friend.

Dream of an **octopus** and it shows just what a spirit of adventure you have. But see one killed and you're taking a very moral stand over something. If an octopus attacks, trouble is in store.

In its shell, an **oyster** is a sign of jealousy that could cause arguments with your mate. If it has a pearl inside you're about to make a worrying mistake at work. Buying oysters is a warning to watch your health. Eat them and the family simply won't understand something you're involved with. It's bound to cause tension.

Fresh **salmon** and a lovers' tiff can be made up if you really care. See it in a tin, and you're in for a bit of an adventure.

Sardines in a tin are a sign you're trying to hide feelings of resentment. Try talking them over with someone. Eat fresh ones and someone is jealous of you.

Things will improve if you eat **scallops**. Raw, they predict a surprise trip.

It's a sign you have made a false friend if you're aware of fish **scales.**

A few pleasant social events are around the corner if you see **shrimps**.

See a toothy **shark** and you could be in danger from your friends. Be extra careful, especially where money is concerned.

Spot a big fish or a **whale** on the end of a harpoon and a pay rise is on the cards. If you're injured by it, then it could spell financial disaster. Don't overspend.

FLAGS Dream of a flag flying and you can expect a few party invites. Raising a flag means money on the way. Lowering a flag means money luck as well. A display of flags means someone out there fancies you. I wonder who it is?

FLASH Any kind of flash in a dream means a momentous change in lifestyle thanks to a really creative idea you come up with.

FLEET *See also*: Sea/Water/Travel. Dream of a fishing fleet in harbour and life will be peaceful. If it puts out to sea, worries are on the horizon. A naval fleet means you will be released from some tiresome responsibility. A fleet of sailing ships means you will get another chance to try something you thought you had failed in.

FLOATING *See also*: Sea/Water/Travel. Dream of floating and you'll soon see sparkling success. Everything is going your way. Use a plastic or rubber float and it means a reconciliation.

FLOOD Dream of a small flood and your troubles will be short-lived. A raging flood in full force spells worries. Life will be hard for a while. If you're swept away in the flood, you're being used by someone of the opposite sex, don't trust them. Escape from the flood and someone will help you overcome your problems.

FLOOR Dream of a wooden floor and someone will show you sympathy. A marble one means trouble in your love life. A tiled floor is a sign not to be so easily influenced. Try standing on your own two feet. A clean floor means an old flame will reappear. A dirty one means you will get that money back which you thought you had lost. Washing or sweeping a floor is a sign to be more cautious in everything.

FLORIST *See also*: Flowers. Dream of a florist and if you are single a delicious new amour is round the corner. If you are married, it could mean divorce, or at least separation.

FLOUR *See also*: Food. Dream of flour and it's a good sign. You will be healthy, strong and life will be comfortable. Cooking with flour signals good news in the family.

FLOWERS Dream of fresh, colourful flowers and you will soon be happier than ever before. Dead or wilted flowers are a warning that you're getting overconfident and even careless. You will come a cropper if you don't look out. Artificial flowers show you are under pressure to compromise your principles. Don't! Wild flowers are a sign you're in for a bit of an adventure.

Flowers in **bloom** say you should beware of a secret. It could spell danger.

A happy social event is on the cards if you see a fresh **bouquet**. A withered one spells illness or even death. Receive a bouquet and you're in for some pleasure. Give one and you needn't worry about your lover. They're as loyal as they come.

Buttercups show what a delicate state you're in emotionally. Money-wise you need to calm down and take stock. You can solve your problems if you listen to advice. Buy buttercups and your emotional life will be plain sailing.

Fake flowers spell jealousy on the part of a friend.

A neat **garden** without flowers predicts life will be comfortable. Apart, that is, from the odd emotional hiccup. But a neglected or overgrown one signals troubled times ahead. A beautiful garden in full bloom is a spectacular dream. Both love and money will be yours. What more could you want?

A **garland** of flowers says either good news is on the way or you are about to have some short-lived pleasures. Having a garland on your head is a symbol of success although you will be on the rough end of a lot of back-biting once you get to the top.

See yourself in a **greenhouse** and it forecasts success and a star-studded future.

Dreaming of white **heather** is one of the luckiest dreams you could possibly have. Any other kind is an excellent omen for all areas of your life.

See or smell **lavender** and things will go well with the opposite sex. Perhaps even a new affair is round the corner for you.

A **meadow** full of flowers and your happiness and trust in your mate are being reciprocated. A newly mown meadow suggests you're depressed about something.

If it's an **orchard** in bloom it's a sign of good luck.

Pull **petals** from a flower or see them fall and you are in for a love split or about to lose a good friend. You will be sad, but if you put it down to experience it will help in future.

Pick **roses** and great happiness is predicted. Give them to someone and it's a sign someone loves you very much. Receive them and socially you will be a stunning success.

A glass **vase** says you're being indecisive. China is a sign of good luck. Full of flowers, a vase suggests your finances are about to improve dramatically.

Weeds in a garden are a sign you're keeping bad company and it's ruining your reputation. Dig them out and every cloud on your horizon will have a silver lining.

FLYING *See also*: Aeroplane. As with falling, this is a very common dream indeed. Its interpretation is largely sexual. Flying is a kind of boast about sexual powers. Dreaming of flying tends to indicate that you're unhappy and not in control of your life. Your ambitions are not being fully realised. Self-esteem is low, and dreaming of flying is often making up for lack of sexual experience.

The flying represents your **ambitions**. Fly successfully and you can expect to achieve them without too much difficulty. Trying and failing to fly higher means you're hoping for too much. Why not pick an easier goal?

A surprise proposition is on the way from a friend or colleague if you see a **glider**. Listen to advice before making up your mind.

Piloting a plane can also suggest a stimulating new project will keep you busy at work. If it's a jumbo jet, you are in an irritable frame of mind. Don't be impatient or your work will suffer. And if you see yourself at the cockpit of a fighter plane your confidence is high.

A **rocket** is a sign of short-lived success. See one explode and it spells family fortune.

FOG *See also*: Weather. Dream of fog at sea and your love life is in trouble. Fog on land means a business dilemma that will need a lot of patience to handle. Things will turn out in the end if the fog disperses in the dream.

FOOD Dreaming of food is generally a good sign. But if there isn't enough to go round in the dream then you must do some careful planning to make sure you don't go short. Selling food means money luck. Buying it means a family celebration.

Eat **almonds** and you will be lucky and have a long life. Buy them and you will triumph over your enemies.

See **aspic** and your social life is about to take off.

A scrummy **avocado** is a delicious omen for your love life. Having an avocado means you will get a

marriage proposal. Buying them means you will be loved by many people. Eating them spells a visit from a loved one.

Eat **bacon** and your prosperity will continue. Buy it or see it rank and you should have a medical check-up. If you see it frying, a surprise gift is coming.

Raw **beef** is a warning to keep yourself to yourself: don't give away secrets. To turn down a serving of beef means you will soon be needing help. But if you eat and enjoy it business will boom.

Hard work will bring its rewards if you see **beets**. Eating them means your love life will go from strength to strength.

Biscuits are a good omen if you eat them. You will soon win a prize or a distinction which you really deserve. Hand out biscuits and you've been over-indulging a bit lately, haven't you?

You may well be in for a win on the horses if you see **bread**. At least some kind of gamble will prove successful. Eating it is a sign of good health and fitness. If you make bread, a long-distance friend will send you some news. White bread is a sign you're feeling fragile and over-sensitive. Brown bread means your friends will rally round when you need them. A bread roll, and, sadly, your current quiet life is about to come to an end.

For lovers, dreaming of **butter** is a sign of marriage. For others it means welcome guests will soon be coming to stay.

Cake is a lucky sign. Sweet cake spells a legacy or promotion at work. If the cake has thick icing then you're in for a terrific time socially. Baking or buying cake is a sure sign you've got plenty of friends. Eating it spells luck in almost anything you do.

See yourself eating **cheese** and you will be successful in love. Make it and things you're currently working on will turn out better than your wildest dreams. Grated cheese is a sign of money luck.

Cooking **chestnuts** is an omen that someone you trust is exploiting you. Eat them and it's a sign of a successful sex life. Split or open chestnuts, and a mystery that's been bugging you will be solved.

Your love life is looking up if you eat **chips**.

Chocolate reflects your current state of ease and well being. Eat it and you must expect to lose money or have a major expense. Chocolate with nuts is a sign you're bored. Drinking chocolate means a marriage proposal.

You will soon get a surprise gift—probably

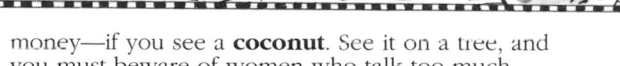

money—if you see a **coconut**. See it on a tree, and you must beware of women who talk too much.

Eating **cucumber** means recovery from illness or the return of a long-lost friend. If they are cooked, you are in danger of making a business boo-boo. Reconsider any decisions.

Life is bound to be boring if you see **custard**. Never mind. Who needs that much excitement anyway?

See yourself on a **diet** and business will boom. A **vegetarian** diet and you have friends you can trust. If you're actually on a diet the dream probably means you are hungry!

You'd better get ready to go on a trip if you dream of **doughnuts**. If you were expecting to, then pack more clothes: you'll be staying longer than you thought.

Eat **eggs** and your health will improve. Find them in a nest and you will get a surprise windfall. But broken, cracked, or rotting eggs mean someone you trust is about to let you down in a big way. Easter eggs predict a celebration.

Eat **fat** and your love life will go well. Cook with it and you will make money in business. The fatter you or others are in your dream the fewer your worries will be.

See yourself having a **feast** and difficulties are on the horizon. Prepare one, and someone else is going to get what you want.

Flour is a good sign. You will be healthy, strong, and life will be comfortable. Cooking with flour signals good news in the family.

Eat food with a **fork** and your worries won't last long.

Put food in a **fridge** and your prosperity will increase. Take it out and unexpected guests are about to arrive.

If it's **frozen food**, then an exciting trip or terrific party is being planned for you.

See a bowl of **fruit** and your home life will be happy. You are also in for a run of good health. Bitter or rotten fruit is a sign of sadness. Wild fruit means you will be comfortable but never rich.

Fry anything in a dream and your love life will soon take a turn for the worse. Burn whatever it is you are frying, and you will quickly be consoled. But it could be a case of out of the frying pan into the fire, so be careful.

Sweet **fudge** is a sign you should cut your spending. Buy it, and your love life is in for some ups and downs.

See **garlic** and you're about to find something you thought you'd lost. Eat it, and be careful, quarrels are in the air. Cook with it, and it's a sign to watch out at work. You're simply not very popular at the moment.

Taste or smell **ginger** and a passionate love affair is on the cards. But sorry, it simply won't last. Gingerbread is a sign of a family party.

Eat or serve **gravy** and you're wasting time. But making it means it's a good time for a flutter.

See yourself in a **grocer's** shop and your current plans should go well. See yourself as a grocer, and some family squabbles are about to erupt. Buying groceries shows you're in a calm state of mind and going through a lucky phase. A closed grocer's shop shows a project of yours will come to a dead end.

A highland **haggis** spells money on the way if you eat it. But cut it or serve it, and you must try to be more discreet.

Ham is a good omen. Smoke it, and a prosperous year is ahead. Bake it, and your worries will soon disappear. Eat it, and business will boom.

A full food **hamper** says happy family times are ahead. But if it's empty it warns of an emotional upset.

Honey in a dream is an unusually favourable sign predicting sweet successes in home and social life.

Feeling **hungry** in a dream signifies good luck and a healthy bank balance. The greater the hunger, the more fortune will smile on you.

Eat **ice cream** and your relationships are secure. Serve, buy or sell it and you're in for some minor successes.

Jam eaten alone shows you are lonely and sad and on the point of having a row with someone close. Eat it with others, and you'll make new friends. Make it, and you could be about to wed.

Lies and deceit are in the wind if you see **jelly.** Eat it and there will be unhappiness in the family.

See yourself pouring **ketchup** on food and a new friend of the opposite sex is about to come into your life—and they could be a bit saucy!

Eat or cook **kidneys** and you should stay away from the betting shop. In fact, don't gamble at all for quite some time.

Cut **lard** and you could lose a dear friend. Cook with it and it's a warning you love money too much. There's more to life, you know.

Your personal affairs are in a bit of a mess if you eat **lettuce**. Buy one and you will soon be in a mess emotionally. Wash a lettuce, and it's a warning not to act foolishly. Take time to think.

Eat or cook **liver** and your health will take a turn for the better.

Macaroni is a sign unexpected guests are about to arrive. Make sure you've got enough food in.

Marshmallows predict an exciting new friend of the opposite sex.

Meat, if you buy or cook it, is an omen of prosperity. Eat it and you're in for a row with someone. Frozen meat is a symbol of deceit, and if it's rotten it's a warning to watch your health.

Read a **menu** and life will be comfortable. Perhaps not luxurious, but you won't want for much. A waiter or waitress seen in an hotel is a lucky sign. If they serve you at home, family problems are looming. Dressed in black-and-white uniforms, they suggest danger is around the corner. Watch out for it.

Mustard, and you're going to deeply regret something. On a table, it predicts petty squabbles. Cook with it, and trouble is on the horizon. Buying it is a sign to beware of false friends.

Eat or cook **noodles** and you will make progress with some cherished plan.

Crack open **nuts** and your current projects will be successful. Eat them, and health will improve.

Grated **nutmeg** and you'd better get those recipe books out: you're going to be doing a lot of entertaining. Taste or smell it, and it's a warning to question people's motives. Don't let them use you to their advantage.

Oats are a successful sign if you are in business. For the traveller they indicate a successful and profitable journey.

Pick **olives** and success at work will follow. Buy them and your emotions are running high. Eat them and an offer you simply can't refuse is about to be made to you. Green olives are a sign of good health. Black ones show your relationships are a bit troublesome at the moment.

Make an **omelette** and it's a sign you are trying hard to save money. Eat it, and it's a warning not to gamble—you simply can't win. If the omelette falls flat, some onerous new task will fall to you. It will prove beneficial in the end.

Get your glad rags on if you make **pancakes**. A social whirl is predicted. Eat them, and your current projects will go well.

A **pantry** well stocked with food says good times are ahead. But if the cupboard is bare, it's time to tighten your belt.

Eat **parsley** and you will get where you want, thanks to a lucky break. Growing, it signifies hard work but eventual success.

Your popularity is about to increase if you see peanuts. See **peanut butter** and you are feeling guilty about something; either confess it or forget it.

Spice up your food with **pepper** and it's time to curb your enthusiasm for a financial venture. It may not be as successful as you think. Grind pepper and it's a good time to take up a new hobby. You are full of beans, so why waste your energy?

Take food on a **picnic** and a secret could spell danger.

Make a **pie** and you are in a strong position. Eat one, and you suspect one of your friends may be being disloyal. You're right!

A **pizza** piled high with toppings is an indication your relationships are going from strength to strength. A burnt one says you're about to score a success with the opposite sex. Make one, and you are entering a very favourable period. Eat pizza and it's a sign you are about to throw yourself wholeheartedly into a new project.

Eat **quail** and you will suffer from a bad attack of remorse.

Swift success is about to be yours if you see **radishes.** But eat them and you will have to put up with some stiff competition before you get what you want.

Raisins say you'll soon be spending faster than you can earn. Simply see them and a few pleasant social events are around the corner.

Plate 10 · The Flying Dream

Dream of a **recipe** and it's a warning that all work and no play is likely to lead to a nervous breakdown! But all play and no work is the road to ruin. Try and strike a happy medium. Give someone a recipe, and it shows you are pretty unflappable right now.

See a **restaurant** in town and someone is keeping something from you. In the country and problems are round the corner. If it's crowded you will run into trouble with your partner by being too timid. Empty, and your partner is about to behave unpredictably. An attractive proposition is about to be made if you see yourself eating food in a restaurant.

Eating **rice** is a very good omen for romance. Cook it and something you thought impossible will prove easy. Pick it and business profits are forecast.

Any **roast** food is a sign of good luck. Carve or serve a roast and the family will soon have something to celebrate.

See **rye** bread and you will make an interesting new friend.

See **salad** and it's a healthy sign. Your talent is about to be spotted at work. Toss one, and happy family times are ahead.

Eat **salmon** and a lovers' tiff can be made up if you really care.

Sprinkle **salt** and it's an excellent omen. All your troubles will be little ones.

Eat or make **sandwiches** at home and you will soon have a chance to improve yourself. Eat them in a restaurant, and it's a warning to keep your secrets to yourself. Toasted or picnic sandwiches mean you should think again before embarking on that new love affair.

Sardines say someone is jealous of you. In a tin, they're a sign you are trying to hide feelings of resentment. Try talking it over with someone.

A tomato **sauce** predicts a letter. If it's curry, it's a warning not to give full reign to your feelings in one particular emotional attachment.

Simply see **sausages** and you're in for a happy surprise. Tuck in to tasty bangers and you could be responsible for a broken marriage or love affair.

Eat **scallops** and things will improve. Raw, they predict a surprise trip.

Snails are not a good omen: you're being a bit unreliable and moody.

Hot **soup** says things will turn out better than you had hoped. Cold and it's a bad omen for your love life. If it's over, face up to it or things will get worse. Vegetable soup means family problems.

See **spaghetti** and it's time to get out the glad rags. Party time is round the corner. If the spaghetti is in sauce, you can expect a real celebration soon.

A wooden **spoon** predicts a secret liaison with someone of the opposite sex. Eat food with a tablespoon and it shows you're adaptable. A teaspoon suggests you are over-critical.

Cook a juicy **steak** and your social life is about to perk up. Eat it, and you can expect a pay rise. Brew a stew and you could get news of a birth. Eating it predicts a reunion with an old friend.

Sugar is a happy omen. Success is just round the corner. And if you indulge in a sweet sugary sundae you're about to score a big hit with the opposite sex.

Sweets symbolise bitterness. Give them away and you could be in for a break with your partner. Eat them, and it's a warning not to make any rash decisions. They could cost you dear.

Tabasco sauce says you're hot stuff at the moment. An exciting new romance is on the cards.

See a **tart** full of cream and some good news is on the way. An apple tart predicts a reward, and a cherry one is an omen of money luck. Chocolate is a sign you're exhausted.

Cook a **turkey** and it's a sign of prosperity. Eat it, and you could be about to make a serious error of judgement.

Tomatoes are a happy omen for future success and contentment.

Vegetables are not a good sign. Dried or cooked they spell family arguments. Eat them, and you're about to lose money. See vegetables growing and you're worrying about something. Pick them and you're the butt of a lot of criticism. Rotten veg spell disappointment.

Venison is telling you not to be so full of yourself. People will dislike you for it.

Check your diet if you see **yams**. Or perhaps even have a medical check-up.

Your ambitions are pitched too high if you see egg **yolk**. Beat one and an attractive business proposal is about to come your way.

Stop flirting if you dream of **watercress**. And be careful who you tell your secrets to.

A **wafer** biscuit is a sign that for some reason you're feeling like a fish out of water.

FOOTBALL Dream of playing football and a windfall is coming. Now is the time to bet, or really chance your arm in money matters. You could end up filthy rich! Dream of watching a football match and you must try and chose your friends more carefully.

FOOTPRINTS Dream of a woman's footprints and a new venture will prove successful, but a man's mean think carefully before you plan any changes. See children's footprints and your worries will vanish. Seeing your own footprints is a sign of success.

FOREIGN PLACES/PEOPLE Dreaming of a foreign country is a sign you're going to be deceived. See yourself going to one and you can bet your real happiness lies at home. See yourself emigrate to a foreign country and it's time to tighten your belt. Unexpected demands on your cash are coming.

Meeting foreigners suggests you're about to discover lost valuables. Marrying one means your love life will go well.

An **aborigine** bodes well. You can look forward to increased energy and some exciting new experiences.

Africa on a map predicts your status is about to improve. Go there and a great joy is about to be yours. Returning from Africa signals a big disappointment.

America means many people are jealous of you. Take a trip there alone and you will marry soon. Go with others and you will have an unsettled future. If you see America in May then something very delicious is about to happen! But if you are deported from America, you will be guilty of foolish actions.

An **Arab** is a warning to take care. You could well be molested while on a trip. If you appear as an Arab, the tide of fortune is about to swing in your favour. See a group of Arabs in your dream and love is on the cards.

See the frozen **Arctic** and your deepest desires are about to be achieved.

Asia forecasts some surprising romantic developments are on the way for you and your family.

Travelling to **Australia** signifies social events are planned. Being there means you are being cheated by a friend. Simply see Australia and you should get your affairs in order. There are important changes on the way.

Canada is a sign business will boom. Go there, and it's a warning that you are spending too much time enjoying yourself. Buckle down to some work. Living in Canada means you have an enemy who is out to see your downfall.

See an **Eskimo** and money is going to be tight. But count those pennies, and you will get yourself straight. You will have to—no one else is going to offer to help.

A **geography** book is an omen you're about to be turned down by someone you really fancy. See a geography lesson, and travel is on the cards.

Indians on the warpath are a sign to watch out for treachery among your friends. If they're not on the attack, it's a good omen.

If you find yourself castaway on an **island** it suggests you are bored and lonely. But if the island is inhabited, interesting new developments are under way to cheer you up. Palm trees are a sign of hopeful new prospects.

Dream of **Jerusalem** and it's a sign you're lonely. Make an effort to call up friends. Someone has to make the first move.

Get lost or stuck in a **jungle** and you will soon run into major problems. Make your way through it, and you will sort things out.

See the **Sphinx** and you will soon have the answer to something that's been troubling you.

FOREST *See also*: Trees/Plants. Dream of being alone or frightened in a forest and someone you trust is going to let you down. If you are lost in a forest, one of your pet projects will be a success. Hide in a forest and something that is difficult now will pay dividends in the end.

FORGE Dream of a forge and you will make steady progress. Work in a forge yourself and a bit of extra effort can solve those money troubles. See sparks in the forge and there will be rows in the family if you don't control your temper.

FORK Dream of a fork in the road and you will soon have to make a decision. Eat with a fork and your worries won't last long. A garden fork is a sign that those hangers-on in your circles should be given the old heave-ho. See someone stabbed with any kind of fork and it's a warning not to gossip.

FORTUNE-TELLING Dream of having your fortune told and your love life will go well but business will be poor. But if you were doing the fortune-telling, your plans will be successful.

FOUNTAIN *See also*: Water. Dream of a flowing fountain and happiness will be yours. A dry fountain predicts a period of frustration.

FRECKLES Dream of freckles on yourself or others and it shows just how popular you are with the opposite sex. Enjoy it!

FROST *See also*: Weather. Dream of frost on a wall or window and you are in for an unusual but exciting experience. Lucky you! Dream of frostbite and it's a warning to be extra cautious in everything you do in order to avoid problems, especially in business.

FROZEN FOOD *See also*: Food. Dream of frozen food and an exciting trip or terrific party is being planned for you.

FRUIT Dream of a bowl of fruit and your home life will be happy and you are also in for a run of good health. Bitter or rotten fruit is a sign of sadness. Wild fruit means you will be comfortable, but never rich.

Ripe, sweet **apples** are an omen for a favourable event. Sour ones mean you will cause trouble for yourself by being foolish. If you simply see apples, you are about to earn big money and have a good life. Apple sauce spells change for the better.

Eat **apricots** and you will be lucky in everything except love. If they are dried, beware of a meddling hypocrite in your circle.

Buying **bananas** predicts prosperity. Eat one and you will be imposed on to perform some kind of duty. See bananas growing on trees and you will have a few small strokes of luck. Rotten bananas forecasts your friends will disappoint you.

Eat **berries** and you could be in for some health problems. Pick them, and your finances will improve. Strawberries and raspberries symbolise a saucy, secret love. Simply see berries grow and your social status will improve.

Dates predict a marriage. Buy them and it's a sign someone somewhere fancies you. See dates grow and business will boom.

See **figs** and you're about to get into a deeply embarrassing situation with the opposite sex. Try and avoid it whatever you do!

Your love life is going to clash with your business interests if you see **grapefruit**. Rely on your intuition to see you through and help you make the right choice. **Grapes**, and you're spending too much time having frivolous fun. See them growing or harvested, and the future will be comfortable.

Suck a **lemon** and you will soon find yourself in an embarrassing social situation. Squeeze one, and it's time to economise.

A **melon** is an omen of hope or surprise. Something you want will turn up when you least expect it. It's a fruit of faithfulness: it's time to commit yourself to your mate—you can guarantee they are loyal to you.

Slow but steady progress is the message if you see **oranges** growing or boxed for shipment. Eat one or drink its juice and a short-but-oh-so-sweet love affair is on the horizon.

Peaches predict small personal pleasures. They may only be little things, but they will certainly cheer you up.

Tinned **pears** are a symbol of an unexpected profit. Fresh ones are a sign you will hear some scandalous gossip—and you can use it to your advantage.

Eat **pineapple** and you will be a social success. See it growing, and a passionate affair is set to get your temperature soaring.

Eat **plums** and appreciation at work is coming your way. Tinned or sour plums signal a disappointment due to bad planning.

A move is on the cards if you dream of **prunes**. Stewed, they're a sign your health will improve.

Rhubarb, if it's growing, is a sign of new friends. Eat or cook it and it's time to check the situations vacant column: you're very unhappy at work.

Growing **watermelon** is a warning not to get involved in a casual affair. Eat it, and it predicts travel.

FRYING *See also*: Food. Fry anything in a dream and your love life will soon take a turn for the worse. But burn whatever you are frying and you will quickly be consoled. But it could be a case of out of the frying pan into the fire. Be careful.

Plate 11 · Everyday Objects

FUGITIVE Dream of being a fugitive and a violent family row is looming. But keep your temper and an argument could clear the air. Dream of helping or simply seeing a fugitive and a cash shock is coming.

FUNNEL *See also*: Sea/Water/Transport. Dream of a funnel and you will have to try and sort yourself out. What a confused little body you are! If it was a ship's funnel, you will be praised for a good job well done.

FUR *See also*: Clothes. Dream of buying a luxurious fur and you'll run into major problems, thanks to others' jealousy. Put on a fur coat and you will get involved with an important relationship at work. All that sucking-up to the boss could well pay off at last. Give a fur as a present and you're wasting time on risky ventures. A white fur means you will lose a friend. A black one means your ideas simply won't work, and a brown one means emotional dramas. Dream of fur in shop window and your plans will succeed because this time at least you have thought them through.

FURNITURE Tatty old furniture is a sign of love troubles. Dream of buying new furniture and you'll have to adjust to changes you don't much like. Sell furniture and there will be a few financial headaches.

Separate items of furniture can have their own meanings:

See a strange **bed** and business will be better. Making a bed suggests a major move. Being in bed signals a new love in your life. See your own bed and you will start to feel more secure.

Any kind of **cabinet** (apart from the political kind!) and someone you trust is sure to let you down. Buy one and money is coming your way. Open one and that long-awaited letter is about to arrive.

An empty **chair** spells surprise news. A rocking-chair is a sign you will gain from other people's hard work. Sitting in one means you're starting to face up to things you should have faced long ago. Not so bad, are they?

A closed **desk** signals a disappointment, probably on the romantic front. An open desk is a sign not to make hasty decisions. Keep your mouth shut for the time being. Rummaging through a desk means you will soon make some influential friends.

See a closed **drawer** and you're going to have to outwit a rival for something you want. An open one suggests a new opportunity, and a full drawer predicts it's the right time to start a new venture. An empty drawer is a sign of hard work on the way, and a locked one suggests a few unforeseen problems. But patience will overcome them.

A **mattress** is a symbol of ease and tranquillity. An old one, and you will be given a useful piece of advice at work. A new one, and easy times are ahead. A double mattress means you have been having a few problems with your partner and are anxious to sort them out. Try talking it over.

See a large **mirror** and it's a sign you're being a bit flighty lately. Watch out or you could upset your mate. A small mirror means you are shy about doing something. Don't be—it will work like a dream. A broken mirror predicts sad news and troubled times ahead. See yourself in a mirror and you simply can't trust one of your friends.

A round **table** suggests unexpected guests. A square one is a sign you're about to make an interesting new friend. An extending table predicts a misunderstanding with someone close. But a marble-topped table is an omen of an exciting new love affair.

AG A typical obstacle dream. If you get rid of the gag or talk in spite of it, you will overcome your problems. If you gag someone else, or see others gagged, it is a warning to be more discreet or nasty gossip will do the rounds about you.

GAIN *See also*: Money; Success. The greater the gain, the bigger the warning to look after your money. But if you make gains dishonestly, business will boom or you can expect to recover a loss.

GALLERY *See also*: Pictures/Painting. Paintings in a gallery are a sign you can expect to rekindle an old flame. See sculpture and it's a warning not to bet. An observation gallery means your current projects will go well but falling from one means a lovers' tiff is round the corner.

GALLOPING On a horse and you're in for a hard time emotionally. See a jockey galloping and good times are on the horizon. Several galloping horses mean your hopes will soon succeed.

GALLOWS A contrary dream. See gallows and it's a sign of happiness. Die on them and you will shortly receive an honourable position. See someone you know on the gallows and it's a warning to steer clear of your rivals.

GAMBLING Winning is a warning not to risk anything you couldn't bear to lose. But see yourself losing and an opportunity for a quick profit is about to come your way.

Place a **bet** and the wind of change is blowing your way. Watching others betting is a signal to look out for sharp practice among your business competitors. Win a bet and good times are coming. Lose one, and an enemy is out to get you.

Cards mean loss of prestige.

Gambling with **dice** is a sign of an inheritance. For a woman, simply seeing dice means that love affair you're thinking of is a mistake—and you know it really, don't you? For a man it's a sign that the money success you're after will cost in the long run. Throw a winning dice and a small windfall is on the way.

Hit the **jackpot** and you're in for some hard work with precious little reward. See someone else win a jackpot, and you can gain something with a lot less effort than you thought.

Any kind of **lottery** is a bad omen for romance. The future with your mate looks a bit uncertain. See a lottery ticket and family troubles are on the cards.

Play **poker** and a happy social life is forecast.

See a **racecourse** and it signifies new surroundings. If it's a racehorse then it's time to economise.

Win a **raffle** and you're going through a lucky phase. Lose, and some kind of date in your diary is about to be cancelled.

Roulette and all your hopes are in vain, I'm afraid. You're also doomed for disappointment if you gamble on a slot machine.

Gamble on the **stock market** and it's a warning not to gamble in reality if you see gains. Losses predict money luck.

GAMES Dream of playing in a game of any sort and some heated rows with your partner are on the cards. Win, and some of your ambitions aren't being realised. Lose, and you will soon beat your enemies. See yourself selling games in a shop and you're deluding yourself in love. Your mate is telling you porkies, I fear. Try to face reality. Play a friendly game and your relationships with the opposite sex are a bit unstable.

Play **backgammon** and you will soon be faced with a test of character. Win and you can expect an inheritance. Lose, and you must expect a business loss. See others playing backgammon and you will rout your rivals.

Any kind of **ball game** is a sign of happy news. Bowling is generally a lucky omen—especially if you are playing.

Playing **billiards** is a sure sign legal action and family squabbles over property are brewing.

Football, and a windfall is coming. Now is the time to bet or really chance your arm on money matters. You could end up filthy rich. Dream of watching a football match and you must try and choose your friends more carefully.

Golf relates to the opposite sex. If the game goes well, so will your love life. If not, you can expect problems in affairs of the heart.

Hockey says hard work will prove successful.

Posh **polo**, either played or watched, says your wealth will increase, probably through a legacy.

Play **pool** and it's time to take up a new interest or make new friends.

Dream of **scoring** any kind of goal and new friends and opportunities are ahead.

A **tennis court** shows you're feeling a sense of responsibility. See someone playing and promotion at work is just around the corner. Play yourself, and it suggests you crave more independence.

GANG Being a member of a gang shows you're simply drifting with the tide. See yourself as a gang leader and it's time to show some initiative. If you're intimidated by a gang, then you are depressed. Shake yourself and do something positive. If you are mugged by a gang it's a warning to keep a tight hold on your wallet.

GANGWAY *See also*: Sea/Water/Travel. This represents a period of transition for you. If the surroundings are happy, e.g. the gangway of a cruise ship, then the future will prove easier for you. Walk up the gangway and you can expect progress. Down, and things will stay bleak for some time. Cross a gangway and you will have to face up to something from your past before you can go on.

GARAGE One full of new cars is a sign an older person is going to help you with a problem you thought you'd never solve. If the cars are old, you must co-operate with someone else, it will help in the long run. See an empty garage at a private house and someone you trust is about to do the dirty on you. Put your car in your own garage and you will win security through your own efforts.

GARDEN *See also*: Flowers; Trees/Plants. A neat one without flowers predicts life will be comfortable, apart from the odd emotional hiccup. But a neglected or overgrown one signals troubled times ahead. A beautiful garden in full bloom is a spectacular dream, both love and money will be yours—what more could you want?

GARGLING This is a sign that you are in for a period of awkward changes. But try and be flexible, it will all come good in the end.

GARGOYLE These bizarre figures show your sense of humour is about to get you into trouble.

GARLIC See also: Food. You are about to find something you thought you'd lost. Eat it and be careful, quarrels are in the air. Cook with it, and it's a sign to watch out at work. You're simply not very popular with your workmates at present.

GARTER See also: Clothes. This relates to your love life. For a man, it shows you have the hots for a particular lady right now. For a woman, it's a sign of faithfulness.

GAS See also: Smells. See someone overcome by it and you are about to hear of a scandal. Light a gas burner or stove and you had better start economising. Someone in a gas mask is a sign of money troubles. Wear one yourself and it's time to talk to your bank manager before he loses his patience! A gas man is a sign not to lend anyone anything.

GATES An open one spells major changes on the way for you. Closed, it's a sign to stop putting off your problems. You simply have to face them. A wooden or iron gate signifies a scintillating social life. Golden or metal gates are a warning to be more careful in everything you do.

GAUZE See also: Doctors/Hospitals. Your worries are over if you see this in a medical context. But see any other form of gauze and it's a warning to get all your resentments off your chest. If you don't, they will simply fester and cause more trouble in the end.

GEM See also: Colours/Gems. Finding, stealing or being given a gem indicates a period of unhappiness and depression. But lose one and you will make unexpected gains. A fake gem is a sure sign some vicious gossip is going round about you.

GENITALS This is a clear sexual dream. See your own sex organs as healthy and it's a sign you have a satisfactory sex life. Dream of diseased sex organs and you've either been overdoing it, or sleeping around. Try and be a bit more faithful. Unusual sex organs are a symbol of a starved sex life. You're not happy about that or it wouldn't be playing on your mind. Dream of pain in the genitals and a medical check-up would not go amiss.

GEOGRAPHY See also: Foreign Places/People. A geography book is an omen you are about to be turned down by someone you really fancy. See a geography lesson and travel is on the cards.

GERMS A contrary dream. If germs are featured in any way, some new activities will reactivate your zest for life.

GETTING UP The meaning here depends on the circumstances. Arise early in the morning and you will make plenty of money. Arising from bed is an omen of sickness. From a chair it means good news and from a couch you will get a surprise letter. Arise from the floor and it spells trouble.

GEYSER A change of direction is on the way for you. It won't all be smooth sailing but things will turn out well.

GHOST See also: Supernatural. A walking ghost indicates set-backs and money worries. A talking ghost is a sign you're deluding yourself about things. Face facts. Good health is forecast if the apparition wears white, but if it's black, your lover is about to behave totally out of character and it could cause bitter recriminations. If you don't run away from the ghost both business and love will go well.

GIANT A danger sign. But kill the giant and you will overcome your difficulties. See yourself as a giant and it's a warning not to get involved in any risky ventures.

GIFT Be careful where you are placing your trust if you receive one of these. Give a gift and an unexpected personal success which spells plenty of pleasure is on the way. Buying one is a sign you are emotionally upset about a surprise event. A gift of money says you are being put upon whether you give or receive it.

GINGER See also: Food; Smells. Taste or smell it and a passionate love affair is on the cards. But sorry it simply won't last. **Gingerbread** is a sign of a family party.

GIRDER Someone is simply waiting for you to make a mistake if girders feature in any way. Don't let them catch you out; be extra careful.

GIRLS A beautiful girl is a good omen for romance, and an ugly one is a sign you are spoilt for choice in some area of life. A girl laughing means an unexpected expense, and a crying one heralds major money problems. If she is asleep, a problem is on the way at work. See a girl at a window and a big row is looming.

GLACIER See also: Places/Settings. Important news from a distance, or news that will take you on a

Plate 12 · Of Games and Play

long journey is predicted. Fall into a crevasse in a glacier and it's a warning not to make any changes or it could be dangerous. Cross a glacier crevasse and your problems aren't as serious as you think.

GLADIATOR A fighting one means money on the way. Several signify a house move but see a gladiator being killed and it is a sign of unhappiness.

GLASS *See also*: Drink. You will have to lower your sights. Coloured glass is a sign you can't trust one of your friends. Cut yourself on it and one emotional relationship is about to be severed.

GLIDER *See also*: Flying. A surprise proposition is on the way from a friend or colleague. Listen to advice before making up your mind.

GLOWING Any bright or pleasant, warm glow predicts improvements in the areas that matter most to you. A glowworm is a sign you have a very faithful friend.

GLUE Look after your money and re-check your investments if you see something mended with this. Get it on your fingers and you can be certain you have loyal friends. In fact they will stick to you like glue! Buy a tube and your ambitions will be realised.

GOAL *See also*: Games. Do a Gary Lineaker and score one of these and new friends and opportunities are ahead.

GOBLET *See also*: Drink. A metal one is a sign of good news. Coloured spells the loss of a friend. Break a goblet and a business loss is forecast.

GOLD *See also*: Metals. Gold cloth, embroidery or trimmings signify honour and recognition. Find gold or work with it and you must remember that old saying 'All that glisters…' Don't take things at face value. Stealing or counting gold is a warning that there is more to life than material things. Don't regard them so highly. Medals, jewellery, or coins forecast financial gain.

GOLF This relates to the opposite sex. If the game goes well, so will your life. If not, you can expect problems in affairs of the heart.

GONDOLA Your love life is boring you if you dream of these romantic vessels. It's time to change partners.

GOSSIPING Good news is on the way if the gossip is about you. But listening to others gossip predicts domestic tiffs or squabbles over property. If you are accused or caught doing it then don't betray a confidence. It will bounce back.

GOVERNMENT See yourself affiliated to any particular party and it's a warning to beware of your enemies. Current plans will all go well if you see an election. Vote and you are lacking in self-confidence. Try and assert yourself a bit more. Remember you are just as good as the rest.

GRAIN A grain of sand indicates an unstable situation. A grain of salt shows you are bored with life. Why not try something new to cheer yourself up? Cereal, and it's time to knuckle down, you are wasting too much time. Grain growing is a good sign for your finances. Sowing or harvesting are signs of good health in the future.

GRASS Cutting it is a sign of money troubles ahead. Yellow or dried-up grass means watch the health of someone close. It could take a turn for the worse. Green, well-kept grass predicts success in all your undertakings.

GRAVEL This represents obstacles. Walk on it and you will have to make an effort to overcome problems. Drive over it and problems will soon be solved. Spread gravel and your troubles are all your own fault, I'm afraid. Try and reconsider things.

GRAVY *See also*: Food. You're time-wasting if you eat or serve this. But making it means it's a good time for a flutter.

GREASE See grease on you or your clothes and something you are planning will turn out to be a huge mistake. Greasy dishes or other items are a warning not to meddle in other people's affairs. Even if they ask you, don't offer any advice.

GREENHOUSE *See also*: Flowers. If you are in a greenhouse, it forecasts success and a star-studded future.

GRILLING *See also*: Food. You are thinking about indulging in a clandestine affair if grills of any kind feature. Think it over carefully, these things aren't as glamorous as you imagine.

GRINDING Prosperity and happiness are on the way if you grind grain, coffee or any type of food. It suggests you are the sort who is happy with the simple things in life. But watch out if you grind pepper, a worrying piece of news is round the corner.

GROCER *See also*: Food. If you are in a grocer's shop, your current plans should go well. See yourself as a grocer and some family squabbles are about to erupt. Buying groceries shows you are in a calm state of mind and going through a lucky phase. A closed grocer's shop shows a project of yours will come to a dead end.

GROWING *See also*: Change/Transformation. See natural things grow and you're in for a promotion at work.

GUARD You could well be robbed or the victim of a burglary if you see him on duty. If you are on guard, then expect a pay rise.

GUESSING Get the answer right in a guessing game and an invitation is on its way. If someone else does the guessing, then guard your back. There's a Judas in your social circle.

GUIDING Interesting new opportunities, perhaps through an influential friend, are on their way if you act as a guide, are guided, or consult a guide book.

GUILLOTINE Don't be childish or you could lose a friend, is what an ancient guillotine is telling you. The paper-cutting variety is a warning to stop shirking at work or you will lose out.

GUILT *See also*: Shame. See yourself guilty of something bad and it's not necessarily a poor omen. It usually means your prospects are about to improve. See others found guilty and if you're a man you're going to have to get used to a few unusual situations in the near future. For a woman, it's a sign you're being over sensitive. See the character **Judas** and it's a sign to be careful of new friends. Let them prove their worth before you get too involved. See the lady with the scales of justice and a successful fixture is assured.

GULF A split with a lover is indicated here. But it can be prevented. Try paying them a bit more attention.

GUN *See also*: Death. A loaded gun is a symbol of misfortune. Unloaded, it shows you've been a bit cantankerous lately. A machine-gun is a sign you feel weak at the moment. Fire a revolver and it would be a good time to start any new projects. Hear one fired and you are full of bright ideas at present. Why not do something about them? If the gun kills someone, then it is time to put an unpleasant period of life behind you and start afresh. If you fire the fatal shot, then you are in for a disappointment with the opposite sex.

GYM An indoor gym is an omen for material prosperity and a respected place in society you little yuppie, you! A trip abroad is forecast if you see an open-air gym. See yourself exercising and you've made a good match. You and your partner will be together for some time to come.

GYPSY A period of uncertainty is coming up if the gypsies are camping or near a caravan. Buy things from them and good luck will come but only after a few trials and tribulations. One female gypsy indicates news from a distance or a sudden trip. A male, and you're in for some amorous adventures.

 ABIT A bad one, like smoking, is a sign you're trying to wriggle out of an awkward situation. Give it up and the problem will be solved. A religious habit, such as a nun's, suggests you have to be firm about breaking off a relationship. It is boring you, so be honest and quit.

HAG You are highly strung and about to enter a period of bad luck if you see her. If she is riding on a broomstick, you will be involved in a scandal that could cost you your job.

HAIR **Black** hair and you will renew old acquaintances.

Blonde is a warning to stop putting things off.

Cut **curls** spell exciting changes for the better on their way. For a woman curls mean the arrival of a new man in your life. For a man it means it's time to break off a relationship. It could harm your reputation.

Dyed hair means you will suffer through your own silliness.

Denis Healey-style bushy **eyebrows** suggest money is coming your way. Arched eyebrows mean a surprise for you. Thin ones predict a business disappointment. If your eyebrows fall out or you're worried about them your lover is two-timing you.

Long lustrous **eyelashes** predict a red-hot love affair. False ones mean you will discover a secret and need advice on what to do about it. See someone with no eyelashes and you must give nothing away. Keep those confidences to yourself.

Dream of a **hairbrush** and if you want that sexy new partner you are going to have to make a few sacrifices.

People are gossiping about you if you see a men's **hairdresser.** A women's is a sign of unrequited love, I'm sorry to say—the one you adore simply doesn't feel the same about you. Going to a hairdresser means something exciting but a bit risky is on the cards. See yourself as a hairdresser and there will soon be a family row.

Hairpins mean the future looks bright.

Long hair is a sign of good health.

A **moustache** is a warning not to let petty irritations explode into major problems. Shave one off and a break with your partner is likely. But don't fret, there's someone new on the horizon.

Having your hair **pulled** indicates friends you simply can't trust.

See someone **shaving** and a colleague is trying to provoke you. Don't rise to the bait. See yourself shaving, and a business loss is on the cards.

Short hair is a sign of lively enthusiasm.

If your hair starts turning **white** you aren't in peak physical shape. Have a check-up.

Wigs are omens of change. New faces, new places all are just round the corner.

HALL A long narrow one predicts a period of worry. If it's grand, changes are coming. A public hall warns it's time to make that decision you have been trying to put off.

HALLMARK A false or missing hallmark is a warning to watch for treachery from colleagues. But a correct one promises success in current projects.

HALO Sad news is on the way if you see someone wearing a halo. Wear it yourself and travel abroad is forecast.

HALTER Obstacles are ahead. But put it on a horse successfully and you can overcome your problems.

HAMMER See a metal one and things are about to go wrong at work. A wooden one is a warning you are being too irritable lately. Try and calm down. Simply hear a hammer and you will achieve something that will make you feel pleased with yourself.

HAMMOCK A minor loss is predicted if it's empty. See yourself in it and it's a warning not to be so selfish. You could lose a friend. Your social life will take a turn for the better if you are in a hammock with someone of the opposite sex. Fall out of one and you must not take your mate for granted.

HAMPER *See also*: Food. An empty one warns of an emotional upset. A full one and happy family times are ahead.

HANDBAG Find one and you will have good luck in love. An empty one is a sign you don't like routine. But remember, sometimes it is the only answer or you'll end up in a muddle. Lose a handbag and it shows you are dithering over a decision. Make your mind up. Buy one and you're about to be extremely busy.

HANDCUFFS *See also*: Police/Prisons. Being handcuffed is a contrary dream and means your worries will soon be over. See others handcuffed and it is a sign of security and protection. Snap them on someone and your life is about to improve unexpectedly.

HAND GRENADE Throw one and you will soon be humiliated thanks to your own hasty behaviour. Simply see one and it is a warning to rely on your own judgement.

HANDKERCHIEF A dirty handkerchief and a quarrel is on the way. A cotton one is a sign you should start to assert yourself. Go on, be bold! A linen one is an omen of hidden hostility. Silk means good times are round the corner. A torn handkerchief indicates a sticky situation at work and a lost one spells a broken romance. You'll take a step up socially if you blow your nose, and if you wave a handkerchief you are about to make an important new friend.

HANGING *See also*: Death. See yourself hanging from a gallows and you are about to rise up the social scale. See someone else hanged and money is going to be tight for a while.

HARBOUR *See also*: Sea/Water/Travel. Enter a harbour and the future is secure. Leave one and you are about to discover a friend isn't as loyal to you as you had thought.

HAREM *See also*: Sexuality. Whether you are in one, or simply see yourself surrounded by one, this is a sign you are going to be busy with the opposite sex. Don't exhaust yourself!

HARPOON *See also*: Fish/Fishing. A pay rise is on the cards if a whale or big fish is on the other end of this. But if you are injured by it, then it could spell financial disaster. Don't overspend.

HARVESTING *See also*: Food. Harvesting fruit is a signal that most everything in life is going your way at the moment—enjoy it. If it's grain, you will soon reap rewards for your past hard work. A poor harvest is a warning you are being exploited—don't be soft, stand up for yourself.

HATCHET Chop anything but wood with this and trouble lies ahead, both at home and at work. If you chop wood you are in for some kind of reconciliation. Sharpen a hatchet and a pay rise is predicted.

Plate 13 · The Hissing Snake

HAY An unexpected stroke of luck is about to be yours if you see a haystack or loft full of hay. But troubled times are ahead if the hay is wet.

HEALTH *See also*: Ill-health. A healthy man forecasts a brilliant career. But a healthy woman suggests bitterness and resentment over a past mistake. Poor health is a warning not to gamble.

HEART A good sign for your love life. It is set to sparkle. Having a heart attack is a contrary dream and predicts a long, active life.

HEAT Cross the **Equator** and life will change for you completely soon. See it, but fail to cross it and it's a sign you are dithering over something. Be brave: make that decision.

Trying to reduce heat with a **fan** refers to your love life. Fan yourself and you are in for an embarrassing entanglement. See others fanning themselves and you're playing the field too much. Dream of losing a fan and you will lose your mate by being too much of a flirt.

See hot **lava** and your social life is about to take off in a big way. But take care it doesn't break the bank.

Dream of anything **melting** and it's not a good omen. If it's gold it's a sign of sadness. Silver indicates money problems. Melting ice is a sign a certain situation is getting out of control. Try to keep a tight rein on it.

A warm **oven** is a sign of good fortune.

Shade yourself from the heat with a **parasol** and it's a lucky omen for your love life. Open it indoors, and someone is going to give you some money.

A hot **radiator** suggests temporary tensions. If it's off, you're about to uncover a nasty secret.

If **steam** burns you then you're being deceived. Hear it escaping and you're in for a row. Turn it off and something you thought impossible is about to happen. See steam from a kettle and you could be feeling a bit off-colour.

A coal **stove** predicts an important new relationship. Gas, and your health will improve. If it's electric it suggests you can't quite decide what to do next. Switch one off and you're about to miss a valuable opportunity.

The heat of **summer** says you're about to hear some surprising news. And some unexpected family responsibilities are looming if you dream of **sunstroke**. But don't panic. You'll cope.

Changes are on the horizon if you check a **temperature** with a thermometer. Buy one and a work project will go well.

HEAVEN Changes are on the way which you don't take to at first. But stick with it, things will turn out for the best in the end.

HEDGE Cut this and you are in for some good luck. Jump over it and something you have been hankering for will soon be yours—but it will prove a bit of an anti-climax. A blooming hedge is a sign of success in your love life. A prickly one predicts someone is out to thwart you. With a bit of determination you can win through.

HELL A bad omen. Bad luck, illness and money losses are predicted. But escape from hell and the future looks brighter.

HELMET Try and be a bit more organised or you'll get in a muddle if you see people wearing helmets. Wear one yourself and it's a warning not to be extravagant.

HERBS Peace and contentment are predicted. Simply smelling herbs is a sign you are about to embark on an exciting adventure—possibly abroad.

HERMIT It's time to take a few risks if you see this character. You'll never get anywhere if you are afraid to try. See yourself as a hermit and the road ahead will be rough but it will lead to happiness in the end.

HIDING Do this and one of your schemes will give you regrets later—and deep down you know it, don't you? Dream of hiding something and it's a warning not to be secretive about your problems. Confide in someone and they may be able to help you.

HILL This represents a difficulty to overcome. Stand on top of it and your troubles are behind you. Struggle up and it's a sign you are tired and have been overdoing things.

HISSING Hear it from a snake and it's telling you to try and control your temper. Human hissing means you will make progress if you hear it. Doing it yourself is a sure sign you are about to make an embarrassing faux-pas.

HITCHHIKING Try to be a bit more self-reliant. If you pick up a hitchhiker, it's a warning to be careful with your money—most of all, don't lend any.

HOLE Fall in and you are keeping bad company lately. A hole in clothes is a sign of money luck. Dig a hole and a sudden trip is on the cards.

HOME *See also*: Family. Home is a symbol of financial security. See your own and it spells happiness within the family. Dream of any **alterations** to your home and you will shortly be able to make pleasant changes. A lavish **estate** is a warning to stop trying to keep up with the Joneses. They can afford it— you can't! A bright tidy **kitchen** spells happiness in the family. The newer and cleaner it is, the greater the joy. See the **lavatory** and an important issue currently hanging in the balance will be successfully concluded. See a luxury **mansion** and you will have to accept some changes you don't much like. But a run-down one and the coming changes will be for the better. See a **mat** at the front door and some unwelcome visitors are about to arrive. Any other kind of mat predicts obstacles. The bigger the mat... **Move** home without a hitch and all will go smoothly in real life. But if it was difficult or even disastrous, you will be faced with a big decision. Carry on as you are or try something completely different. The choice is yours. See a ritzy **penthouse** and it's a sign you are living beyond your means.

HOOK *See also*: Fish/Fishing. Hang something from a hook and you are feeling generous. Injure yourself on it and it's a sign one of your friends isn't happy with your behaviour lately. A fish hook shows you have a secret passion for someone you've known for a long time. Screw a hook into a wall and it's a warning that you are sometimes very obstinate.

HOPS See them grow and money is coming to you. Pick them and a passionate love affair is on the cards but it will quickly fizzle out, I'm sorry to say.

HORN *See also*: Music. A good luck sign. A bull's horns are a sign of calm confidence. A goat's and promotion is on the way at work. See yourself with horns and you have strong will-power. Hear a horn and you'll soon be caught up in a social whirl.

HOROSCOPE Read it and a happy event is about to cheer you up. If it is good, you are feeling a bit nervous over a recent failure to agree on something, probably at work. If it is bad, don't despair, a hope you have been nurturing will soon come to fruition. Reading someone else's horoscope predicts a row with your mate.

HOSE Squirt it and you are in for a little adventure. Use it for a fire and an explosive new love affair is just round the corner. Hose a garden and you are about to make some new friends.

HOTEL Stay there alone and it relates to work. Stay with someone of the opposite sex and it concerns your love life. If it's a luxury hotel then failure or

disappointments are predicted. A modest one and things will turn out well for you.

HOURGLASS This is a warning to think carefully before you act—don't rush into anything.

HOUSE *See also*: Buying/Selling. An old one predicts a reunion with someone. A new one is an omen of financial security. See a house being built and you will get an unexpected gain. Buy a house and a short, but pleasant, love affair is on the horizon. Sell one and you will be released from some responsibility. Watch a house being demolished and you are grieving over a loss, probably a broken relationship. You'll get over it quicker than you think.

HUMAN BODY Simply seeing the **human body** is a happy omen. If it's a female body, then you're in for social success. A male body means business will boom.

The human body is made up of many parts and each has its own interpretation:

Your own **ankles** are a sign a friend is trying to help you secretly. Broken ankles signify success after a struggle. The ankles of someone of the opposite sex suggest an unwise love affair.

Your own **arms** mean you will beat your enemies. If you have an arm cut off you will lose a relative. Pain in the arm spells bad luck in business. A broken arm for a man means a family fight, but for a woman it means the loss of her husband. Breaking an arm signifies danger ahead. Having any other accident with the arms means ill-health in the family.

A bad **back** should prepare you for some reverses or loss of status. If someone turns their back on you it means your colleagues are jealous of you. But if they turn round again, their envy will only be temporary. Seeing a man's back is a sign of short-lived traumas. A woman's back is a sign of emotional instability. A broken back is a warning of ulcers.

A **bladder** suggests you should get a medical check-up. You are over-exerting yourself.

Human **bones** show that someone dear is going to be away for a while.

Rest your head on someone's **breast** and you will soon make a new and lasting friend. Seeing a naked breast signals some kind of minor pain or illness. If you see a baby suckling at the breast joy and happiness will follow.

Buttocks are generally a good omen! If they are a man's, business will go well. A woman's and love is winging its way to you.

Cheeks are a sign your personal relationships will soon improve.

Shock news is on the way if you see other people's **ears**. If it's your own, then watch for a snake-in-the-grass around you. Big ears mean help from a surprise source.

A swollen **elbow** is a sign of a nasty experience. A grazed one shows just how much you care about a certain person. Break an elbow and you will adapt to changes that are on the way.

See **eyelids** and you are in danger of splitting with your partner. And it will be a trivial tiff. Try and bury the hatchet. Is it really worth rowing over the toothpaste? Fluttering eyelids mean you are very generous—a bit too much so at times.

Something in your **eye** suggests someone is trying to trick you at work. Crossed eyes means money luck, but a squint is warning for you not to get involved in an illicit love affair—it'll damage your reputation. Wide eyes predict an inheritance. Blue ones are an omen for finding a new friend. Dark eyes mean you're on the brink of an exciting new love affair.

See your own **face** in a mirror and one of your secrets is about to be discovered. See a happy, smiling face and life will be the same. A sad face spells trouble ahead. The face of someone you know signals a celebration. A stranger's face foretells upheavals and travel. See a man's face and it means you're confident about the future. See a woman's, and it shows you have doubts.

Dream of big **feet** and you are in for good health. Small ones mean you are worrying for nothing. Itchy feet predict travel. Strange feet mean new friends. Bare feet and watch out—you're going to have a new experience with the opposite sex. Dirty feet are a sign not to lend any money. A broken foot means you could lose a relative. Dream of having your feet stepped on and it is a warning not to gossip.

See a **finger** pointing and you will move house. Dream of a bandaged finger and you will narrowly avoid a disaster. A cut finger means you are going to have to work extra hard for a while. A missing

finger means legal trouble, probably over money. Short stubby fingers signify new friends.

Long, luxurious **fingernails** say you are about to have trouble with the opposite sex. Short nails mean a surprise gift. Dream of varnishing your nails and it's a warning not to be impulsive. It could have scandalous results. A broken nail means you will be discontent with life for a while. Cut your nails and your prestige will soar. Bite your nails and you should get a medical check-up.

Your own **forehead** says you simply can't rely on others for help. You will have to go it alone. Soothe someone's brow and your love life will perk up. A wrinkled forehead means your worries are about to disappear.

See yourself covered in **freckles** and it shows just how popular you are with the opposite sex. Enjoy it!

See **genitals** and it's a clear sexual dream. See your own as healthy and you have a satisfactory sex life. Dream of diseased sex organs and you've either been overdoing it or sleeping around. Try and be a bit more faithful. Unusual sex organs are a symbol of a starved sex life. You're not happy about that or it wouldn't be playing on your mind.

Sore **gums** are an omen of family problems. If they are treated, a quarrel that could lead to a parting is on the cards.

A woman's **hands** predict a brief feeling of depression, both at work and in your love life. But it will soon clear up, thanks to help from a close friend. A child's hands predict financial success. Dirty hands are an omen that a relative is at risk in some way. A clean, well-groomed pair means a period of satisfactory events is round the corner. Waving hands predict a separation. Hairy ones and a stroke of luck is on its way at work. Shake hands and a friendship is about to be renewed.

A **head** is a good omen for all that's important to you. A disembodied one is a warning not to lose your own! Stay calm when confronted with a new situation. See yourself with more than one head and promotion is predicted. An accident or bang on the head suggests you've been overworking; try and take a break.

The **hips** of someone of the opposite sex are a

warning not to embark on a new love affair. Big hips predict some unexpected gains.

See your own **jaws** and you will be the target of spiteful gossip. Fight it or it could damage your reputation. If the jaws belong to others, someone is going to help you make money.

A swollen **knee** says business looks a bit risky at the moment. A grazed one predicts a long journey. See a bandaged knee and it's a sign to take things easy for a while.

Knuckles say you're wasting your time and energy on something that will come to nothing. Why not redirect your ambitions?

Sit on someone's **lap**, and if they are of the opposite sex an exciting new love affair is on the horizon. Fall off and some silly behaviour will lose you prestige.

Skinny **legs** are a warning to take care in romance. Injured ones spell money troubles that simply can't be avoided. See a pretty pair of pins and a happy change of circumstances is forecast.

Don't judge others too harshly if you see thin, cruel **lips**. Lovely lips spell success in your love life. Thick, full lips mean you will fail in love but succeed in business. Chapped or sore ones predict business losses.

Have trouble with your **liver** and things will improve for you. But dream of **lung** trouble, and it's a warning to see your doctor.

A round body **mole** is a sign of good luck. A hairy one predicts difficulties.

An open **mouth** is a warning you've been using your own a bit too much lately. Shut up and listen. If the teeth are showing, one of your friends can't be trusted. A small mouth and money is coming to you. A large one predicts a valuable new friend.

The **neck** says money is on its way to you. If it's broken you are mismanaging your affairs. Pay more attention to them.

Nipples sucked at for nourishment by an adult are telling you your debts are getting out of hand. Pay them off and try and stop spending so much. A baby suckling means at least one of your worries will vanish. Painful nipples are a warning to get a medical check-up, and if you see yourself with more than the statutory pair it's a sign you're not being very discriminating in your choice of partner.

See your own **nose** and you have more friends than you think. Blow it and you are about to be relieved of an irksome duty. Don't lend money if you see a nosebleed. You will lose an important piece of paper if you see a red nose. A turned-up nose means a promise simply won't be kept.

A cut **throat** is a sign you could be in some sort of danger soon. Swollen, and your imagination is running riot. Have your tonsils out and a series of disappointments will make you gloomy.

If you see your **tummy** exposed, it's a warning of unfaithfulness or treachery by someone you trust.

Your own **waist** is a sign your finances are being stretched. Someone else's and a friend is going to ask for your help.

Warts on your hands are a sign of money to come. The more the merrier. But your generosity could land you in a tight spot if you see them on any other part of the body. Warts on others are a sign of hidden hostility.

HUNCHBACK Pleasant news is about to arrive. Touch the hunchback and good luck is yours. See yourself as a hunchback and it would be wise to have a medical check-up.

HUNGER *See also*: Food. A contrary dream. If you or others are hungry, it signifies good luck and a healthy bank balance. The greater the hunger, the more fortune will smile on you.

HUNTING It's an obstacle dream. Success in the hunt and you will soon sort out your problems successfully. If not you will have to carry on coping with them for a while. Hunting or shooting **antelope** means you have an untrustworthy business associate. Kill a **fox** and you will be able to outwit someone you dislike, or even a love rival. See a **spear** and your love life is going to take an exciting turn, especially if it's used to catch fish.

HURDLES A sure sign you should stop trying to give a false impression. Honesty is by far the best policy for you at the moment.

HUT If you are in it then a catastrophe is just round the corner. But see a low hut and your future will be more secure.

HYPNOTISM Let sleeping dogs lie is the warning if you are the one hypnotised. If you hypnotise someone else then tighten your belt. Money is about to be a bit thin on the ground.

HYSTERIA See someone in hysterics and you must be careful not to be forced into doing something you really don't want to do. If you have hysterics, then follow the advice of your friends.

**I**CE *See also*: Weather. Not a good omen. A vast expanse of ice and snow invariably signals dangers or difficulties. An icy road or path shows you are restless and waiting for something more exciting to happen. If you break through ice, your fears are groundless. Ice in a drink means you are wasting your time and your money.

ICEBERG Hidden obstacles lie in your path but you can get round them if you go carefully.

ICICLES Your deepest anxieties will soon disappear. If the icicles are dripping, hang on to your money at least for a couple of months.

IDIOT Dream of being or seeing one and your own intelligence will help you make a success of things.

IDOL *See also*: Religion. Worship one and you are in for a major disappointment. A wooden one is a sign to take more care. A gold one and watch out for jealousy.

ILL-HEALTH *See also*: Affliction; Health. See yourself sick and perplexing problems are predicted. See others ill and a promise is about to be broken.

An **abscess** is a signal to get rid of bad friends. Having an abscess means an immediate recovery unless it's on the neck, which spells sickness. Seeing an abscess being operated on means a mystery will be solved.

Dream of having your **adenoids** removed and some new friends will greatly admire you.

Anaemia is a contrary dream. Your health will be good.

Any **antidote** warns of a scandal in the offing. Taking one means you must be more circumspect in relationships.

Any sign of **appendicitis** is a warning not to blab. Be more careful with your confidences.

Arthritis says your ailments are only minor.

If you suffer from **asthma** and dream of it, then it's of no significance. If not, however, it's a warning against loss through risky speculation.

Feeling **bilious** is a warning against high living in low company!

Bronchitis is an obstacle dream. If the illness is shortlived, then try hard and you will solve your problems. If you don't recover, you will need to ask friends for help. Don't be afraid to ask.

Dream of **cancer** and your health will be fine and your life long if you cut down on high living and stop burning the candle at both ends.

Chilblains are again a contrary dream. Something that's been causing you pain will soon be cleared up.

Cough and it's time to check your insurance. This is a prediction of fire, theft or even flood.

Dream of your own **fever** and you're worrying too much. It will never happen, so try and enjoy life. Fever in others signals exciting times ahead.

Poor health in general is a warning not to gamble.

If you are afflicted by **insanity** good news is on the way. See others in this condition and you can expect an unpleasant surprise.

Success will come but not as quickly as you'd hoped if you see yourself as an **invalid**. See others thus and a friend or relation is about to ask you for help.

See yourself with the **measles** and it's time to stop fretting. Worrying will only make things worse—especially at work. See others with measles and affairs of the heart won't run smoothly. But if it's children, happiness is round the corner.

Lose your **voice** and it's a warning not to gamble or take any unnecessary risks for a while.

ILLUMINATIONS *See also*: Darkness/Light. Whether they are in Blackpool or anywhere else, bright illuminations are an omen of good fortune in the things you care about most.

IMPATIENCE Don't make any hasty decisions. You are in for a confusing time, take it steady.

IMPERSONATION *See also*: Deception. You are going through a jealous phase if you imitate someone. This is not a very lucky omen.

IMPOTENCE *See also*: Sexuality. A contrary dream. Success is starred in your love life and your other interests will go well too.

INCENSE Smell this and your troubles are over. See the smoke and your hopes can be put into practice.

INCEST Don't give in to temptation no matter who tries to persuade you otherwise. You will regret it forever if you give in.

INCISION If you are not a doctor, then you could be in for legal troubles. Check all your paperwork.

INCOME *See also*: Money. A dream of opposite. Money troubles are on the way if you dream of a large income. A low one and your financial burdens will soon be lifted.

INCOME TAX *See also*: Money. You won't be able to help that friend you hoped you could support and if anyone tells you 'the cheque's in the post'—don't believe them!

INCUBATOR You are worrying too much; relax and all will be well.

INDEX Compile one and you're in for promotion. Looking at one is a sure sign your sex life is about to improve.

INFIDELITY *See also*: Deception; Relationships. Dream your partner or a friend is being unfaithful to you and all is well. It actually means you can trust them. But if you are unfaithful yourself, you are going to face a few temptations. Try and resist.

INHERITANCE *See also*: Money. A straightforward prediction that a legacy is on its way.

INK A loss or separation could be on the cards, particularly if it is spilt. An ink stain is a sign of possible illness. The larger the stain, the more serious the illness. Pour ink into a pot and travel is predicted.

INOCULATION Money may be tight but don't worry. Everyone, including the bank manager, will rally round until you are on the up and up again.

INQUEST New responsibilities are forecast. They may be tough but you will enjoy them.

INSECTS An obstacle dream. Get rid of them or kill them and your troubles are easier to sort out than you think.

Ants at work mean business matters will go well. Ants in the house and there could be an illness in the family. But see ants on food and your happiness is assured.

See **bedbugs** and some unpleasant news is coming. Kill them and your situation will eventually improve.

Bees symbolise hard work and success. If you are stung by one, you are in for a petty tiff with someone. If you kill a bee or see dead bees, a so-called friend will do you out of something. Buzzing bees signal good news.

There is jealousy and hostility around you if you see **beetles**. Kill them and your difficulties are only temporary.

A colourful **butterfly** and your life will soon be so full you won't know which way to turn. If it's flying around a light, one of your victories will be short-lived. A dead butterfly is a sign of danger.

Caterpillars are omens of jealousy. Someone is out to humiliate you if you dream of them.

Someone out there doesn't like you and is out to cause trouble if you see **earwigs**.

Fleas mean someone around you is being malicious. But if you managed to get rid of the fleas you can beat the backstabber.

Dream of **flies** and there is jealousy in your life that will cause some petty annoyances. Get rid of the flies and you will get rid of the trouble-makers.

Gnats also spell petty troubles from jealous friends. But get rid of them and your troubles will disappear.

Mosquitoes flying high predict good fortune. If they bite you, it's a sign you are jealous of someone. Hear them buzzing and you are the subject of some vicious gossip.

Try and catch a **moth** and someone is jealous of you. Kill one and you will outwit your rivals. Moth holes in material predict sadness in the family.

Spiders are a good luck sign. Kill one and good news is coming. See it spinning and money is on the way. Climbing a wall and the things that matter to you most will go well. A spider in a web warns that someone close to you is simply using you.

A **wasp** says one of your relationships is holding you back. It's time to break it off.

Worms used as bait are a sign of material gain. Kill them and your efforts will be successful. Otherwise worms warn of illness.

INSIGNIA *See also*: Uniform. Despite hostile competition, you'll make progress. Wear insignia and an exciting new love affair is round the corner.

INSTRUMENT *See also*: Music. A medical one, like a scalpel, is a sign the family is putting obstacles in your way. Navigation instruments mean you've made a bit of a blunder, probably at work, and you need some understanding right now. Most musical instruments are omens of harmony and happiness.

INSULT If this is done to you, then you have emotional problems. Your partner has just betrayed you in some way. Insult someone else and an unhappy phase will only end if you make a major change—like a new job or a house move.

INSURANCE *See also*: Money. If you collect it, you will be faced with a set-back. Buy it and your plans are sound. The future looks bright.

INTERCOURSE *See also*: Sexuality. If you enjoyed it, you will happily adjust to new circumstances. If you see others having intercourse, contentment and success are coming to you. But if any feature of the dream is unpleasant, you're probably repressing an emotional problem. An expert counsellor could help.

INTERPRETER *See also*: Speaking. Money problems are to the fore if you act as or use one of these.

INTERROGATION See yourself doing this and it's a sign you are not very good at forming lasting relationships with those around you. If you were on the end of interrogation, a pleasant surprise probably in the form of a journey, is coming.

INTERVIEWING If you are talking to celebrities, a pleasant meeting is round the corner. Interview a politician and it shows you have a rebellious streak. A job interview suggests a major change, though not necessarily of career.

INTRIGUE An element of this and you are about to be blushing when a so-called friend breaches a confidence. It is a warning to be more discreet in the future.

INVALID *See also*: Ill-health. Success will come but not as quickly as you hoped if you see yourself as an invalid. See others thus and a friend or relation is about to ask you for help.

INVENTION Your dearest wish is about to be granted.

INVISIBILITY Quick and unexpected changes are round the corner. But never fear, they are for the better.

INVITATION This is a dream of opposite. Receive one and you are about to enter a boring phase that will make you rather depressed. But if the invitation is verbal, things could look up in your social life.

IODINE All your troubles are of your own making, I'm afraid. But a bit of effort will put things right.

IRON *See also*: Metals. If it is rusty, it is a sign of physical strength. Molten iron is a good sign for happy times ahead in your love life. Beaten and it shows you are a bit on the grumpy side lately. Any iron object brings good luck with it. A clothes iron means it's time to solve those little irritating problems before they get bigger.

IRONING For a woman, this mundane chore signifies a happy release from some burden. For a man, it means a quick profit or pay rise.

ISLAND *See also*: Foreign Places/People. If you are a castaway on one, it suggests you are bored and lonely. But if the island is inhabited, interesting new developments are under way to cheer you up. Palm trees are a sign of hopeful prospects.

ITCH Itchy feet are a clear sign you are yearning for new horizons and experiences. Itchy hands mean money luck and if it's your nose, you should be careful not to make mistakes at work. A general feeling of itchiness is an omen you are worrying too much—try and lighten up!

IVORY *See also*: Jewellery. A good luck sign. A single girl who dreams of this will marry a kind, gentleman and have a happy family life.

IVY Outdoors, this is a sign of faithful friends. Indoors, it predicts personal happiness. Money is coming in the future if you see it growing on a house. Twining round a tree, it is a symbol of good health.

JAB You are underestimating yourself if you feel or are given this. Try and be a bit more confident. Jab others and you must try not to be so aggressive. Try a softer approach.

JACK A car jack is a sign of a change for the better. But if you are using it yourself, then look out for spiteful gossip.

JACKPOT A contrary dream. Win it and you are in for some hard work with precious little reward. See someone else win and you can gain something with a lot less effort than you thought.

JAIL *See also*: Police/Prisons. An obstacle dream. Release or escape means your problems will be short-lived. If not, the road ahead will be long and hard. See others in jail and your worries will soon disappear.

JANUARY *See also*: Time. If it isn't the first month of the year, then some perplexing problem will soon be solved. If it is, then money is coming to you.

JAR Your social life is about to spice up with lots of invites in the offing. If the jars are empty, you can expect a letter from abroad.

Plate 14 · The Journey

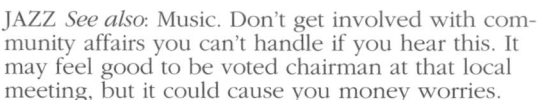

JAZZ *See also*: Music. Don't get involved with community affairs you can't handle if you hear this. It may feel good to be voted chairman at that local meeting, but it could cause you money worries.

JEALOUSY *See also*: Anger/Confrontation. This emotion is a sign you'll soon be involved in problems in your love life or with your friends. But if the jealousy is directed at you, things will soon turn out to your advantage.

JERUSALEM *See also*: Foreign Places/People. A sign you are lonely. Make an effort to call up friends. Someone has to make the first move.

JESUS *See also*: Religion. Consolation in adversity is the message here. If you spoke or prayed with Him or He touched you, true peace of mind will be yours.

JEWELLERY If the jewellery is real then your current interests will go well. If it is only costume your vanity could lead you astray. Steal it and it's a warning to take care in business. Give or receive it and you're about to be lucky. Wear jewellery and you must try not to be so impulsive.

A **bracelet** is a happy sign. See one on your arm and your love life will go well. If someone else puts it on for you, then expect to fall in love and marry soon. Find a bracelet and it's a warning that you will shortly meet someone who will cause you confusion. Lose one and you are in for a disappointment.

Wearing a **brooch** predicts an inheritance. Buying one means someone is deceiving you. Sell one and watch your wallet—you could lose a great deal of money.

Gold **earrings** spell some temporary set-backs on the way. Silver ones suggest you are being judged a bit harshly by others. Diamonds or other gems in the earrings mean you are a bit below par or even lazy right now. Buy earrings and your ideas are a bit too extravagant. Lose them and the road is rocky financially. Finding earrings is a warning not to have that flutter. Wear them and you are not pulling your weight at work.

Ivory is a good luck sign. A single girl who dreams of this will marry a kind, gentle man and have a happy family life.

A **necklace** predicts marriage or promotion at work if you put one on. See one in a shop and it's a sign you are jealous of someone. A pearl necklace predicts a period of gloomy despondency. A broken necklace and there are family rows brewing.

Lose a **ring** and it's a sign your relationship with your partner is hanging in the balance. Take one off

and your love life problems will be short-lived. Receive a ring and you're in for a night of passion. Put one on and you will soon go to a wedding. It might even be your own.

A religious **rosary** says someone influential is supporting and protecting you. If it's ivory you aren't showing much initiative at the moment. Wooden and it's a sign you are feeling sentimental. Buy a rosary and you have high hopes for a new project.

JIG *See also*: Music. Dance it alone and happy times are ahead. Dance with a partner and it's time to curb your sex life! See others jigging and you are being a bit over-generous with money.

JILT *See also*: Weddings. A contrary dream in your love affairs. They will be constant if you dream you are jilted.

JINGLE *See also*: Music. Hear this and a harmless flirtation is just round the corner. Jingling bells signify social activity.

JOCKEY An auspicious sign, especially if he is riding in a race. A very good omen if he wins. Then your hopes and desires are about to come true. But if he falls off, one of your projects is doomed to failure.

JOKE A funny one and you are about to have a spat with a friend. Tell a funny joke yourself and business will boom. But if it falls flat, a personal disappointment is on the cards. Dirty jokes are a sign of fat profits.

JOURNEY *See also*: Arriving/Leaving. This predicts changes. A pleasant journey and they will be favourable. An unpleasant one and the changes will be for the worse.

JUDAS *See also*: Guilt. Be careful of new friends if you see this character. Let them prove their worth before you get too involved.

JUG *See also*: Drink. Full ones are a sign of good friends. Drink from one and you can look forward to good health. A broken jug predicts an influential new friend or exciting new love affair.

JUGGLER *See also*: Performing. A new opportunity involving a quick profit or promotion is about to present itself. Don't hesitate, all will be well.

JULY *See also*: Time. Be cautious of all new offers if it is not in fact July. Delve into them deeply before deciding.

JUMPING Patience is the key. You will overcome

your difficulties if you persevere.

JUNE *See also*: Time. Dream of June when it isn't and an exciting new romance is predicted.

JUNGLE *See also*: Foreign Places/People. Get lost or stuck here and you will soon run into major problems. If you make your way through the jungle, you will sort things out.

JUNK A difficult decision is looming. Don't make it alone, sound out advice.

JUSTICE *See also*: Guilt; Legal matters. See the lady with the scales and a successful future is assured.

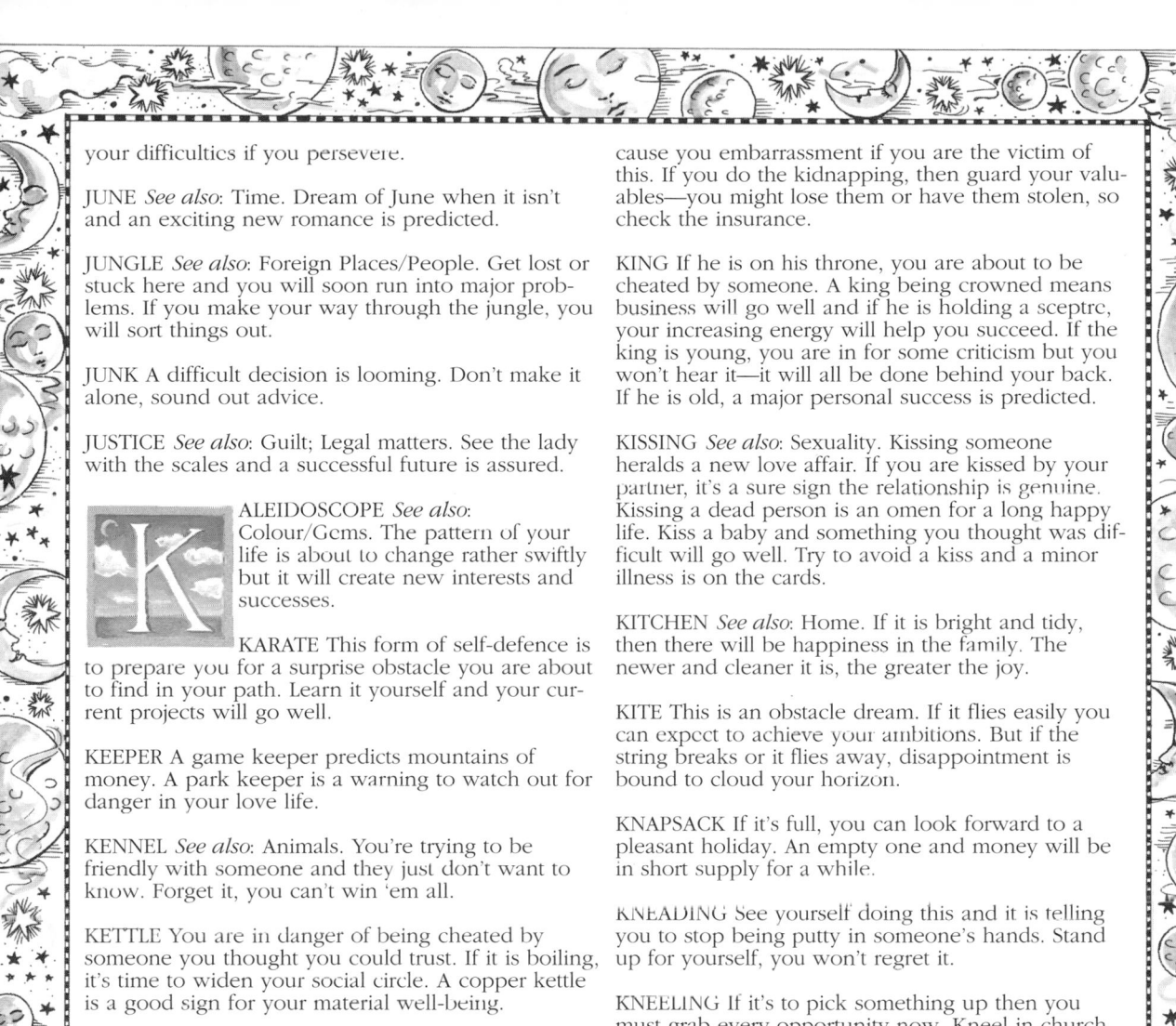

ALEIDOSCOPE *See also*: Colour/Gems. The pattern of your life is about to change rather swiftly but it will create new interests and successes.

KARATE This form of self-defence is to prepare you for a surprise obstacle you are about to find in your path. Learn it yourself and your current projects will go well.

KEEPER A game keeper predicts mountains of money. A park keeper is a warning to watch out for danger in your love life.

KENNEL *See also*: Animals. You're trying to be friendly with someone and they just don't want to know. Forget it, you can't win 'em all.

KETTLE You are in danger of being cheated by someone you thought you could trust. If it is boiling, it's time to widen your social circle. A copper kettle is a good sign for your material well-being.

KEY/KEYHOLE *See also*: Doors. Find one and a pressing problem is about to be solved. Lose one and a disappointment is inevitable. Fit a key in a lock and your love life will run smoothly. A broken key is a sign you have lost a good opportunity. A bunch of keys indicates business profits.

If there is no key in a keyhole, this is a warning one of your friends can't be trusted. Peep through a keyhole or see someone else do it and you are being a bit impulsive lately. Try and think before you act.

KICKING If someone does it to you, then you are afraid of competition. Do the kicking and things will improve. You may even get promoted soon. Kick a ball and good news is on the way. A kick in the buttocks means a steady rise in status. But if you did the kicking someone, somewhere is jealous of you.

KIDNAPPING Change your friends or they could

cause you embarrassment if you are the victim of this. If you do the kidnapping, then guard your valuables—you might lose them or have them stolen, so check the insurance.

KING If he is on his throne, you are about to be cheated by someone. A king being crowned means business will go well and if he is holding a sceptre, your increasing energy will help you succeed. If the king is young, you are in for some criticism but you won't hear it—it will all be done behind your back. If he is old, a major personal success is predicted.

KISSING *See also*: Sexuality. Kissing someone heralds a new love affair. If you are kissed by your partner, it's a sure sign the relationship is genuine. Kissing a dead person is an omen for a long happy life. Kiss a baby and something you thought was difficult will go well. Try to avoid a kiss and a minor illness is on the cards.

KITCHEN *See also*: Home. If it is bright and tidy, then there will be happiness in the family. The newer and cleaner it is, the greater the joy.

KITE This is an obstacle dream. If it flies easily you can expect to achieve your ambitions. But if the string breaks or it flies away, disappointment is bound to cloud your horizon.

KNAPSACK If it's full, you can look forward to a pleasant holiday. An empty one and money will be in short supply for a while.

KNEADING See yourself doing this and it is telling you to stop being putty in someone's hands. Stand up for yourself, you won't regret it.

KNEELING If it's to pick something up then you must grab every opportunity now. Kneel in church and your wishes are about to come true. Otherwise it's a warning you are being cheated.

KNIFE If it's sharp, some personal disputes are in view. A rusty one spells family troubles. A broken one, failure in love. A penknife predicts legal troubles and a table knife new successes. Cut yourself and it's a warning to pay your debts.

KNIGHT *See also*: Uniform. A lucky symbol. It is an omen of protection and security.

KNITTING Do this and peace of mind will soon be yours. But drop stitches and your domestic scene won't be exactly blissful for a while. An intricate pattern predicts renewing an old friendship or starting an interesting new one.

KNOT An obstacle dream which could spell a spat with someone close. Untie it and you will reach a compromise. Cut it and a split is likely.

LABEL Your investments are about to pay dividends if you see this. Luggage labels spell a surprise, probably a visitor. A label on a bottle shows how practical you are.

LABORATORY You could be in danger here. Perhaps it's your health. Are you exhausted because you've been working too hard? Or it could be your state of mind. Could it be you're depressed? Perhaps you are going through a bad patch with your mate. But whatever it is, take heart, it will only be temporary.

LABOURER *See also*: Work. Seeing a man doing any kind of heavy work means a lucky coincidence is round the corner. It will bring both money and respect. If he is having a rest it shows your enthusiasm is lacking at work. Try and shape up.

LABYRINTH An obstacle dream. Find your way out and your problems will be easily solved. Get lost or be frightened and some surprise opposition may force you to change direction.

LACE Who's popular with the opposite sex then? You are at your most magnetic right now. Make lace and a dodgy deal will rake in a profit. But mind you don't get caught. Lace curtains are a warning not to squander your time on frivolous fun and paper lace is telling you not to put too much store on appearances.

LADDER If you're climbing it then the higher the ladder the greater will be your achievement. But if a rung breaks under you then you will fail to achieve your greatest ambition. Climb down a ladder and disappointment is round the corner. Fall from it and you've bitten off more than you can chew, I'm afraid. Walking under a ladder, despite the old superstition, is in fact a good luck sign. See one fall and you will have to deal with a few unexpected obstacles. Carry one and you will be called on to rescue a friend in some way. A rope ladder spells success in business. A step ladder and a stroke of good luck is predicted.

LADLE Use one and you will hear news from an absent friend. Simply see one and some sort of secret spells danger.

LAKE *See also*: Water. A clear, calm lake is a symbol of future happiness and success. But if the water is rough or dirty, a difficult period in life is just ahead. Cross a lake in a boat and you will rise in others' estimation. Jump into it and it is a sign of unhappiness. You're worrying too much if you wade or walk into a lake. Try to take things easy.

LAND Own it and your fortunes will take a turn for the better. If you are ordered off it you should brace yourself for a disappointment.

LANDSLIDE See it from a safe distance and you are handling your current problems with intelligence. Get caught up in it and there is deception between you and someone close. But whose side is it on?

LANE A narrow country one is a sign to be more discreet in your affairs with the opposite sex. If it is blocked off then you are troubled by personal dilemmas and doubts. A dark lane is an omen for a major money problem.

LANTERN This is a warning not to play the field in your sex life. Try and stay faithful. If the lantern is blown out you are in for legal trouble.

LAP An exciting new love affair is on the horizon if you sit on the lap of someone of the opposite sex. Fall off and some silly behaviour will lose you prestige.

LATE *See also*: Time. Don't make promises you can't keep is the warning if it is you that is late. If it is others then it's time to tighten your belt. You simply can't afford those luxuries for a while.

LATHER *See also*: Washing. News from a distance will sort out your problems if you find yourself in this.

LAUGHTER *See also*: Sounds. Hear a man laugh and you are about to learn a lot from a new work project. A woman is a sign you are being a bit anti-social. News will arrive from a long way away if you hear children laughing. And if you make people laugh it is time to face the fact that you and your partner aren't really suited.

LAUNDRY *See also*: Washing. Wash by hand and you are in good shape physically at the moment. Hang it out to dry and you are on the boil mentally. Clean laundry is a mark of good fortune. If it's dirty, problems are in store.

LAVA Your social life is about to take off in a big way. But take care it doesn't break the bank.

LAVATORY An important issue currently hanging in the balance will be successfully concluded.

LAXATIVE Take this and you will be asked to do something difficult but you will come out of it well. Administer one and you will gain in areas where you expected a loss.

LEAF *See also*: Trees/Plants. If it's green and healthy everything is going your way, both at home and at work. Fallen or dried-up leaves are a sign of difficulties and illness.

Plate 15 · The Ladybird and the Wasp

LEAK *See also*: Water. You are wasting your time here. A leaky pipe is a sign to try and find wider scope for your activities—branch out. A roof leak and misfortune is ahead. See a leaking radiator and you will soon hear news of a birth.

LEANING A dream of contrary. Lean on someone or something and you are about to become more independent. If someone leans on you then you are going to need help soon.

LEARNING *See also*: School. It's a sign you have taken on too much if you are learning a new skill. Learning to sing means a temporary sadness. If it's dancing you are about to get involved in a new activity.

LEATHER *See also*: Clothes. Anything made of this is a lucky omen. Buy it and it indicates family happiness. But give leather as a gift and you are in for some family squabbles. You will beat your enemies if you see a leather shop.

LECTURE *See also*: School. Hear one and it is a sign of limited successes. Give one and you could be in for a move.

LEECH A big bill that you didn't expect is about to land on your mat. But don't fret, you'll raise the dosh.

LEFT The left side of anything or a left turn is a signal not to be discouraged by a set-back. You'll get there in the end. Dream you are left-handed when you are not and you should watch your back. You have a dangerous rival.

LEGACY *See also*: Legal matters. A very lucky omen especially where money is concerned.

LEGAL MATTERS Anything involving the law or lawyers is a sign of trouble in business or money matters. Don't take risks or lend anything. See yourself as a lawyer and your inner strengths will see you successful. Defend someone and friends have lost their faith in you for some reason. You are feeling very guilty about something if you simply see lawyers.

If you are **acquitted** in court, you're heading for a rough time from hostile competition. But calm down. Suddenly you will win through.

Become an **advocate** and you will have safety and money. Hiring one to defend you means a project you are involved with will not have good results. If you are introduced to an advocate in your dream prepare for some bad news.

If you dream of giving someone an **alibi** then give a wide berth to quarrelsome friends. But if it's some

one else's alibi, an unexpected good time is approaching.

See your own affairs subject to **arbitration** and you will gain something you want. If you are the arbitrator, tact is the only tool to get you out of a tight spot.

Needing or offering to pay **bail** means you are thinking of committing yourself to an unwise partnership. Try and sidestep it for your own sake.

Sign a **contract** and you will be promoted. Refuse to sign and you'll get there but it will take longer than you thought.

Watch your pocket if you see a **court** building. But don't worry, if you don't waste so much time it won't be empty for long.

Give **evidence** in court and someone is going to ask you for help. Hear someone else give evidence and you must watch your back—or you will get stabbed there.

A **judge** is an ill prediction for the future. Obstacles and difficulties are round the corner. You may be involved in an argument or be accused of something you didn't do. But keep cool and all will turn out well.

Some sort of recognition will be yours if you see yourself before a **jury**. But serve on a jury yourself and it's a warning to rely more on your intuition and stop listening to others.

If a **magistrate** finds you guilty nothing will go according to plan for a while. Innocent and you are in for happy times. See yourself as a magistrate and you can get what you want if you work hard for it.

See **stealing** and you should look after your money or you'll be out of pocket. Get caught at it and it's a sign of good luck.

If you are on **trial** it's a warning to stick to the tried and tested for a while. Don't attempt anything new.

LEPER A period of hardship is on the cards. A man dreaming of having this illness should have a check-up. For a woman it is a sign she will be helped by a rich man. See others with leprosy and the only way to solve your problems is on your own. Don't listen to advice, however well meant.

LETTER Write one and everything is going well for you emotionally. Receive one and news is on the way to you from a distance. Post a letter and your current problems will soon be solved. An anonymous letter is a sign of danger. A love letter indicates you are regretting a foolish affair. A chain letter predicts an unusual new experience. Finding a letter is a warning that a friend is being disloyal.

LIBRARY See also: Reading/Writing. A good omen. It is a sign you are full of self-confidence and ready to take on all-comers.

LICKING Lick your lips and it shows you have been greedy lately. Lick your fingers and it indicates you have a phobia you must overcome. If it's a spoon, you are in for some pleasant changes.

LIFEBOAT See also: Sea/Water/Travel. If it's on a ship you are about to run into opposition at work. See it at sea and you will beat your enemies. If it is damaged changes are on the way and they will be for the better. See a lifeboat save people and it predicts a long happy life.

LIGHTHOUSE See it at night and both business and love affairs will run smoothly. Seen in daylight it predicts a long journey. If you are in it, life will be long and healthy.

LIGHTNING See also: Weather. If something is struck by lightning your future plans will meet with success.

LIPSTICK You are being a bit selfish at the moment if you see this. Choose it in a shop and money troubles are ahead. Give someone lipstick and you are feeling in a confident frame of mind.

LOCK If it's a padlock you will soon need some legal advice. Pick a lock and you are about to be involved in someone else's embarrassment. Unlock something and happiness is on the way. But trouble lies ahead if you fail to unlock it.

LOCKJAW See also: Speaking. A straightforward warning to keep your mouth shut! Remember what they say about careless talk…!

LOG See also: Trees/Plants. Things will improve at home if you see logs. Stack them and it is a good omen for whatever concerns you most. If the logs are floating in water it is a signal to grasp every opportunity now. If they are burning, a family celebration is on the cards. Sit on one and you will soon feel more content with life. A log cabin means you will have to work hard but will get there in the end.

LOOM A step backwards is indicated here. But don't panic. You'll soon be able to take another two in the right direction.

LOSS Lose something and unexpected changes are afoot. Lose a bet and it is a sign you are being a bit arrogant over something. If it's a race or a game you are getting into bad habits.

LOTTERY A bad omen for romance. The future with your mate looks a bit uncertain. See a lottery ticket and family troubles are on the cards.

LOUDSPEAKER Hear this and you are in for a worrying time. But manage to turn it down a decibel and you will be thanked for a bit of useful social or charity work.

LOVE See also: Relationships. Dream of falling in love and someone somewhere loves you—and is about to tell you so. If love passes you by it is in fact an omen that you will soon marry.

LYING DOWN A short illness or some unhappiness is predicted.

ACE You'll be recognised for doing some kind of community work if you see or smell this.

MACE-BEARER See also: Uniform. If you carry it yourself it spells danger in love affairs. See someone else bear it and you will receive some kind of distinction.

MACHINERY Watch it or inspect it and work will go well. Despite differences of opinion you will be successful. If you are worried or frightened by the machinery a serious problem will crop up because you keep putting things off. If you see machinery in a factory it is a good sign for your health.

MAGAZINE See also: Reading/Writing. If they are on a newsagent's shelf then news is coming from a distance. Buy one and your troubles will soon be over. Sell one and it is a sign of loneliness.

MAGIC See also: Supernatural. Unexpected changes are coming. They may be hard to understand at first but all will make sense in the end. See a magician doing his act and you could rekindle an old flame or bump into an old friend.

MAGNET You are going to be very popular with the opposite sex. In fact, your attraction will be quite magnetic!

MAGNIFYING GLASS A sudden stroke of money luck or even a pay rise is indicated here. Buy one and you will rediscover lost valuables.

MAHOGANY Life is about to look up if you see this wood. You may even receive an inheritance.

MAID *See also*: Tidiness. If you actually have one this is a good omen. If not, it predicts a loss of status. For a woman dreaming of being a maid is a sign she is about to step up the social scale.

MANICURE Some unexpected expenses are on the way. Budget for them now or you will be caught short of cash.

MANSION *See also*: Home. A dream of contrary. A luxury mansion and you will have to accept some changes you don't much like. But a run-down one and the coming changes will be for the better.

MANURE Shovel this and it is a favourable sign. Money luck or some sort of profit is on the way.

MAP Not surprisingly, these signify journeys and changes. The bigger the map the longer the journey or greater the change. Draw on a map and the trip or change will be lucky for you.

MARBLES *See also*: Childhood/Children. Love troubles or a personal disappointment are predicted.

MARCH *See also*: Time. Dream of this month when it isn't and you are in for a disappointment. Something you expected simply won't happen. See people marching and it predicts sad news.

MARIJUANA Something you are planning doesn't do you any credit. Think carefully before going ahead. If you are caught smoking this illegal substance it is a sign you are playing around too much.

MARKET Particularly favourable for the unattached. You could soon be falling in love and, even better, a few other pleasant little surprises are just round the corner. For a married woman a market is a symbol of betrayal.

MARRIAGE *See also*: Relationships. If you are single and dream of marriage you are involved in something that will come to no good. But good news is on the way if you see yourself at someone else's wedding. A secret marriage suggests you are confused because of a love let-down.

MARSH Don't get involved in other peoples' problems is the message here. Give advice by all means but stay well out of it.

MARTYR You've been making too many sacrifices lately if you see yourself as one of these. Try and be more decisive and aggressive. You can still be generous but it's about time charity started at home for you. See someone else as a martyr and it is a warning not to get your troubles out of proportion or

exaggerate your problems.

MASCOT Any type of mascot is an omen of beneficial changes. Whatever they are they will work out well.

MASS *See also*: Religion. If it is outside then good news is coming. Inside a church predicts up-coming difficulties.

MASSACRE You could be robbed or burgled if you see this. Check your security.

MASSAGE Have one yourself and your doubts about someone's loyalty are unfounded. Stop being so paranoid! Give one and you can expect some good news.

MAT See it at the front door and some unwelcome visitors are about to arrive. Any other kind of mat predicts obstacles. The bigger the mat…

MATCH *See also*: Fire. Strike one and a pay rise is on the cards. Make some kind of match and it is a good time for a little flutter.

MATTRESS This is a symbol of peace and tranquillity. An old one and you will be given a useful piece of advice at work. A new one and easy times are ahead. A double mattress means you have been having a few problems with your partner and are anxious to sort them out. Try talking it over.

MAY *See also*: Time. If it is not the month of May then you are in for a few money troubles.

MEADOW *See also*: Flowers. See it full of flowers and your happiness and trust in your mate is being reciprocated. A newly mown meadow suggests you are depressed about something and thick grass is a sign your hopes are in vain, I'm afraid.

MEASURING A sign of gain. Measure your own body and your material wealth will increase. Measure the temperature and good times are ahead. Measure ingredients and you should take extra care with everything for a while. If it is a house be careful—you could lose more than you save.

MEDAL Wear one and the boss is finally going to start appreciating you at work. See others display them and it is a warning to curb your vanity or even that jealous streak.

MEDICINE *See also*: Doctors/Hospitals. Take it yourself and your troubles are trivial. Administer it and after a lot of effort you will enjoy success.

MEETING Hold one and you are kicking yourself over a lost opportunity. Attend one and you are at your decisive best. Now is the time to make those

Plate 16 · The Mermaid and the Fish

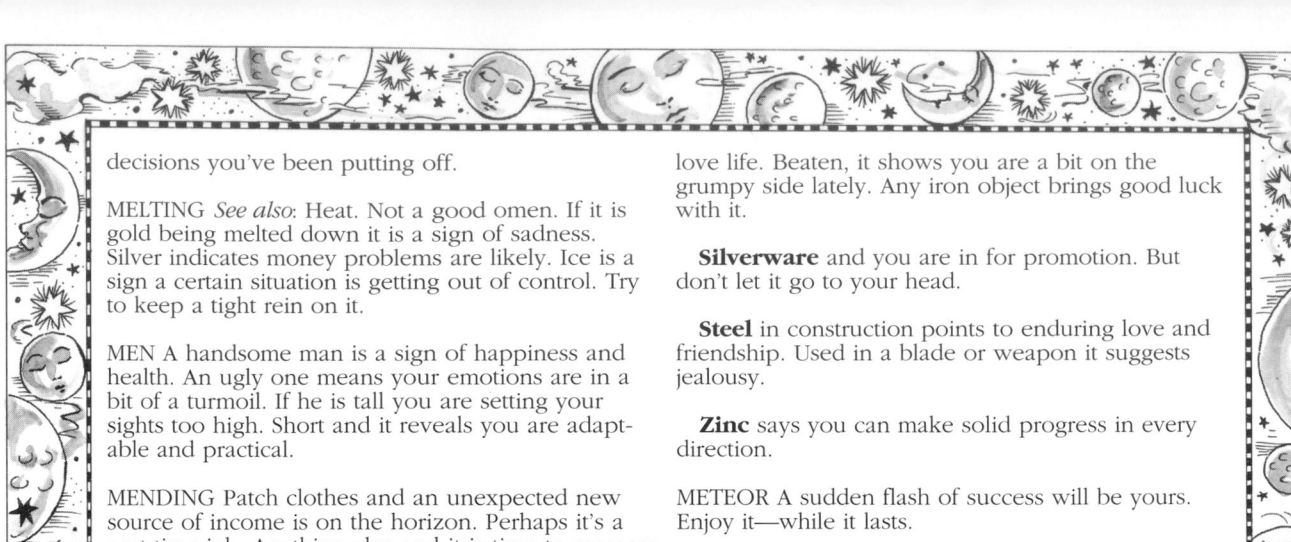

decisions you've been putting off.

MELTING *See also*: Heat. Not a good omen. If it is gold being melted down it is a sign of sadness. Silver indicates money problems are likely. Ice is a sign a certain situation is getting out of control. Try to keep a tight rein on it.

MEN A handsome man is a sign of happiness and health. An ugly one means your emotions are in a bit of a turmoil. If he is tall you are setting your sights too high. Short and it reveals you are adaptable and practical.

MENDING Patch clothes and an unexpected new source of income is on the horizon. Perhaps it's a part-time job. Anything else and it is time to reassess your plans—just to make certain you are doing the right thing.

MENU *See also*: Food. Read this and life will be comfortable. Perhaps not luxurious but you won't want for much.

MERMAID She relates to your love life and the exact meaning depends on the atmosphere of the dream. Pleasant and things will go well. But a feeling of confusion and you're in for a disappointment.

MESS A dream of contrary. Whatever is worrying you will soon come to a clean-cut conclusion.

MESSENGER Act as one and you are about to get a lucrative offer. Receive one and you can be sure your job is safe.

METALS Just like the substance, this dream indicates you're being cold and hard at present. Try to be a bit softer in your dealings with people. Molten metal suggests obstacles in your path. It would be better to try and change direction.

Watch new friends if you see **brass**. Rely on your own judgement.

See something made of **copper** and it's a sign your fears are groundless. If it's engraved it shows you have expensive taste.

A metal **engraving** says you are about to change jobs.

Find **gold** or work with it and you must remember that old saying 'All that glisters…'. Don't take things at face value. Stealing or counting gold is a warning that there is more to life than material things. Don't rank them so highly. Medals, jewellery, or coins forecast financial gain.

Rusty **iron** is a sign of physical strength. Molten iron is a good sign for happy times ahead in your love life. Beaten, it shows you are a bit on the grumpy side lately. Any iron object brings good luck with it.

Silverware and you are in for promotion. But don't let it go to your head.

Steel in construction points to enduring love and friendship. Used in a blade or weapon it suggests jealousy.

Zinc says you can make solid progress in every direction.

METEOR A sudden flash of success will be yours. Enjoy it—while it lasts.

MICROSCOPE Use this and you will suddenly discover you have a hidden talent for something. If it is broken, someone is going to challenge your integrity.

MIDGET A new acquaintance will develop into a valued friendship.

MILDEW Someone you care about is going to disappoint you. Unless you see it on food. That predicts a lucky escape from danger.

MILK *See also*: Drink. Cow's milk is an omen of good health. Goat's and you could be in for promotion. Mother's milk is one of the luckiest omens of all; long-lasting happiness is about to be yours. Sour milk predicts set-backs and if you spill it you are setting your sights too high, I'm afraid. See yourself milking and it signifies prosperity.

MILL A working wind or water mill suggests you are about to complete an important work project and earn respect and job satisfaction. But if it is not working you are in danger of stagnating both at work and in your current relationship. Try and sort things out. Or both could come to a sticky end.

MILLIONAIRE *See also*: Money; Success. Dream you are one and you are about to profit from a past favour. Meet one and it is a warning to seek advice before making any commitment.

MINE Work down one and your own hard work will eventually bring in the money. Simply see one and there could be a break with someone of the opposite sex.

MINISTER *See also*: Religion. The political kind is a sign you could soon be promoted at work.

A church minister means you should try and spend more time alone to think things through. You could be in for a disappointment if you don't take time to reflect.

MINT If it is the herb, both your health and happiness are about to improve. A money mint means you will get that promotion—you've waited long enough for it.

MIRROR A large one is a sign you are being a bit flighty lately. Watch out or you could upset your mate. A small mirror means you are shy about doing something. Don't be, it will work like a dream. A broken one predicts sad news and troubled times ahead. See yourself in a mirror and you simply can't trust one of your friends.

MISER *See also*: Money. Your financial future is a bit on the shaky side. And if you are contemplating an illicit affair think twice. Your partner is bound to find out.

MISSIONARY One of your long-term plans is doomed to failure if you see yourself as one of these. But if you are converted by one, things will be successful.

MISTLETOE Patience is the key word here, especially at work. But at least you can bet your love life will go well.

MOLASSES A warning not to gossip. Or you could find yourself in a sticky situation.

MONEY Money is a good luck sign. Give it away and you can expect a period of financial stability and prosperity. Receive some and a major development, possibly a birth, is on the cards. Finding money means changes for the better are coming either at work or in your relationship. See yourself collecting money for charity and it suggests you're feeling a bit unloved. Spend it, and you'll make an unexpected profit. Steal it, and it spells a surprise stroke of luck. Worry about money luck and it sparks off a run of good money luck.

Receive **benefits** and you must guard against uninhibited actions. Calm down. If you are the benefactor, your current plans will be lucky.

New social contacts will prove unexpectedly useful if you get a **bonus.**

Borrow money and you're in for some domestic tiffs. Pay it back and things will soon go smoothly. If others borrow from you, it predicts the death of a friend.

Buying is a contrary dream. The more you buy the more you should tighten your belt. But if you are buying carefully, expect a stroke of money luck.

Put away that **credit card** if you see a cashier. Money will soon be in short supply.

Pay **debts** and you are entering a lucky period. If someone repays you, then be prepared for a loss. Don't gamble.

Make any **gains** and the greater they are the bigger the warning to look after your money. But if you make gains dishonestly business will boom and you can expect to recover a loss.

Income in a dream is one of opposites. Money troubles are on the way if you see a large one. A low one and your financial burdens will soon be lifted.

You won't be able to help that friend you hoped you could support, and if anyone tells you 'the cheque's in the post', don't believe them if you dream of **income tax.**

An **inheritance** is a straightforward prediction that a legacy is on its way.

Dream you are a **millionaire** and you are about to profit from a past favour. Meet one and it's a warning to seek advice before making any commitment.

See a **miser** and your financial future is a bit on the shaky side. And if you are contemplating an illicit affair, think twice. Your partner is bound to find out.

Pay off a **mortgage** and an unexpected bill is looming. Dream you can't manage to pay it and you will get a lucky break. Apply for a mortgage and your worries will soon disappear.

A shiny new **penny** is a warning not to trust one of your friends. Give them away and money luck is on the cards. Receive them and you are about to make a loss.

Find a **purse** and a debt long overdue to you is about to be repaid. Lose one and a friend or lover is going to disillusion you.

Give or receive a **receipt** and better times are round the corner.

Collect **rent** and money will be tight. Pay it and you are in for some unhappiness. If you can't afford to pay, then a pleasant surprise is round the corner.

You are going to have to pay out in some way if **taxes** worry you. If not you can expect to prosper.

Pay **wages** and a good opportunity for change is round the corner. Receive them and you could be the victim of theft. Make sure things are secure.

A leather **wallet** is a sign you are having second thoughts about something. Full of money, and you have serious problems to overcome. Find a wallet and an unexpected meeting is on the cards. Lose one and it's time to stop being so indecisive. It's a good time to have a flutter if you see an empty wallet.

MONOCLE This is a warning not to put on airs and graces. Try being yourself. Honesty is the best policy.

MONSTER Not a good sign. You are making life difficult for others by being depressed and pessimistic. If a monster attacks or chases you it suggests you have been bitterly disappointed lately. You'll get over it.

MOON *See also*: Darkness/Light. This symbol of peace and harmony is a very hopeful sign especially for your love life. A crescent moon indicates you have problems with your partner but they are easily and soon solved. A half moon means a hazardous journey but a full moon predicts great happiness and a wonderful new romance.

MOP You are about to take up a new hobby that could prove lucrative if you see a clean mop. A dirty one is a sign you've been slacking at work. It could cause embarrassment if you don't pull your socks up.

MORGUE *See also*: Death. Difficulties and disagreements are in the air. See your own corpse and it's time to take better care of your health. Have a check-up just to be sure.

MORTGAGE *See also*: Money. Pay it off and an unexpected bill is looming. Dream you can't manage to pay it and you will get a lucky money break. Apply for a mortgage and your worries will soon disappear.

MOSS Dry moss means you are in for a disappointment. But if it is soft and green your love life will simply sizzle.

MOTOR *See also*: Driving. If it's running smoothly you will make good progress. Trouble starting it is a warning to change direction. Your current plans simply won't work out.

MOTORCYCLE Buy one and you are in for notoriety or even fame. Sell one and a debt is about to be repaid. Driving a motorbike suggests problems at work and if you fall off one your financial situation looks sticky. A motorcycle race is a sign you will get surprise help to solve a problem.

MOUNTAIN See yourself at the top and work will go well. See yourself coming down a mountain and you are being far too timid over something. Stand up for yourself.

MOUSTACHE *See also*: Hair. This is a warning not to let petty irritations explode into major problems. Shave one off and a break with your partner is likely. But don't fret. There is someone new on the horizon.

MOVING HOUSE All will go smoothly if the move went without a hitch. But if it was difficult or even disastrous you will be faced with a big decision. Carry on as you are or try something completely different. The choice is yours.

MUD A lucky sign, this. But walk in it and there will be trouble in the family.

MUSEUM Go to one and you are going through a phase of unhappiness and boredom. Try and find some new interests or things will go from bad to worse. See statues in the museum and your problems are caused by overwork.

MUSIC Tuneful and harmonious music predicts fabulous fortune in all that deeply concerns you. But if it's out of tune, trouble is in the wind at work. Play an instrument and a surprising change of lifestyle is on the cards. But a broken musical instrument is a warning to watch your health.

Most musical instruments are omens of harmony and happiness:

Hear an **accordion** and if it sounds sad then you must expect some sadness, though not for long. If it sounds bright and lively then a social whirl is on the horizon. Play the accordion and your love affairs look good.

Bagpipes can signify loss of money. But if you are playing them it shows you are greatly loved. And if you see others playing them someone is going to ask you to marry him. Och aye!

Play the **banjo** and it's a sign of poverty to come. But if you see others strumming, then joy will be yours.

Hear a **bugle** and you can expect good news from a distance. Play it and your hard work will be rewarded.

Plate 17 · Chased by Monsters and Enemies

Put new strings on a **cello** and good news is on the way. Play it with a broken string and there will be a bust-up in your love life.

See a **choir** in church and a few frustrations are on the way. Somewhere else, and good news is round the corner.

Attend a **concert** and you'll get some surprise good news. But if you don't enjoy it then it's a sign of illness.

Hear a **flute** play and happy times are ahead in the household. Dream of playing it yourself and your love life could prove embarrassing.

Play the **guitar** and it's a sign you are being a bit unreliable lately. Try and be a bit more stable. Hear someone else play it and your problems will come to a quick conclusion.

Buying or playing a **harmonica** says money is on its way to you. Hear one and a fight is brewing, probably in the family.

Hear a **harp** played and good times are coming. But if the instrument has a broken string you could be in for a rough time. See yourself playing it and it's a warning not to be so trusting.

You'll soon be caught up in a social whirl if you hear a **horn.**

Don't get involved with community affairs you can't handle if you hear **jazz**. It may feel good to be voted chairman at that local meeting but it could cause you money worries.

Hear a musical **jingle** and a harmless flirtation is just round the corner. **Jingling bells** signify social activity.

Cut down on your favourite vice, be it smoking, drinking or even the opposite sex, if you see **kettle-drums**. It isn't doing you any good.

A lovely **lute** predicts a lingering love affair. Or good news from an absent friend.

Enjoy **opera** and it reveals you are deceiving someone. If you get caught—and you surely will the blushes will be yours, I'm afraid. Use **opera glasses** and you will have to defend your reputation.

An ancient **organ** shows there are grounds for new hope in your love life. A modern electric one predicts an unexpected income. See an organ in church and long-term plans will have to be revised.

Play an **organ** and a problem that has troubled you

for quite a while is about to be solved.

Play the **piano** and all your hopes will succeed. Unless it's out of tune in which case you must expect some difficulties. Shift a piano and you will achieve something solid. Tune one and good news is coming.

Sing and though you may be cheerful at the moment worries are right around the corner. Still, they won't last long.

That decision you've been putting off will have to be made if you see a **string quartet**. Play in one and you will lose out at work.

Play a **tambourine** and a shock rumour is about to reach your ears. Try to find out the truth. Otherwise this instrument predicts a nice surprise.

See or hear a **trumpet** and you are about to accomplish something you never thought possible.

See a **violin** out of tune or with a broken string, and a row with your partner is on the horizon. Otherwise your social life will flow smoothly.

Important news is on the way if you hear a **xylophone**. See yourself playing and it is a warning to avoid your rivals.

Lots of outings are on the cards if you see a **zither.** You're sure to be a social success.

MUSK Smell this and you are in for a passionate new love affair. Your sex life will simply sizzle.

MUTE Finding yourself struck dumb in a dream especially if it means you are unable to cry for help—is common. It's a sure sign you are about to let the cat out of the bag—and deep down you know it. An inability to cry out for help says it's time to keep your own counsel and don't take chances on revealing your secrets or those juicy bits of gossip to anyone, however plausible they may seem. Don't trust anyone for a while, and keep mum! Gambling's out, too. Keep a low profile for the foreseeable future.

MYTH Any mythical character is telling you that flattery can get you everywhere. Go on, flirt like crazy, suck up to the boss and you can be sure you'll get what you want!

AIL Hammer them in and something you thought was out of your reach can be yours—but it will take a lot of effort. Shiny nails forecast surprise news. Rusty ones are a sign of slow progress.

NAKEDNESS Nakedness in a dream is quite common. If you see yourself naked then things are about to improve. You may even have a stroke of money luck. See others naked and you will uncover some kind of deception among those close to you. Walk naked in the street and you are in for a disappointment. If others are naked it can be a great time for love.

See a **stripper** on stage and it suggests you are thinking of something that is a bit indiscreet. Don't do it; you could pay a high price if you do.

See a child **undressing** and it's time to stand up for your rights. A man is a sign of an unfaithful relationship. A woman shows you are being unscrupulous. You have misplaced your affections if you see yourself undress. If you do it in public, it's a sign you need a rest.

NAME If you can't remember your own or that of someone you know it is a warning you are involved in a dodgy deal. Can you really justify it? If you are called by the wrong name personal problems are looming but they will lead to a better understanding. Use a false name and it suggests you haven't been concentrating lately. Be more careful or you could make a serious mistake.

NAPKIN Use one and somehow you will complete a task you didn't think you'd have the strength to finish. Fold one and a special invitation is about to be issued to you.

NARROW An obstacle dream if you are aware something is narrower than it should be. It is a sign you have bitten off more than you can chew. Ask for help.

NAVY See also: Sea/Water/Travel; Uniform. Dreaming you are in the navy predicts illness. See sailors and a loss at work is on the cards. High-ranking officers predict love troubles.

NECKLACE See also: Jewellery. Put one on and it predicts a marriage or promotion at work. See one in a shop and it is a sign you are jealous of someone. A pearl necklace predicts a period of gloom and despondency. A broken necklace and there are family rows brewing.

NEEDLE Prick yourself and you will soon run into emotional problems with a friend or relative. Thread one and something you are working on will require a lot of patience. Find a needle and it's a sign you are worrying unnecessarily. Lose one and it is a warning not to be careless.

NEIGHBOUR Help one out and a surprise gift is on the way. Quarrel with one and it is a warning to keep that temper of yours in check.

NET See also: Fish/Fishing. A big trawling net is a sign you are squandering your money. A small one suggests a bumpy period in day-to-day life. See a net laid out to dry and your health is excellent. Throw one into the water and you are being unfairly suspicious of a new friend.

NETTLES Be brave and you will be successful. But you will have to work hard as well. Get stung and it is a warning you must protect yourself from a disloyal friend or deceitful lover.

NEWS See also: Communicating. Waiting for news suggests you need to change direction because you are simply not getting the results you'd hoped for. Receiving news is a dream of contrary. The worse the news the better things will be for you.

NEWSPAPER Read one and distant events are working in your favour. Buy one and a swift promotion is on the cards. Wrap something in one and a happy reunion with absent friends is predicted.

NICKNAME Don't attempt anything new is the warning here. Stick to the tried and tested for a while.

NIGHT See also: Darkness/Light; Time. Obstacles and delays are predicted. A really dark night is a sign you are hiding your resentment towards someone who harmed you in the past. A starlit night suggests you are going to make an interesting discovery.

NIGHTMARE It is rare to dream of having a nightmare but if you do it suggests you have a deep-rooted emotional problem and should talk it over with someone you trust or even a professional.

NIGHTSHADE Time to take chances if you see this poisonous article. New ventures, new relationships… all will work out well.

NOBEL PRIZE Win it and it's a warning not to try and be such a smart Alec. No one likes a cleverclogs. See someone else receive this prestigious prize and some happy family news is coming.

NOISE See also: Sounds. Hear children making a noise and it is a warning to be patient. Unusually loud noises are a sign you aren't relaxing enough. Try to slow down.

NORTH Be aware of this direction and it is a sign

you are about to find the right path in life at last.

NOVEL *See also*: Reading/Writing. Write one and trouble is brewing. Read one and your social life is about to look up.

NOVEMBER *See also*: Time. Dream of this month when it isn't and the latter years of your life will be happy and content.

NUGGET Made of precious metal, this predicts a spectacular change which will turn your life around. But you will have to grab the opportunity. It won't be handed to you.

NUMBERS Write them down and someone's unpredictable behaviour has put you in an odd situation. Talk to them about it. Read numbers and you can be confident in your hopes for the future. Rub them out or change them and you are being too shy with your partner. You are only feeling lonely because you don't communicate enough.

NUTSHELLS Empty shells are a sign of futile efforts. No matter how hard you try things just won't work out.

NYLON *See also*: Clothes. This is a reminder that things aren't always what they seem. Don't be taken in by appearances.

NYMPH An exciting experience in your love life is about to knock you for six.

AR *See also*: Sea/Water/Travel. Use these and an important matter needs sorting out pronto. Lose them over the side and some bad news could irreparably damage your relationship with your partner. Broken oars mean only the goodwill of others can help you now.

OASIS A stunning success in an exciting new venture. You've a lot to look forward to.

OATH *See also*: Speaking. Hear one or take one and you will either be promoted or rise up the social scale a notch.

OBSERVATORY This is a warning to guard against impulsive relationships. You could regret them sooner rather than later.

OCCULT *See also*: Supernatural. Some secret info is about to come your way. You can use it to your advantage.

OCEAN *See also*: Sea/Water/Travel. A good omen as long as it's calm. An important project at work is about to be concluded and you are about to make a

useful friend. Romance is also well starred. See a stormy ocean and exciting news is around the corner.

OCTOBER *See also*: Time. Dream of October in another month and someone is trying to persuade you to make a change you don't much like. Be firm. Don't listen to them.

OCTOPUS *See also*: Fish/Fishing. What a spirit of adventure you have! But see one killed and it's a sign you are taking a very moral stand over something. If an octopus attacks, trouble is in store.

OFFERING Make or receive an offer of some kind and things will improve. There may be delays at work but in the long run you could be in for promotion.

OFFICE Strangely, this relates to emotional rather than business matters. See yourself in your own office and your love life is about to change. A strange new office predicts an important new friend.

OFFICER *See also*: Uniform. A police officer is a warning that a friend is going to be careless with money and you will be caught up in their predicament in some way. An officer in the services is a sign of security and protection.

OIL Strike oil and you will soon be in the money. Oil something and the boss is about to give you a pat on the back. Castor oil suggests you are being a bit argumentative. Olive oil predicts a bright future at work. Sun-tan oil means you and a colleague aren't compatible. Spill oil and problems are about to crop up.

OIL PAINTING *See also*: Pictures/Paintings. Try not to be such a snob. You are missing out on a lot of fun.

OINTMENT Remember the film *Now, Voyager?* As Bette Davis said, 'Why ask for the moon when we already have the stars?' She was right, you know.

OPERA *See also*: Music. Enjoy this and it reveals you are deceiving someone. If you get caught—and you surely will—the blushes will be yours, I'm afraid. Use opera glasses and you will have to defend your reputation.

OPERATION *See also*: Doctors/Hospitals. Undergo surgery and your lifestyle is about to change dramatically. Watch an operation and some surprise news will arrive. A heart transplant is a sign your plans will succeed. Brain surgery means you still have to overcome a major obstacle to get what you want.

OPIUM You are mixing with a bad lot. And although it may not be fair, others judge you by the company you keep.

Plate 18 · Performing

OPTICIAN This is telling you to pull your socks up at work or you could be passed over.

ORCHARD *See also*: Flowers; Trees/Plants. In bloom this is a sign of good luck. Your deepest wish is about to be granted if it's full of fruit. See it bare and you will have a small success.

ORGAN *See also*: Music. An old one shows there are grounds for new hope in your love life. A modern electric one predicts an unexpected income. See an organ in church and long-term plans will have to be revised. Play an organ and a problem that has troubled you for quite a while is about to be solved.

ORNAMENT Selling your house, car or some other asset is bound to make a profit. Break an ornament and a stroke of good luck is coming.

ORPHAN Selfishness is about to lose you a valued friend, if you see an orphanage. But see an orphan and some unexpected gain will add to your material wealth. Dream of being an orphan and some kind of promise has not been kept.

OVEN *See also*: Heat. A warm one is a sign of good fortune. If it's switched off then a few rows are looming. You could be about to lose a friend.

OXYGEN Whatever is standing in your way is about to disappear. Your path ahead is clear and easy.

OYSTER *See also*: Fish/Fishing. In its shell this is a sign of jealousy that could cause arguments with your mate. If it has a pearl you are about to make a worrying mistake at work. Buying oysters is a warning to watch your health. Eat them and the family simply won't understand something you are involved with. It's bound to cause tension.

PACKAGE Carry one and you are shouldering a responsibility you feel is really down to someone else. Tell them so! Receive one and someone out there loves you madly. Post one and something a child does will cause unhappiness.

PAGE *See also*: Reading/Writing. Turn these and small investments will reap rich rewards.

PAGEBOY *See also*: Weddings. Holding a bride's train is a sign your love life is going your way. Things are swimming in your direction at work too. Take advantage of it.

PAGODA Go in and you will soon solve a long-standing problem. Come out and it's a warning not to forget to keep a promise. Simply see one and unexpected travel is forecast.

PAIL Carry it and things will improve. Spill one and it's time to be a bit more careful with money. An empty pail means you will get what you want eventually and a full one predicts a minor achievement.

PAIN Any kind of pain suggests you are suffering small, short-lived problems and irritations.

Pain in the **abdomen** means success will come.

Dream of a trivial **ache** and you should see a doctor. A severe ache signifies an important event that will be good for you.

Agony is a dream of contrary: the greater the agony, the greater the joy coming your way.

See yourself in a plaster **cast** and you will have to defend your reputation—but it will be your own fault.

An **earache** predicts unwelcome news.

If your **eyes** hurt a relative is off-colour.

A **headache** means things won't be going your way for a while. And it suggests you should keep your secrets to yourself.

An irresistible **itch** is a clear sign you are yearning for new horizons and experiences. Itchy hands mean money luck, and if it's your nose you should be careful not to make mistakes at work. A general feeling of itchiness is an omen you are worrying too much: try and lighten up.

If someone **kicks** you then you are afraid of competition. Do the kicking and things will improve. You may even get promoted soon.

Toothache suggests you are not happy about a certain situation.

PAIR Pairs of anything predict a very unusual event is about to take place in your life.

PALACE Seen from the outside this predicts improvement. But if it's inside it is a warning not to be so vain. A crumbling palace spells the end of one romantic liaison.

PANTOMIME There's a word for what your friends are handing out to you these days—but I'm too polite to use it. Basically they are filling you up with false praise when they are really trying to catch you out. Try and choose more trustworthy chums.

PANTRY *See also*: Food. Well stocked, and good times are ahead. But if the cupboard is bare it's time to tighten your belt.

PAPER *See also*: Reading/Writing. A clean sheet and you must renew your efforts to get where you are aiming for. Waste paper is a sign not to waste time accepting a new offer. It's absolutely right for you.

PARACHUTE *See also*: Aeroplane; Falling. Use this successfully and your love life will run smoothly. But if it fails someone you were relying on is about to let you down.

PARADE Lead one and your efforts are about to be recognised, probably at work. March in one and unexpected, unwelcome visitors are on their way. Watch a parade and a pay rise is due.

PARASOL *See also*: Heat. Open it indoors and someone is going to give you some money. Outdoors and it is a lucky omen for your love life.

PARK An exciting love affair is around the corner if you see a public park. Walking in one is a warning not to set your sights too high. Get lost in a park and you have made an error of judgement at work. Park a car and it's time to quit a relationship that doesn't draw you any more.

PARSLEY Growing this signifies hard work but eventual success. Eat it and you will get where you want, thanks to a lucky break.

PARTY You'll have a lot of fun but won't make much money if you attend one of these. Throw one and quarrels are around the corner.

PASSPORT Apply for a new one and your love life will blossom. Lose it and you are in for a disappointment with the opposite sex. Find one and it is a sign you are worrying about someone's health. There really is no need. They are fighting fit.

PATH A wide one predicts happiness through friends. A narrow one and you are in for some kind of struggle. Take care and you will come out of it well.

PAVEMENT See a new one laid and your current interests will go smoothly. But a bumpy one is a warning to fight those jealous feelings. You could lose a valued position.

PAWNING *See also*: Money. A pawnbroker or pawnshop is an omen of good luck. Your troubles will soon be over.

PEBBLES Pick them up and a broken relationship or affair will leave you lonely and depressed. Tossing them is a warning not to gossip. Walk on them and now is the time to get your own back on an old enemy.

PEELING *See also*: Food. Peel fruit and you will uncover a useful secret. If it is vegetables some disappointing news is coming.

PEN *See also*: Reading/Writing. A gold one and you will hear good news about a relative. A silver pen shows you are in the mood to put up a fight. A ballpoint means someone somewhere resents you. A fountain pen predicts an important letter. An old-fashioned quill says it's time to stop being so shy.

PENCIL *See also*: Reading/Writing. These relate to love and romance. A lead one is a warning not to tell tales about your love life to people you've just met. A coloured pencil predicts a new affair.

PENDULUM *See also*: Time. Changes are about to upset your routine. Accept them gracefully and all will be well.

PENNY *See also*. Money. A shiny new one is a warning not to trust one of your friends. Give them away and money luck is on the cards. Receive them and you are about to make a loss.

PENTHOUSE You are living beyond your means if you see one of these ritzy establishments.

PEPPER Curb your enthusiasm for a financial venture. It may not be as successful as you think. Grind pepper and it's a good time to take up a new hobby. You are full of beans, so why waste your energy?

PERFORMING Dream you are acting and your plans will not succeed. You must assert yourself. Be more positive. Watching actors acting says your friends will cheat on you. Watching children acting predicts good news.

If you are introduced to an **actress** you will have trouble at home and if it is an actor, don't repeat gossip or you could lose a friend. A comedy actor or actress spells success in business. A group of actors means major satisfaction in your life.

Being watched by an **audience** means you are feeling insecure about something, but don't worry. A surprising distraction will come your way. If you are in an audience in your dream, a good friend will have a stroke of luck.

A **juggler** suggests a new opportunity involving a quick profit or promotion is about to present itself. Don't hesitate. All will be well.

An empty **theatre** is a sign of boredom. But see a performance and your social life is about to be busy.

PERFUME For a woman this is a sign an exciting new love affair is on the horizon. For a man it predicts a misunderstanding at work. Simply smell it and a passionate new partner is about to come into view.

PERISCOPE Surprise news from a distance is about to give you a shock.

PETAL *See also*: Flowers. Pull them from a flower or see them fall and you are in for a love split or about to lose a good friend. You will be sad but if you put it down to experience it will help in the future.

PHARMACY Go in and it is a warning to be more selective where friends are concerned. A minor illness is predicted if you go in during the day. But if it's an all-night chemist it could be a bit more serious. See the pharmacist and you will make a successful investment but it will set tongues wagging.

PHOTOGRAPH *See also*: Pictures/Paintings. See your own and it spells unhappiness in your love life. Look at snaps and you will renew an old friendship. Take photographs and you have a rival for your lover's affections.

PICKING Hard work is ahead but there will be rich rewards.

PICNIC *See also*: Food. A secret spells danger if you throw or attend one of these.

PICTURES/PAINTING Pictures of yourself are an unhappy sign for your love life. See yourself painting and something you are planning would be best kept secret. But is it really wise? Paint a house and something that has been kept from you is about to be revealed.

See an **artist** with an **easel** and life will be plain sailing sooner than you think. Important changes are brewing if you see yourself as an artist.

Paintings in a **gallery** are a sign you can expect to re-kindle an old flame.

An **oil painting** is telling you not to be such a snob. You are missing out on a lot of fun.

If someone paints your **portrait** it's a sign flattery is going to your head if you then give it or receive it as a present. Simply having it painted says you will be disappointed in love. See someone else sitting for a portrait and a rise in your status is predicted.

See **sculpture** and it's a warning not to bet. Sculpture is a warning to pay more attention to your personal affairs. See a sculptor at work and an opportunity to make an exciting change is round the corner.

PIE *See also*: Food. Make one and you are in a strong position. Eat one and you suspect one of your friends is being disloyal. You're right!

PILES You have forgotten to do something if you see piles of anything.

PILLS *See also*: Doctors/Hospitals. Take or give these and you will be faced with new responsibilities. Buy them and you could be moving house.

PILLOW A crumpled one is a warning that your own foolish behaviour is about to cause trouble.

PILOT *See also*: Aeroplane; Flying. Fly a plane and a stimulating new project will keep you busy at work. If it's a jumbo jet you are in an irritable frame of mind. Don't be impatient or your work will suffer. And if you see yourself at the cockpit of a fighter-plane your confidence couldn't be higher. Pilot a boat and you have narrowly escaped danger.

PIN Minor disappointments and petty squabbles predicted. Sit on a pin and you're in for a happy surprise! Prick yourself and you will have to sort out someone else's problems. Find one and you are in for good luck. A pin-cushion is a sign of achievement.

PIPE Smoke one and you will be able to solve your own problems. Plumbing or other pipes mean you are making things worse by being pessimistic. Things will look up if you cheer up.

PIRATE *See also*: Sea/Water/Travel. You are tempted to start an exciting new venture. But check it out thoroughly before you do.

PLACES/SETTINGS An **amusement arcade** means you should use your time more wisely. Walk through any other arcade and intriguing temptations will be put in your way. See an arcade and don't give away any secrets or your own could be betrayed.

An **arena** is advising you to be cautious in all business matters. There will be hidden snags. If you are in an arena watch out for a false friend. Spectators in an arena spell misery.

If you are young and dream of an **attic** it is a warning against flirting and even being sexually promiscuous. But if you are older it means comfort in old age.

See yourself standing on a **balcony** and you could lose your job. But if you see yourself on a balcony

Plate 19 · The Prince and Princess

with someone of the opposite sex—my, are you in for a big love affair! If the balcony collapses or looks dangerous, sad news from a distance is likely.

Going into a **barn** means good luck in your current projects. If it falls down or catches fire there will be trouble with your daily routine.

A strange **bedroom** is a sign of a change for the better. Your own bedroom suggests all will go well in your current affairs. If you see a hotel bedroom some stupid gossip will soon be going the rounds. Watch out. It could concern you.

A high **belfry** spells good news. But if you see a crumbling old one things will have to change, as you won't have as much money in future.

A big **building** forecasts changes in your lifestyle. A small one spells problems in your affairs. A very tall building means you will shortly be very successful. Old dilapidated buildings are a sign to start saving for the rainy days ahead.

You must summon up all your tact to avoid a squabble if you see a **canyon**. It could well be a row over money. Postpone any business discussions.

That temper of yours is going to cause some arguments if you see a **castle**. An ancient one is a sign to check your investments. Visiting one means you are about to travel a bit. A ruined castle is a warning to curb your passions. They could lead to trouble.

A **cellar** says you are a bit depressed. But if it's full of wood or coal you'll soon snap out of it. Bottles of wine in a cellar mean you're going to feel gloomy for a while yet, but an empty cellar is a much more cheerful sign. You will shortly feel refreshed, relaxed, and ready to take on the world.

A big **city** shows you have big ideals. Dream of living here and they are about to be realised.

An empty **closet** is a warning not to get into debt. A full one means your business profits will soar. A linen closet is a sign of happy times ahead at home.

See a **corner** and it is an obstacle dream. It is a warning not to force an issue. If the corner is outside, say in a street, a new opportunity is going to change your life. Turn a corner and you will get a nice surprise.

Live in a **cottage** and better times are round the corner. An empty one spells loneliness, and a

derelict cottage is a sure sign it's time you sorted out your personal life. You are in a muddle emotionally, aren't you?

A **crossroads** means exactly what you would imagine. You will soon have to make an important decision. Listen to advice.

See a **cupboard** and it is a straightforward dream. If it was bare, lean times are ahead. A full cupboard and things are looking up. Put things away in a cupboard and you can make up your losses but it will take a lot of hard work.

Cross a **desert** and a difficult period is coming up in your life. If there is a sand storm your problems will take a long time to solve. An oasis means it won't be all that bad. There'll be a few laughs along the way.

A **ditch** is another obstacle dream. It spells money troubles if you were in it and love troubles if you fall in. But your troubles will be small, and if you manage to get out you'll soon be able to put it all down to experience.

Someone close will get an unexpected honour or some kind of well-deserved recognition if you dream of a **dome**.

You'll soon be mixing with influential folk if you see an **embassy**. If you are on official business there you have to go all out for what you want. It won't come easily to you.

As with other dreams, if you see an **escalator**, up indicates success and down means reverses. But if you dream of going down on an escalator you can succeed in the end if you are determined about it.

Dream of a **factory** and you will have a struggle on your hands but success in the end. See yourself working in the factory and some good changes are on the way.

See green healthy **fields** and you will be happy and make money. Dry fields predict reverses. A newly ploughed field means you can get what you want but you will have to make a few sacrifices.

An open **gate** spells major changes on the way for you. Closed it is a sign to stop putting off your problems. You simply have to face them. A wooden or iron gate signifies a scintillating social life. Golden or metal gates are a warning to be more careful in everything you do.

Important news from a distance is predicted or news that will take you on a long journey if you see a **glacier.** Fall into a crevasse in a glacier and it is a warning not to make any changes or it could be dangerous. Cross a glacier crevasse and your problems aren't as serious as you think.

An indoor **gym** is an omen for material prosperity and a respected place in society—you little yuppie, you! A trip abroad is forecast if you see an open-air gym. See yourself exercising there and you've made a good match. You and your partner will be together for some time to come.

Dream of a long narrow **hall** and a period of worry is on the way. If it's grand changes are coming. A public hall warns it's time to make that decision you have been trying to put off.

Any **hill** represents a difficulty to overcome. Stand on top of it and your troubles are behind you. Struggle up and it's a sign you are tired and have been overdoing things.

Fall in a **hole** and you are keeping bad company lately.

Stay alone in an **hotel** and it relates to work. Stay with someone of the opposite sex and it concerns your love life. If it's a luxury hotel then failure or disappointments are predicted. A modest one and things will turn out well for you.

See yourself in a **hut** and a catastrophe is just round the corner. But see a low hut and your future will be more secure.

You could be in danger if you dream of a **laboratory**. Perhaps it's your health. Are you exhausted because you've been working too hard? Or could it be your state of mind. Could you be depressed? Perhaps you are going through a bad patch with your mate. But whatever it is—take heart. It will only be temporary.

A **labyrinth** is an obstacle dream. Find your way out and your problems will be easily solved. Get lost or be frightened and some surprise opposition may force you to change direction.

See **land** that you own and your fortunes will take a turn for the better. If you are ordered off it you should brace yourself for a disappointment.

A narrow country **lane** is a sign to be more discreet in your affairs with the opposite sex. If it's blocked off then you are troubled by personal

dilemmas and doubts. A dark lane is an omen for a major money problem.

Dream of a **library** and it is a good omen. It means you are full of self-confidence and ready to take on all comers.

Any kind of **market** is favourable for the unattached. You could soon be falling in love and, even better. A few other pleasant little surprises are just around the corner. For a married woman a market is a symbol of betrayal.

Marshes mean you shouldn't get involved in other people's problems. Give advice by all means but stay well out of it.

A working wind or water **mill** suggests you are about to complete an important work project and earn respect and job satisfaction. But if it is not working you are in danger of stagnating both at work and in your current relationship. Try and sort things out, or both could come to a sticky end.

Work down a **mine** and your own hard efforts will eventually bring in the money. Simply see one and there could be a break with someone of the opposite sex.

See yourself at the top of a **mountain** and work will go well. See yourself coming down and you are being far too timid over something. Stand up for yourself.

Go into a **museum** and you are going through a phase of unhappiness and boredom. Try and find some new interests or things will go from bad to worse. See statues in the museum and your problems are caused by overwork.

A stunning success in an exciting new venture is on the cards if you dream of an **oasis**. You've got a lot to look forward to.

An **observatory** is a warning to guard against impulsive relationships. You could regret them sooner or later.

An **office** relates to emotional rather than business matters. See yourself in your own office and your love life is about to change. A strange new office predicts an important new friend.

Go into a **pagoda** and you will soon solve a long-standing problem. Come out and it's a warning not to forget to keep a promise. Simply see one and unexpected travel is forecast.

The outside of a **palace** predicts improvement. But if it's inside it is a warning not to be so vain. A

crumbling palace spells the end of one romantic liaison.

An exciting love affair is around the corner if you see a public **park**. Walking in one is a warning not to set your sights too high. Get lost in a park and you have made an error of judgement at work.

Dream you're at a **party** and you'll have lots of fun but won't make much money. Throw a party and quarrels are around the corner.

A wide **path** predicts happiness through friends. A narrow one and you are in for some kind of struggle. Take care and you will come out of it well. See a newly laid pavement and your current interests will go smoothly. But a bumpy one is a warning to fight those jealous feelings. You could lose a valued position.

Go galactic and see other **planets** and it's a sign you are feeling restless and bored. Study them like an astronomer and your current projects will be slow but successful.

Stand on a **platform** and promotion is coming. But if it is shaky you still have to impress the boss before being considered.

The romantic **pyramids** spell success at work and a new romance. Climb one and you are at your confident best. See one inverted or damaged and money trouble is looming.

A **quadrangle** courtyard means the time is coming when your troubles will be over.

Don't rest on your laurels if you see a **quarry**. There is still a lot of work to be done. A chalk quarry spells financial problems. Stone predicts a journey.

Pull someone out of **quicksand** and your salary will steadily rise. Sink into it and it is a warning not to meddle in other people's affairs.

Hold any kind of **reception** and business will go well and make money. Go to one and there will be an exciting development on the romantic front. A reception held in your honour is a sign something unusual is about to happen in your life.

Dream of a waiting **room** and you are uncertain about a work project. A ballroom and emotional problems are looming. A games room is a sure sign certain suggestions and proposals aren't what they seem. A dining room is a warning not to be so obstinate. A living room predicts unexpected gains.

See a **town square** and your energy is increasing. Walk through a square and you are going to be offered an opportunity you should grab with both hands.

As with an escalator, if you see **stairs** up is good and down not so good. Trip up them and it's a good sign for your love life. Fall down and it's a warning to be less controversial. Cleaning stairs predicts an unexpected change in lifestyle. A wooden staircase suggests you are making mistakes at work.

See a railway **station** and important news is on its way at work.

A strange **street** says a profitable new venture is on the cards. A long street shows you will have to be patient about something.

A **tunnel** is an obstacle dream. If you see yourself struggling through it things may be difficult. Otherwise it is a sign of change. Get through successfully and happiness awaits you.

Sit on a **verandah** and the troubles in your love life will soon vanish. Sleep on one and it's time to keep your back to the wall. Someone is trying to stab you in it! See flowers on a verandah and you are in for a nice surprise.

See a seaside **village** and you will have to face a few difficulties. A mountain village predicts unexpected gains. In the country and you are about to make a big achievement. See a village in the distance and be careful of that 'golden opportunity'. It may not be as good as you think.

A **warehouse** indicates good luck and prosperity. Hard work and a few sacrifices will soon lead to major successes. If you are single your future partner is just around the corner.

A working **windmill** is a sign of contentment. But if it's damaged it is a warning you are wasting your time on something. Cut your losses and try a new approach.

PLAN Building plans suggest an important new friend. Draw them yourself and there is a hidden snag to some deal you are about to get involved in. Check it out carefully.

PLANET You are feeling restless and bored with routine if you see other planets. Study them like an astronomer and your current projects will be slow but successful.

PLANK Robbery could be around the corner. Take extra precautions. Walk on a plank and you will soon be faced with a choice you find hard. Don't be hasty and you will make the right decision.

PLASTER Mix this and you will be in the money. Plaster a wall and you've got that pay rise. Crumbled or cracking plaster is a sign of family troubles. A medical plaster or cast means you will have to defend your reputation. But it will be your own fault.

PLASTIC A new friendship will make you happy and be very useful to you.

PLATFORM Stand on one and promotion is coming. But if it was shaky you still have to impress the boss before being considered.

PLAY See also: Childhood/Children; Games. Children playing are an omen of a successful romance. A stage play means good times are ahead.

PLOUGHING For a woman dreaming of this is a sign your husband, or even future husband, is a solid hard worker. For a man it suggests an adaptable personality that will stand you in good stead especially in your social life.

PLUMBING If it's new, an unexpected opportunity will help you achieve a long-held ambition. Old or leaky plumbing spells a misunderstanding at work.

POCKET A hole in one and you'll soon be blushing, thanks to a hasty decision. A full pocket suggests you will have an easier time than you thought with someone in authority. An empty pocket and one of your friends has a mean streak.

POETRY See also: Reading/Writing. Write it and a fascinating new friend is about to be made. Read or listen to it and your popularity with the opposite sex is about to soar.

POISON Take this and it is time to compromise. Administer it and a broken friendship or love affair is predicted. Throw poison away and you will discover a deceitful friend—and save a lot of money.

POKER See also: Cards. A happy social life is forecast if you play the card game. Poke a fire and it is a warning not to try and re-kindle an old flame.

POLICE/PRISONS Spot a friendly copper and help is on the way from someone you love. It will mean you can regain your self-confidence. See yourself as a policeman and it's a sign you've been meddling in other people's affairs. Go to a police station and you are involved in a tough project at work. Come out of one and a friendship with the opposite sex will be misunderstood by your mate.

Get **arrested** and you will have sadness followed by joy. If you see others being arrested a surprise gift is coming to you. If you are released from arrest sudden success will be yours.

Seeing yourself behind **bars** is a sign of good luck. Simply see a prison and there will be happiness in the family.

Get locked in a **black maria** and your status will improve. If you see others being taken away you must expect temporary set-backs.

A **convict** says your worries will soon disappear unless he escapes. Then you must steel yourself for some ups and downs as someone is trying to block your moves. See yourself convicted and you will prosper.

Detectives mean exactly what you'd think. You will soon solve a mystery.

Being **handcuffed** means your worries will soon be over. See others handcuffed and it is a sign of security and protection. Snap them on someone and your life is about to improve unexpectedly.

See yourself **interrogating** someone and it's a sign you're not very good at forming lasting relationships with those around you. If you were at the end of the interrogation, a pleasant surprise probably in the form of a journey is coming.

An old-fashioned **jail** is an obstacle dream. Release or escape means your problems will be short-lived. If not, the road ahead will be long and hard. See others there and your worries will soon disappear.

If you are **raided** by police it is a sign you have a few minor personal problems, but avoid arrest and all will work out well. You're confused emotionally if you see a bank raid.

POLO Play or watch this Royal game and your wealth will increase—probably through a legacy.

POOL See also: Games. There'll be plenty of parties if you see a swimming pool. But if it's empty or dirty don't dream of gambling. Your tips and systems are all failures, I'm afraid.

POPE See also: Religion. See him on a throne and you should follow up those new ideas of yours. They

will be a success. See him surrounded by cardinals and you are doing something that is going against the grain with your friends. See yourself as the Pope and the future will be peaceful and happy. Speak to him and problems with your partner will soon disappear.

PORTRAIT *See also*: Pictures/Paintings. Flattery is going to your head if you give or receive this. Have your own painted and you will be disappointed in love. See someone else sitting for a portrait and a rise in your status is predicted.

POSTCARD Receive one and you will hear a surprising piece of news. Write one and it shows you have put your problems in perspective. Collect them and you can't go back on that decision—no matter how much you want to.

POST OFFICE An empty **envelope** says you will soon snap out of the doldrums. Sealed envelopes are a sign of just how busy you are. Put a letter in one and you'll find something you thought you'd lost.

Write a **letter** and everything is going well for you emotionally. Receive one and news is on the way to you from a distance. Post a letter and your current problems will soon be solved. An anonymous letter is a sign of danger. A love letter indicates you are regretting a foolish affair. A chain letter predicts an unusual new experience. Finding a letter is a warning that a friend is being disloyal.

Act as a **messenger** and you are about to get a lucrative offer. Receive one and you can be sure your job is safe.

Carry a **package** and you are shouldering a responsibility you feel should really be down to someone else. Tell them so! Receive a package and someone out there loves you madly. Post one and something a child does will cause unhappiness.

Spot a **postman** and it's a straightforward sign news is on the way.

Rare **stamps** predict good profits. And your status will improve if you stamp letters. Buy stamps and you are in for a rise. Collect them and you are about to rise higher up the social scale.

POT If it's a flower pot you might not have much money but there will be plenty of fun. Cooking pots are a warning not to be so trusting. Broken pots spell sadness.

POWDER Spill it and you are confused over conflicting advice. Work things out for yourself. Gunpowder predicts a lucky escape from danger.

PRAYER *See also*: Religion. Say one and peace of mind is promised. Hear one and it's a sign of loyal and lasting friendships.

PREGNANCY You are going through a hard time. For a girl it is an omen that others are going to help solve problems. For a woman, only patience can help you achieve your ambitions. A man dreaming of being pregnant is going to have to fight hard to achieve the success he hopes for.

PRINCE/PRINCESS Meet one of these Royals and your prestige is on the up and up. But some of your friends will try and take advantage of it. Don't let them.

PRINT *See also*: Reading/Writing. See yourself as a printer and you will always have enough to cover your needs. See a printer at work and only hard graft can make you successful. Read something printed and your problems will soon be over.

PRIZE Win one and it spells success. Give one and you will soon be in the money.

PROFESSOR *See also*: School. Things are bound to improve if you see yourself as this learned chap. Listen to him and you are about to discover you have a hidden talent.

PROSTITUTE *See also*: Sexuality. Fear of sexual failure is the message in this dream. If you are solicited by one try not to be so easy with your flattery. It's meaningless if you offer it all the time. See yourself as a prostitute and some news to cheer you up will arrive. Visit a prostitute and trouble is brewing at home.

PUBLISHING *See also*: Reading/Writing. You are bored and depressed at work if you have something published in a book. If it's a newspaper or magazine jealous people are gossiping about you. See yourself as a publisher or meet one then trust your own judgement where money is concerned or you could lose it.

PUDDLE *See also*: Water. Get splashed and you will be blushing at some social event soon. Keep dry or step round it and someone will help you out of a sticky situation.

PUMP Business will boom if it's automatic. A hand pump shows life is getting you down. A bicycle pump is a warning not to ask for help with your problems. Only you can solve them.

PUNCTURE Try not to be so inflexible. Listen to others. They may have a point.

PUPPETS Happiness is assured if you see these. Hold a puppet show and it is a sign your organising skills are at their best. Use them to your advantage.

PURSE *See also*: Money. Find one and a debt long overdue is about to be repaid. Lose one and a friend or lover is going to disillusion you.

PUSHING A dream of contrary. Push anything and you will be able to overcome your troubles by your own efforts. The harder you push the greater will be your success in solving problems.

PUTTY You are wasting money and time on trivial pursuits.

PYRAMID Success at work and a new romance are predicted. Climb one and you are at your confident best. See one inverted or damaged and money troubles are looming.

 UADRANGLE See this courtyard and the time is coming when your troubles will be at an end.

QUADS You are in for double trouble. But it will be shortlived.

QUARANTINE This isolation period is not a good sign. Put someone in it and a project that was going well will soon come to end. See yourself in quarantine and a split with your partner is on the cards.

QUARRY Don't rest on your laurels. There is still a lot of work to be done. A chalk quarry spells financial problems. Stone predicts a journey.

QUARTET *See also*: Music. That decision you have been putting off will have to be made if you see a string quartet. Play in one and you will lose out at work.

QUAY *See also*: Sea/Water/Travel. Ships here are a sign of travel. But an empty quay is a warning not to be lazy or it could lead to disappointments.

QUEEN Business will boom if she is sitting on her throne. Waving from a balcony and it's an omen of distant news. See a queen in her carriage and your lust for power and fame are making you a laughing stock, I'm afraid.

See her in a pack of cards and you are being over-confident. A queen bee is a good sign for your health.

QUESTIONNAIRE Irritating delays will thwart your plans if you fill this in.

QUEUE Wait in one and a bit of family advice is going to help you out. See one and an important event will be beneficial.

QUICKSAND Pull someone out and your salary will steadily rise. Sink into it and it is a warning not to meddle in other people's affairs.

QUILT The luxury down variety is a sign of increased prosperity. A patchwork quilt is a omen of domestic bliss.

QUININE Old habits or even old friends are stopping you from making progress. Try and break free and move on to new pastures.

QUIVER See one full of arrows and you must pay attention to your target—otherwise you will miss it.

 ABBI *See also*: Religion. If you are Jewish you will prosper through your own efforts. If you are not Jewish a rabbi is a sign your friends are going to help you achieve your ambitions. See yourself as a rabbi and your financial future looks bright.

RABIES Someone is trying to undermine you and it is probably a so-called friend. Take a look at your close circle and try and spot who it is before it's too late.

RACE Run in one and you can expect an exciting new offer. Watch one and you will have success. See a racecourse and it signifies new surroundings. If it's a racehorse then it's time to economise.

RACKET Curb your tongue. You have a tendency to be outspoken.

RADIATOR *See also*: Heat. If it is on there will be temporary tensions. Off and you are about to uncover a nasty secret. A car radiator is a warning not to be too hasty.

RADIO Listen to this and a pleasant meeting is around the corner. Turn it off and it's a sign you are feeling restless with your partner. Mend one and you could lose money. Buy one and you're in for some criticism. An old valve radio predicts a trip where you can mix business with pleasure.

RADIUM Loads of money but very little personal happiness, I fear. Avoid anything risky if you see a radium burn.

RAFFLE Win one and you are going through a lucky phase. Lose and some kind of date in your diary is about to be cancelled.

RAFT *See also*: Sea/Water/Travel. Float on one and it is a warning not to be lazy. Someone else will profit from it. Build one and you can achieve a great deal through your own efforts.

RAGE *See also*: Anger/Confrontation. Fly into one and a temper tantrum could lose you an influential friend. If someone else is in a rage, calming them down suggests you could do with a change of pace or even a move.

RAGS *See also*: Clothes. Clean ones predict prosperity. Dirty ones and it's time to be more selective in your choice of friends. Ragged clothes are a sign you are about to make a wise decision.

RAILWAY Socially things couldn't be better. An underground railway shows someone or something is getting in your way. It will take all your strength to shift this particular obstacle. A rail crash is an omen one of your plans is about to go wrong.

RAIN *See also*: Water; Weather. If you are out in the rain an ailing love affair is about to draw to a close. Get drenched in a heavy storm and you are going to come into some money.

RAINBOW *See also*: Weather. A sign of good luck even if you don't find the pot of gold at the end! Pleasant changes are on the way.

RAKE A metal one shows how hard you are working. A wooden one and you'll soon be faced with a tricky situation. Step on one and you are in for a smashing surprise. Rake over something and you will be invited to a happy family celebration.

RAPE *See also*: Sexuality. Careless behaviour could cost you your reputation. Think carefully or you are bound to disappoint people.

RAZOR An electric one is a warning to take more care. A cut throat and you are feeling calm and content. A broken razor shows you are hiding your pain and a blunt one is a sign you are confused by someone you love. Buy one and it's time to face up to the differences between you and your partner. Shaving is a sign you simply can't put up with a certain situation any longer. Try and change things.

READING/WRITING Read and you are about to make some progress. Read aloud and you will get help from an outside source. Hear someone else read and peace of mind is at hand.

Read an **agreement** but refuse to sign means beware of friends cheating on you. Signing an agreement means success in your plans.

An **author** is a sign that your interests are about to widen. Watch them write and it is a warning that financial difficulties are ahead. Most of all don't lend money to anyone.

Collecting **autographs** means a quick profit. Signing them means you will eventually get the success you seek.

Read a **book**, buy one or receive one and it is a hopeful omen. But lend or borrow a book and your love life is in for a few disappointments. Books in a library predict an unexpected experience. A torn or worn one shows just how anxious you are feeling.

An **editor** says you are letting things slide too much. Buck up and pay attention to detail. See yourself as an editor and you must expect delays in projects.

Reading an **epitaph** is a sign your problems aren't as bad as they seem. If the epitaph is faded, happy family news is coming.

A **library** is a good omen. It is a sign you are full of self-confidence and ready to take on all comers.

Writing articles for a **magazine** is a warning to avoid some kind of loss.

Read a **newspaper** and distant events are working in your favour. Buy one and a swift promotion is on the cards. Wrap something up in one and a happy reunion with absent friends is predicted.

Write a **novel** and trouble is brewing. Read one and your social life is about to look up.

Write **numbers** down and someone's unpredictable behaviour has put you in an odd situation. Read numbers and you can be confident in your hopes for the future. Rub out or change them and you are being too shy with your partner.

A gold **pen** and you will hear good news about a relative. A silver pen shows you are in the mood to put up a fight. A ballpoint pen means someone somewhere resents you. A fountain pen predicts an important letter. An old-fashioned quill says it's time to stop being so shy.

Pencils relate to love and romance. A lead one is a warning not to tell tales about your love life to people you've just met. A coloured pencil predicts a new affair.

Write **poetry** and a fascinating new friend is about to be made. Read or listen to it and your popularity with the opposite sex is about to soar.

Read something **printed** and your troubles will soon be over.

Plate 20 · The Twelve Signs of the Zodiac

If you manage to get something **published** in a book you are bored and depressed at work. If it's a newspaper or magazine jealous people are gossiping about you. See yourself as a publisher or meet one, then trust your own judgement where money is concerned or you could lose it.

Sign anything and it is a symbol of security. See other people signing and you can be sure your friends are loyal.

See yourself **writing** and you must try not to be so impulsive. Think first and act last. See others writing and you should trust your own judgement. Listen to advice but make up your own mind. Handwriting is a warning not to trust one of your friends.

RECEIPT *See also*: Money. Better times are around the corner whether you give or receive this.

RECEPTION Hold one and business will go well and make money. Go to one and there will be an exciting development on the romantic front. A reception held in your honour is a sign something unusual is about to happen in your life.

RECIPE *See also*: Food. All work and no play is likely to lead to a nervous breakdown! But all play and no work is the road to ruin. Try and strike a happy medium. Give someone a recipe and it shows you are pretty unflappable right now.

RECORD *See also*: Music. Your love life is on the skids if you see this on a turntable. Buy one and your confidence could do with a boost. Break a world record and you are fighting for your independence. Don't worry. You'll get your freedom.

REEDS One of your friendships is on very dodgy ground. Your chum simply can't be trusted.

REFLECTOR On a bike this suggests you are unreliable especially where relationships are concerned. Try not to let people down so much.

REFRIGERATOR *See also*: Food. Put food in and your prosperity will increase. Take it out and unexpected guests are about to arrive.

REFUGEE The needs of others are going to have to come before your own for a while. See yourself as a refugee and a past favour is about to reap its reward.

RELATIONSHIPS See yourself **admired** and you could lose useful friends thanks to your own vanity. Admiring others spells unhappiness.

Any dream involving **adultery** predicts problems in your love life. You are undergoing traumas and probably, if the truth be known, at your wits' end. If your wife is committing adultery then quarrels with the neighbours are coming. If it's your husband then you could receive an inheritance. If you commit it guard against telling your friends your secrets. Resist temptation and some disappointing set-backs will be short-lived.

Showing normal signs of **affection** in a dream indicate a happy family life and pleasant personal relationships. But embarrassing displays of affection which are not the type you would normally offer suggest your current plans are influenced by ulterior motives. Lack of affection predicts a long life.

See your own marriage **annulled** and there will be cause for a family party. Someone else's marriage and you will have to put up with some petty annoyance.

If a man dreams of **bigamy** it can mean a loss of virility so go for a medical check-up. For a woman it spells a need to be more discreet in your choice of men.

If you are married and dream of **divorce** you can rely on your mate. If you are single it's a warning you are misplacing your affections.

You're in for a rough ride romantically if you see an **engagement**. Try and be philosophical. Put it all down to experience. See an engagement ring and you have rivals out there somewhere.

Dream of **falling in love** and someone somewhere loves you—and is about to tell you so. If love passes you by it is in fact an omen that you will soon marry.

Jealousy is a sign you'll soon be involved in problems in your love life or with your friends. But if the jealousy is directed at you things will soon turnout to your advantage.

If you are single and dream of **marriage** you are involved in something that will come to no good. But good news is on the way if you see yourself at someone else's wedding. A secret marriage suggests you are confused because of a love let-down.

Help out a **neighbour** and a surprise gift is on the way. Quarrel with one and it is a warning to keep that temper of yours in check.

Separate in a dream and you will reach a better understanding with your partner.

If you are married and see yourself **single** again it is a warning not to get involved with dodgy companions.

See someone **unfaithful** to you and they will shortly display their devotion. See yourself unfaithful and temptation is coming your way. You have been warned.

RELIC You are feeling guilty about something you did in the past. A religious relic—like the Turin Shroud—shows you are very down-to-earth. And others love you for it!

RELIGION If religion is the main theme of your dream you will soon feel content and have much needed peace of mind.

See an **abbey** and it is a particularly good omen for gaining peace of mind. A ruined abbey indicates unexpected good luck—possibly financial. An abbot is a sign you should try to calm your passions. See yourself as an abbot and you will have many disappointments. A group of abbots spells grief and pain.

See yourself as **agnostic** and it is a warning to be more circumspect in your liaisons with the opposite sex.

An **altar** says you could find some lost money. If you are kneeling at the altar then a secret desire will be yours. Decorating one signifies a long trip, and if you see an altar being built you will soon be in the money.

Dreaming of an **angel** is an extremely favourable sign. It indicates a major increase in other people's respect for you. You will have success in love, peace and well-being. If you see yourself in the midst of many angels you can look forward to a happy life with many friends you can trust.

See a **baptism** and that unforeseen circumstance will cause you disappointment. But don't worry, new doors are about to open for you. Seeing a child baptised is an omen of great joy.

A good deed you have done will reap rewards if you see a **Bible**. But see it open on a lectern and it is a sign your mind is in turmoil. Swearing an oath on one means you must assert yourself more.

Spot a **bishop** in church and there will be new developments in an old situation. If he is standing at the altar the future looks bright. If he is giving Communion, a happy event will occur in your family.

Hear **blasphemy** and it is a sign you will realise your ambitions. Use blasphemy and some so-called friends are about to embarrass you.

A **cardinal** spells good fortune round the corner. See him giving a blessing, saying prayers or walking in a procession and new experiences, important changes and promotion at work are on the cards.

Your most special dream can come true if you see the outside of a **cathedral**. The inside is a sign of failure. But don't fret—some good will come out of it all.

A **chapel** is a very lucky sign. You will soon be very happy indeed.

Seen from the outside a **church** is a good omen but go in and you are clearly plagued with worries. But never mind. All your troubles will turn out to be blessings in disguise. A churchyard is a sign of better things to come.

Any of the ten **Commandments** is a warning to change your ways. You know what you are doing is wrong, so why carry on?

A wooden **cross** says you will get a surprise. A gold cross means your bosses are talking about you and it's all good! Any other cross is a sign of comfort and security.

Celebrate **Easter** and good times are coming. An Easter parade suggests temptation is on the way.

Contentment and peace of mind can be yours, if you adjust to circumstances, if you see, hear or are aware of **God**. Pray to Him and you will prosper. Talk to Him and great joy is on the way to you.

Worship an **idol** and you are in for a major disappointment. A wooden one is a sign to take more care. A gold one and watch out for jealousy.

Dream of **Jesus** and consolation in adversity is the message. If you spoke or prayed with Him or He touched you, true peace of mind will be yours.

See a **mass** outside and good news is coming. Inside a church it predicts up-coming difficulties.

A church **minister** means you should try and spend more time alone to think things through. You could be in for a disappointment if you don't take time to reflect.

Curb a tendency to be big-headed at work if you see a **nun.** You are successful but you don't have to keep telling everyone. A young nun is a symbol of unfulfilled desires. An old one points to an experience which will be useful in the future. A singing nun is a sign you and your partner will live happily ever after.

See the **Pope** on a throne and you should follow up those new ideas of yours. They will be a success. See him surrounded by cardinals and you are doing something that is going against the grain with your friends. See yourself as the Pope and the future will be peaceful and happy. Speak to him and problems with your partner will soon disappear.

Say **prayers** and peace of mind is promised. Hear them and it's a sign of loyal and lasting friendships.

If you are Jewish and see a **rabbi** you will prosper through your own efforts. If you are not Jewish he is a sign your friends are going to help you achieve your ambitions. See yourself as a rabbi and your financial future looks bright.

Someone influential is supporting you and protecting you if you see a **rosary**. If it's ivory you aren't showing much initiative at the moment. Wooden and it's a sign you are feeling sentimental. Buy a rosary and you have high hopes for a new project.

Hear a **sermon** inside a church and a pet project will be thwarted by delays. Deliver one and your suspicions about someone are groundless.

A church **spire** is an omen of true love and friendship. But if it was twisted or leaning you will have to overcome some difficulties before achieving your aims.

The **Virgin Mary** is a warning to be careful with your confidences.

A Communion **wafer** is a warning you are taking on too much. Something will suffer if you try and do too many things at once.

RENT *See also*: Money. Collect it and money will be tight. Pay it and you are in for some unhappiness. If you can't afford to pay up then a pleasant surprise is around the corner.

RESCUING Sudden success will be yours if you rescue someone. But watch out if you are on the other end of the rescue. You are approaching an accident-prone phase. You have been warned!

RESERVOIR *See also*: Water. If it's full you'll soon be in the money. Empty, and times will be hard through no fault of your own. If the reservoir was filling up, the wind of change is blowing new opportunities in your direction.

RESIGNATION *See also*: Work. Resign from your job and major changes are on the horizon. If it's anything else then legal matters will be cleared up in your favour.

RESTAURANT *See also*: Food. See one in town and someone is keeping something from you. In the country and problems are around the corner. If it's crowded you will run into trouble with your partner by being too timid. Empty and your partner is about to behave unpredictably. An attractive proposition is about to be made to you if you see yourself eating in a restaurant.

RETIRING *See also*: Time; Work. Dream of this and, sorry, but a lot of hard work is on the way.

REUNION *See also*: Relationships. You will have some much needed outside help if you see yourself getting back together with someone.

REVENGE Seek it and your love life will be hit by a bitter blow. And problems at work are on the way if someone tries to take revenge on you.

REVIEW The theatrical type predicts a visit from someone a long way away. A military review shows you are at your creative best. A naval one spells good news.

REVOLUTION Keep a close eye on business affairs if you see people revolt. If the army is involved, some set-backs in your private life are inevitable. Bloodshed is a sign you are being too rash lately.

REWARD Receive one and you will soon have an unusual stroke of luck. Offer one and it is a warning not to be complacent.

RIBBON This shows just how easily you make friends. If it's pink a long-term project will be successfully concluded. Silver and your enthusiasm is a little excessive. Tie a bow and you are in for some success at work.

RIGHT You will get caught between your pleasure and your principles if you see the right side of anything or a right turn. Let your conscience guide you. Legal matters will go well if you see yourself as right-handed.

RINGING *See also*: Sounds. Hear church bells and it is a sign you are anxious. Ring them yourself and you are about to make a lasting friend.

RINK A fickle friend is going to disappoint you if it is for roller skating. But an ice rink means a social invitation is on the way.

RIOT Curb your extravagance if you see one of these.

RISING Do it from the ground and you will beat the opposition. Rise from a chair and it forecasts a temporary upset. From a couch or bench and you will have to face an unexpected obstacle.

RIVAL A dream of contrary. A business rival relates to your love life and vice versa. Beat them and you will be successful. Fail and trouble is ahead.

RIVER See also: Water. A slow-flowing clean river is a sign of good fortune. If it is rushing or muddy then trouble is brewing. Fall in and danger is around the corner. Bathe in one and money is coming to you. Swim across it and your hopes will soon be realised.

RIVET For a woman this is a sign her current relationship is too restricting. Try telling your lover he shouldn't be so possessive. For a man it shows some sort of sex problem. If it continues seek professional advice or counselling.

ROAD See also: Driving. Straight and broad and good steady progress is predicted. But bumpy, narrow or twisting, and obstacles will have to be overcome. Road signs mean small but pleasant changes.

ROAST See also: Food. Eat roast food and good luck follows. Carve or serve a roast and the family will soon have something to celebrate.

ROBBER You are falling head over heels for someone who isn't really worthy of your affection. Try not to make a fool of yourself.

ROBBERY Organise one and some inner conflict has you so anxious you'd best resolve it as soon as possible. Take part in a robbery and you are suffering from lack of self-control. If you are a victim an unexpected gain is coming.

ROCK See one and an opportunity for promotion at work is about to fall into your lap. Move one and it shows you are in a gloomy frame of mind. Break one and you are feeling a bit lifeless. Buck up! Climb a rock face and your desires are about to be fulfilled. Falling off a rock predicts the loss of a friend.

ROCKET A sign of short-lived success. See one explode and it spells family fortune.

ROD Only your strong will and determination can get you what you want. Steel rods spell unhappiness. Brass ones and someone is being unfaithful to you.

ROLLING Roll downstairs or down a hill and it is a sure sign you are feeling off-colour. Don't take it out on others! Rolling in mud suggests you are loading your problems on to others and it simply isn't fair to them. Rolling something along such as a barrel means it's going to be tough dealing with family members for a while.

ROLLING PIN A happy family reunion is on the cards if it is used in the kitchen. In any other way it is a warning to control your temper.

ROLLS-ROYCE That new offer will turn out to be even better than you think. Grab it with both hands.

ROOF On a house and you should put your new ideas into practice. A tiled roof predicts happiness. Thatched and you are in for a romantic disappointment. Fall off or climb down from one and that success you're so proud of will be just a flash in the pan.

ROOM A waiting room suggests you are certain about a work project. A ballroom and emotional problems are looming. A games room is a sure sign certain suggestions and proposals aren't what they seem. A dining room is a warning not to be so obstinate. A living room predicts unexpected guests.

ROOT The plant or tree variety is warning you to assert yourself more or someone will benefit from your hard work. The root of a tooth predicts family rows.

ROPE Coiled, this is a sign you will complete that difficult task. Uncoil it and a whole new chapter of your life is about to unfold. Walk a rope and it's a good time for a little flutter. Climbing a rope is a good luck sign. See a rope fence and you are being deceived.

ROSARY See also: Religion. Someone influential is supporting and protecting you. If it is ivory you aren't showing much initiative at the moment. Wooden and it's a sign you are feeling sentimental. Buy a rosary and you have high hopes for a new project.

ROYALTY See this family and your financial success is assured. If they are at the Palace you can expect a surprise stroke of luck.

RUBBER Your worries will simply disappear if you see this.

RUDDER See also: Sea/Water/Travel. Confidence is your finest quality if you see the rudder of a ship. Broken, it is a warning to avoid unnecessary travel for a while. If you are at the helm yourself you will attain a difficult goal.

RUIN Ancient ones are a forecast for improving conditions. But unhappy news about a relative is coming if something new is ruined.

RULER Measure with it and only careful meticulous planning can get you where you want to go.

RUNNING You are trying to escape from a tricky situation if you see yourself running. Find yourself unable to run and it suggests a lack of self-confidence. Try and be a bit more pushy. Run scared and you will be cut off from something you enjoy. Running to catch something is a sign of good fortune.

RUST See this and you will make an unexpected profit.

ABOTAGE You are going to need all your tact to prevent family arguments. Be persuasive not aggressive.

SACK A full one forecasts good luck. Empty and there are obstacles to be overcome. Full of coal is a sign that a stimulating new project is round the corner. And a sack of potatoes is a warning against sexual indiscretions.

SACRIFICE *See also*: Death. Sacrifice an animal and a row is brewing at work. A son or a daughter and a serious disagreement with a loved one could spell the end of the relationship.

SADDLE You might have to revise your plans. Check them carefully.

SAFE If it's full then worrying times are ahead. An empty one is a sign of great success.

SAFETY PIN Stick to your guns and you will be successful.

SAGE See the spice and changes for the better are due. If it is a wise man you are in for some luck.

SAILING/SAILOR *See also*: Sea/Water/Travel. Sail across the sea and it's time to use your talents. You are sociable and have considerable initiative. Play on those qualities. A square sail is a sign you must face up to your problems. A triangular one indicates an embarrassing choice. If it is white, money matters need a bit of organising. Any other colour predicts happy news. See yourself as a sailor and you need a change of scene to cheer you up. Sailors on shore predict a new exciting romance. On board ship and some unsettling news from a distance is about to arrive. See a yacht and you are full of confidence.

SALARY *See also*: Work. If the boss turns you down for that rise, money is coming from a surprise direction. If he gives it to you it is a warning to pay more attention at work or you could be demoted. Pay someone a salary and money matters will go well.

SALT *See also*: Food. An excellent omen. All your troubles will be little ones.

SALVATION ARMY You will soon find yourself in a more contented frame of mind.

SAND Walk along it and it's a sign you are jealous. Lie on it and you will have to spring to someone's defence. Sprinkle it on the ground and money is about to slip through your fingers.

SANDWICH *See also*: Food. Eat or make them at home and you will soon have a chance to improve yourself. Eat them in a restaurant and it is a warning to keep your secrets to yourself. Toasted or picnic sandwiches mean you should think again before embarking on that new love affair.

SATELLITE Try thinking for yourself a bit more. Listen to advice by all means but make up your own mind.

SAUCE *See also*: Food. Tomato sauce predicts a letter. Curry sauce is a warning not to give full rein to your feelings in one particular emotional attachment.

SAW If it's electric then you are keeping bad company and it's ruining your reputation. A hacksaw predicts increased responsibility. An ordinary handsaw means you are in for a few problems but the way they will change things will be for the best.

SCAFFOLD On a building this predicts new opportunities. A hangman's scaffold warns of danger through your own indiscretion.

SCALES An important decision will have to be made. Fish scales are a sign you have a false friend.

SCAR A surprisingly positive sign. Dream you have one yourself and you can overcome your difficulties. The larger the scar the greater your ability to sort things out. But see scars on others and you are in for a period of ups and downs.

SCHOOL Different schools mean different things. You are going to have to make a few changes if you see a primary school. A secondary school and you will have to make a choice between a great number of options. A boarding school shows you have supportive friends. A private one and you will face something risky. Go back to school and money plans will go well.

Any kind of **academy** predicts new friends and experiences. But be careful. It could cost you a fortune.

News is on the way if you see a **blackboard**. If it is chalked on it will affect your immediate plans.

Win a **diploma** if you're a man and there'll be mountains of money through your own efforts. For a woman it's a warning not to be so vain. Stop spending so much money on makeup and hairdos. You look fine as you are.

Fail an **exam** and it's a warning your ambitions are aimed a bit too high and you should try changing course. Pass and all your hopes will be fulfilled.

It's a sign you have taken on too much if you are **learning** a new skill. Learn to sing and you will suffer a temporary sadness. If it's dancing you are about to get involved in a new activity.

Hear a **lecture** and it is a sign of limited successes. Give one and you could be in for a move.

See yourself as a learned **professor** and things are bound to improve. Listen to him and you are about to discover you have a hidden talent.

Measure something with a **ruler** and only careful, meticulous planning can get you where you want.

See yourself as a **teacher** and it's a warning you can't ride every horse in the race. Decide what you want to do and stick to it.

For a man, wearing a **uniform** is a sign his status will improve in some way. For a woman it's a good sign for her love life.

Apply to get into **university** and you are feeling particularly strong-willed. If you actually go then it's time to stop being so moody. Work there and a happy period is just around the corner. Graduate and a new challenge is about to present itself at work.

SCISSORS An omen of a broken relationship. But use them yourself and you can mend things by acting quickly.

SCRAPING Scraping anything metal predicts a set-

back at work. Wood means you need your freedom. If it's a wall an ex-lover is about to come back into your life. Use a knife and you are in for a major disappointment in love. Sandpaper and you are being over-ambitious.

SCRATCH A sign of insecurity. If it bleeds someone is working against you. If not there are protective forces working for you.

SCREAM Hear one and distressing news will follow. Scream yourself and it's a good sign for your closest concerns.

SCREEN You are trying to cover up a mistake. Either confess it or forget it.

SCULPTURE *See also*: Pictures/Painting. A warning to pay more attention to your personal affairs. See a sculptor at work and an opportunity to make an exciting change is around the corner.

SEA/WATER/TRAVEL *See also*: Water. Most dreams involving the sea suggest travel is on the horizon.

Find yourself **adrift** and this refers to a problem you can't solve or refuse to face. Land safely and all will be resolved. But if not you will have to tackle serious difficulties because you simply can't make up your mind. See yourself rescued in your dream or swim to safety and success will follow hardship.

See a small boat **afloat** and business will be good. If it's a big ship you will have abundant means. See a fish floating and your earnings will be good. A dead person afloat predicts happiness. If the water is calm and clear a happy event is on the cards. But if it is rough or murky difficulties are ahead.

An **anchor** is telling you to economise on things you don't really need. Raising an anchor from the water means an improvement in earnings.

See an **ark** and important events are on their way.

Take on **ballast** and you must also guard your resources. If it is being thrown overboard a burning desire will be realised.

Barnacles are a sign you will have a comfortable old age.

A loaded **barge** predicts you will outwit your rivals. An empty one is a signal not to make any hasty decisions. Seeing a distant barge forecasts a long trip soon.

A scenic **bay** predicts travel. Rough water in it denotes your money will go out faster than it's coming in. But if you see a calm bay unusual social success is in store.

An empty **beach** is a sign of an opportunity that you should grab with both hands. A busy beach shows you are feeling secure and confident. Sunning yourself on a beach shows your business relationships will improve.

See a **boat** and it symbolises your life, so the other details should be interpreted accordingly. If it is in calm waters life will be smooth. Stormy or murky waters and you're in for a rough ride. A sinking boat suggests a hidden danger round the corner.

See a ship's **cabin** and you're in for a rough ride on the home front. There might even be a legal wrangle on the horizon.

Cargo being loaded on a ship says you'll go on a nice little trip. See it being dropped or thrown overboard and someone else's money problems will bounce back on you.

Cliffs are a warning not to take any risks for quite a while. If you are scaling a cliff your efforts will be rewarded. Going down one means your friends aren't to be trusted.

Dive into the sea and you will soon be faced with a terrific temptation. If the water was clear all will be well. If it was choppy or murky there will be some nasty results.

A **dock** seen from on board a ship and a surprising turn of events is on the way. A dockyard means you now have enough money to start to save. Being alone on a dock signifies some kind of sadness.

Drowning is not a good omen for business matters. But if you or the person drowning are saved you will soon recoup any losses.

Dream of travelling on or seeing a **ferry** and your efforts will be rewarded—probably at work.

Float at sea and you'll soon see sparkling success. Everything is going your way. Use a plastic or rubber float and it means a reconciliation.

See a **fishing fleet** in a harbour and life will be peaceful. If it puts out to sea worries are on the horizon. A naval fleet means you will be released from some tiresome responsibility. A fleet of sailing ships means you will get another chance to try something you thought you had failed in.

A ship's **funnel** says you will be praised for a good job well done.

A **gangway** represents a period of transition for you. If the surroundings are happy, say a gangway to a cruise ship, then the future will prove easier for you. Walk up the gangway and you can expect progress. Down and things will stay bleak for some time. Cross a gangway and you will have to face up to something from your past before you can go on.

See a **lifeboat** on a ship and you are about to run into opposition at work. See it at sea and you will beat your enemies. If it is damaged changes are on the way and they will be for the better. See a lifeboat save people and it predicts a long, happy life.

Dream you are in the **Navy** and it could spell illness. See sailors and a loss at work is on the cards. High-ranking officers predict love troubles.

Use **oars** and an important matter needs sorting out, pronto. Lose them over the side and some bad news could irreparably damage your relationship with your partner. Broken oars mean only the goodwill of others can help you now.

Seeing the **ocean** is a good omen as long as it's calm. An important project at work is about to be concluded and you are about to make a useful friend. Romance is also well starred, but see a stormy ocean and exciting news is around the corner.

Pirates at sea and you will be tempted to start an exciting new venture. But check it out thoroughly before you do.

Ships on a **quay** are a sign of travel. But an empty quay is a warning not to be lazy or it could lead to disappointments.

Float on a **raft** and it is a warning not to be lazy. Someone else will profit from it. Build one and you can achieve a great deal through your own efforts.

Confidence is your finest quality if you see the **rudder** of a ship. Broken, it is a warning to avoid unnecessary travel for a while. If you are at the helm yourself you will attain a difficult goal.

Sail across the sea and it's time to use your talents. You are sociable and have considerable initiative. Play on those qualities.

A square **sail** is a sign you must face up to your problems. A triangular one indicates embarrassing choices. If it is white, money matters need a bit of organising. Any other colour predicts happy news.

See yourself as a **sailor** and you need a change of scene to cheer you up. Sailors on shore predict a new exciting romance. On board ship and some unsettling news from a distance is about to arrive.

Walk along the **sand** and it's a sign you are jealous. Lie on it and you will have to spring to some-

Plate 21 · School Days

one's defence. Sprinkle it on the ground and money is about to slip through your fingers.

Seaweed says don't compromise your principles. Stand your ground and you will come off best.

Ships are a symbol of profit. A model ship predicts a passionate new affair. A fleet of ships forecasts success in business. A shipwreck is a sign you will have to protect your reputation.

Sinking is a sign you have just paid over the odds. Shop around next time.

Surf breaking on the shore is a sign of advances—both in business and your love life.

Swimming is a lucky omen if you do it naked. In a suit and you will soon be blushing socially. Teach someone to swim and money luck is coming. Swim towards the shore and you will have to work hard to get what you want. Things are bound to go well at work if you see a swimming pool, but if it is empty don't make snap judgements of people you have only just met. You could be unfair to them.

The **tide** of money luck will soon be flowing your way if you see **yachts**. And your highest hopes will be realised if you see yourself entertaining on a yacht.

SEANCE *See also*: Supernatural. Don't be too proud to ask for help if you see this hand-holding session.

SEARCHING Searching for a male means your easy time at work will be hit by problems. If it's a female you are in for some criticism. An object and your future plans are over-ambitious.

SECRET Hear this and you will be involved in a bit of intrigue. Repeat it and you will have to defend yourself against gossip.

SECRETARY *See also*: Work. Old habits are holding you back if you see yourself as one of these. Employ one and your status is about to improve.

SEPARATION A dream of contrary. You will reach a better understanding with your partner.

SEPTEMBER *See also*: Time. If it is not September changes for the better are on the way.

SERVANT A dream of contrary. See yourself as one and long-awaited happiness will be yours. Having them predicts money loss.

SEWING *See also*: Clothes; Tidiness. Make plans for the future if you see someone sewing. Do it yourself and an exciting new opportunity is about to present itself. If the sewing is by hand you will have to work hard. By machine and you must be careful who you confide in.

SEXUALITY If you are a woman and dream of changing sex then success in the family is predicted. For a man it's a sign he is about to be an embarrassing failure in bed! Tease someone sexually and you will realise an ambition. But is it really a worthy one?

Visit a **brothel**—whether you're a man or a woman—and your domestic life will really improve.

Dream of being **embraced** and you'd better temper that impulsive streak. It will land you in trouble. Embracing others or watching others embrace means a few family rows are on the horizon.

See yourself in a **harem** or simply surrounded by one and it is a sign you are going to be busy with the opposite sex. Don't exhaust yourself.

If **impotence** features, your love life is starred with success and your other interests will also go well.

Enjoy **intercourse** in a dream and you will happily adjust to new circumstances. If you see others having intercourse contentment and success are coming. But if any feature of the dream is unpleasant you're probably repressing an emotional problem. An expert counsellor could help.

Kissing someone heralds a new love affair. If you are kissed by your partner it's a sure sign the relationship is genuine. Kissing a dead person is an omen for a long, happy life. Kiss a baby and something you thought was difficult will go well. Try to avoid a kiss and a minor illness is on the cards.

Dream of a **prostitute** and fear of sexual failure is the message. If you are solicited by one try not to be so easy with your flattery. It's meaningless if you offer it all the time. See yourself as a prostitute and some news to cheer you up will arrive. Visit a prostitute and trouble is brewing at home.

See **rape** and careless behaviour could cost you your reputation. Think carefully or you are bound to disappoint people.

See your own **sex organs** as healthy and it's a sign you have a satisfactory sex life. Dream of diseased sex organs and you've either been overdoing

it or sleeping around. Try and be a bit more faithful. Unusual sex organs are a symbol of a starved sex life. You're not happy about that or it wouldn't be playing on your mind. Dream of pain in the genitals and a medical check-up would not go amiss.

A **virgin** is a symbol of happiness. Though if she is dead you must expect complications at work. Start a relationship with a virgin and fortune is about to smile on you in everything you do. See yourself as one and you are being a bit naive about something.

SHADE *See also*: Darkness/Light. Lower it and you are aiming too high. Raise it and you will be successful at whatever interests you most. If it shoots up on its own you are in for a surprise.

SHADOW *See also*: Darkness/Light. Legal matters will go well if it is your own. Anyone else's and it is a warning not to travel for a few weeks.

SHAME *See also*: Guilt. Being ashamed means good fortune in business. But if you're ashamed of specific actions, then you're suffering from a guilty conscience, aren't you?

SHAVING *See also*: Hair; Razor. See someone shaving and a colleague is trying to provoke you. Don't rise to the bait. See yourself and a business loss is on the cards.

SHELL Seashells predict an unusual event. Find them and something is about to make you blush. A shell from a gun shows your love affair is burning out.

SHIP *See also*: Sea/Water/Travel. A symbol of profit. A model ship predicts a passionate new affair. A fleet of ships forecasts success in business. A ship wreck is a sign you will have to protect your reputation.

SHOP *See also*: Buying/Selling. Buy something and if you watch the pennies you can sort out your finances. Work in one and you are in for a stroke of money luck.

SHOVEL Your responsibilities are about to increase. But see a grave digger use it and finances are a bit shaky.

SHOWER *See also*: Washing; Water. Take one of these and money is coming your way.

SHY *See also*: Relationships. Suffer from shyness and current projects will go well. Dream others are shy and someone you are relying on is about to let you down.

SIEVE Stop splashing out on luxuries or you won't be able to afford the necessities.

SIGNATURE *See also*: Reading/Writing. Sign anything and it is a symbol of security. See other people signing and you can be sure your friends are loyal.

SILVER *See also*: Metals. See coins and you could lose money. Silverware and you are in for promotion. But don't let it go to your head.

SINGING *See also*: Music. You may be cheerful at the moment but worries are right around the corner. Still, they won't last long.

SINGLE *See also*: Relationships. If you are married and see yourself single again it is a warning not to get involved with dodgy companions.

SINKING *See also*: Sea/Water/Travel. Sink into anything and you have just paid over the odds. Shop around next time.

SITTING Sit up high and your status will improve. If it's on a low seat it's time to assert yourself more.

SKATING On ice and your love affair is being threatened by someone who is jealous of you. Roller-skating is a sign you are anxious about something. Take skating lessons and an opportunity will allow you to make your mark at work. See skaters and so-called friends will turn against you.

SKELETON *See also*: Human body. If it's human serious worries are around the corner. An animal skeleton shows you have a tendency to get depressed and lonely. Try to make more friends. See it as part of a medical display and new events are on the horizon.

SKIDDING Do this and it shows you are reluctant to make a decision. It is the only way to solve things so do it as quickly as possible. Recover from a skid and money matters will go well.

SKIN If it's smooth it's a good sign for your sex life. Blotchy and problems are on the horizon romantically. Peeling skin predicts a period of uncertainty but it will end with an exciting new relationship.

SKIPPING Help will arrive from an unexpected source. A skipping rope is a sign you are doubting yourself. Don't!

SKULL *See also*: Death. Human and you don't trust someone close. An animal's skull predicts an

embarrassing situation.

SKY If it's clear, happy times are ahead. Gathering clouds mean you will have to make more effort. A stormy sky forecasts stress and if it's grey your friends will stand by you whatever the weather.

SLAPPING Do it and you'll be blushing socially. Receive it and it spells social success.

SLEEPING It is quite common to see yourself or others asleep. If it's restless your health is below par. Deep and you will make new business connections. Sleeping with someone else shows you are optimistic and trusting. A man snoring shows the boss at work knows your worth. A woman and a financial project is over-ambitious.

SLEEVE *See also*: Clothes. A slight disappointment is on the way if you see short sleeves. Long ones and your services will be recognised. Tight sleeves are an omen of sexual pleasure. Full ones a warning to control your temper.

SMELLS Smell **camphor** and it is a warning against casual sex. Scandal or illness could result. Don't do it!

Smell **gas** and it's a warning to mind your own business.

Get a whiff of **ginger** and a passionate love affair is on the cards. But sorry—it simply won't last.

Herbs predict peace and contentment, but simply smelling them is a sign you are about to embark on an exciting adventure. Possibly abroad.

Lavender says things will go well with the opposite sex. Perhaps even a new affair is around the corner for you.

Smell **mace** and you'll be recognised for doing some kind of community work.

Musk and you are in for a passionate new love affair. Your sex life will simply sizzle.

Nutmeg is a warning to question people's motives. Don't let them use you to their own advantage.

SMOKE *See also*: Fire. You'll be in the money if it comes from a chimney. But if you don't know the source you are heading for disappointment. Cigarette smoke predicts an important new friend.

SMUGGLING That skeleton in the family cupboard is about to be revealed. But never fear. The fuss will soon die down.

SNEEZING Things will run smoothly for quite a while. But see others sneezing and you will have to fight to get what you want.

SNOW *See also*: Weather. Light and powdery, it shows what a mischievous mood you're in. If it's turned to ice you have doubts about a lover. Slush is a sign you are being discreet. And a snowdrift is an omen of unexpected pleasures and money luck. See snow falling and there will be some interesting changes in your life.

SOAP *See also*: Washing. A good sign for your love life. Soap flakes mean you will have to fight to get what you want. Medicated soap suggest a mystery is about to be solved.

SOLDIER *See also*: Uniform. For a woman this is a warning against a casual affair. For a man it means changes at work.

SORE See them on yourself and things will improve. On others or animals and you.are going to have to shelve your needs in favour of those of others for a while.

SOUNDS Hear an **alarm** and exciting profitable times are ahead.

Receive **applause** and it's a sign you're a bit of a vain one. Beware of jealousy. You can overcome it but you'll need some tact. If you hear others applauding, friends may do the dirty on you.

A lamb **bleating** says business will prosper. Hear a flock of them at it and your home life will be happy.

A **buzzer** sounding says your social life will be such a whirl you won't know if you're coming or going.

You will soon be swelling with pride for some reason if you hear **chanting**.

Chatter is a straightforward warning you've been gossiping too much.

Hear **chimes** and better times are ahead.

A striking **clock** means things will improve if you take positive action.

A cock **crowing** predicts wonderful news.

A **cork** popping says you're in for a bit of a fling.

Cymbals and it's time to hold tight. You're in for a passionate new romance.

Push a **door bell** and you'll meet an exciting new friend. Hear it ringing and a new pursuit will soon entrance you.

Plate 22 · The Sphinx and the Unicorn

Some smashing success will soon be yours if **drums** feature. Play them and things'll be simply wonderful.

Exploding **dynamit**e is a warning to abandon any new plan. It won't work. Any other explosion predicts lasting improvements in every area of life.

The sound of your own **echo** means you're in for a strange experience—probably with the opposite sex. Another kind of echo is a sign you will get a big 'yes' from a proposal you put forward. It could be marriage or a business proposition.

Hear a **gong** and an exciting event is on the way. Simply see it and someone you know is about to experience changes in their life.

Hissing from a snake is telling you to try and control your temper. Human hissing means you will make progress if you hear it. Do it yourself and you are about to make an embarrassing *faux-pas*.

Fortune is about to smile on you if you hear someone **knocking** on a door. Do it yourself and you are feeling nostalgic. But don't try and recreate the past. Going back is never quite the same. Knock on a window and you are in for a row with your mate.

A man's **laugh** says you are about to learn a lot from a new work project. A woman's is a sign you are being a bit anti-social. News will arrive from a long way away if you hear children laughing. Make people laugh and it's time to face the fact that you and your partner aren't really suited.

Tuneful harmonious **music** predicts fabulous fortune in all that deeply concerns you. But if it's out of tune trouble is in the wind at work.

Children making a **noise** is a warning to be patient. Unusually loud noises are a sign you aren't relaxing enough. Try to slow down.

A **rattle** is a sign you are in for a few problems.

Church bells say you are anxious. **Ring** them yourself and you are about to make a lasting friend.

Hear a **scream** and distressing news will follow. Scream yourself and it's a good sign for your closest concerns.

A clap of **thunder** means whatever is troubling you most will soon be cleared up. Rumbling thunder says that the disloyalty you suspect from a friend, well, you're absolutely right. Don't trust them.

SOUTH This direction is a sign of security.

SPEAKING See and/or hear yourself or others speaking in an unfamiliar **accent** and news from a distance could involve a hasty trip.

Utter an **apology** and an old friend will come back on the scene. If you receive one you will be happy with your lover.

You are going through a jealous phase if you **imitate** someone. This is not a very lucky omen.

Money problems are to the fore if you act as an **interpreter** or use one.

See yourself **interrogating** someone and it's a sign you are not very good at forming lasting relationships with those around you. If you were on the end of the interrogation a pleasant surprise, probably in the form of a journey, is coming.

Interview a celebrity and a pleasant meeting is round the corner. Interview a politician and it shows you have a rebellious streak. A job interview suggests a major change, though not necessarily of career.

See yourself with **lockjaw** and it's a straightforward warning to keep your mouth shut. Remember what they say about careless talk.

Hear or take an **oath** and you will either be promoted or rise up the social scale a notch.

Hear a **sermon** inside a church and a pet project will be thwarted by delays. Deliver one and your suspicions about someone are groundless.

Mind your tongue if you **whisper**. A hasty outburst could get you into trouble.

SPEAR *See also*: Hunting; Weapons. Your love life is going to take an exciting turn, especially if it's used to catch fish.

SPECTACLES Wear them and you could miss out on a golden opportunity. Sunglasses predict a period of self-confidence. Buy glasses and you will have to cope with a minor illness.

SPINSTER More than one and some happy social events are on the horizon. If she's the old maid type it's a warning not to be impulsive. See yourself as one and you are in for an unexpected change of circumstances.

SPIRE *See also*: Religion. An omen of true love and friendship. But if it was twisted or leaning you will have to overcome some difficulties before achieving your aims.

SPLINTER If you have it then it's a warning to control that temper of yours. See someone else with one and it's time to pay more attention to your personal affairs.

SPONGE *See also*: Washing. Wash with this and you'll be thanked for a good job well done. Squeeze water out and a pay rise is on the cards. A dry sponge is a warning not to gamble.

SPOON *See also*: Food. A tablespoon shows you're adaptable. A teaspoon suggests you are over-critical. If it's wooden it predicts a secret liaison with someone of the opposite sex.

SPRING *See also*: Time; Water. If it's dried up it predicts bitterness. Drink from a spring and your affection for someone is about to be reciprocated. A bedspring shows you're not the materialistic type. And if you see the season it's a sign you are at your inspirational best.

SPY See yourself spied on and it's a warning not to be rash. Spy on others and an exciting new offer is on the horizon.

SQUARE This shape is a sign of security. A town square shows your energy is increasing. Walk through a square and you are going to be offered an opportunity you should grab with both hands.

STABLE *See also*: Animals. Full of cows it means a major success. See donkeys in it and there are work problems ahead. But horses in a stable predict prosperity.

STAIRS Up is good and down is not so good. Trip up them and it's a good sign for your love life. Fall down and it is a warning to be less controversial. Cleaning stairs predicts an unexpected change of lifestyle. A wooden staircase suggests you are making mistakes at work.

STAMP *See also*: Post Office. Rare ones predict good profits. And your status will improve if you stamp letters. Buy stamps and you are in for a rise. Collect them and you are about to rise higher up the social scale.

STAR A powerful friend of the opposite sex is going to help you achieve your ambitions if you see a bright twinkling star. Lots of stars spell success. A shooting star means you will get there in the end but you're going to have to wait a while.

STATION *See also*: Arriving/Leaving. Important news is on its way at work if it's a railway station. Meet someone at a station and your career will be helped by someone influential.

STEALING *See also*: Legal matters. Look after your money or you could be out of pocket. Get caught stealing and it's a sign of good luck.

STEAM *See also*: Heat. If it burns you then you are being deceived. Hear it escaping and you're in for a row. Turn it off and something you thought impossible is about to happen. A steam train shows a shaky love life. A steam boat and you're in the money. See steam from a kettle and you could be feeling a bit off-colour.

STEEL *See also*: Metals. In construction this points to enduring love and friendship. Used in a blade or weapon it suggests jealousy.

STEW *See also*: Food. Cook it and you could get news of a birth. Eating it predicts a reunion with an old friend.

STOCK MARKET A dream of contrary. See gains and it is a warning not to gamble. Losses predict money luck.

STONE Stepping stones forecast slow but steady progress. Cobbles are a warning not to take any risks. Throwing stones is a sign you are regretting a missed opportunity.

STORM *See also*: Weather. An obstacle dream. You will pull yourself out of the doldrums when you accept that only you can change things.

STOVE *See also*: Heat. A coal one predicts an important new relationship. Gas and your health will improve. If it's electric it suggests you can't quite decide what to do next. Switch one off and you're about to miss a valuable opportunity.

STRAITJACKET An obstacle dream as far as money is concerned. If you are released someone is going to help you out of trouble. Otherwise it's time to tighten your belt.

STRANGLING You'll never get what you want if you don't push for it. See yourself strangled and it's a sign you are being far too timid. Strangle someone else and you should follow your instincts if you don't quite trust someone.

STRAW Piles of it suggest you will soon have money

to save. See it burning and it's a warning not to be careless with your pennies. If it's wet you could be about to do something foolish. A straw hat is telling you that appearances can be deceptive. A drinking straw is a sign of increased responsibility.

STREAM *See also*: Water. This represents life forces. A smooth-flowing clear stream predicts your life will run the same way. Cloudy or rough and that's just how things will be for a while.

STREET If you don't recognise it, a profitable new venture is on the cards. A long street shows you will have to be patient about something. Crooked predicts a surprise.

STRENGTH A strong man is a sure sign you are setting your sights too high. A strong woman and it's a good time for a little flutter. Show unusual strength yourself and a passionate new affair is on the cards.

STRIP *See also*: Clothes; Nakedness. See a stage stripper and it suggests you are thinking of something that is a bit indiscreet. Don't do it. You could pay a high price if you do.

SUCCESS Any kind of **advancement** simply means what it says. It's a good omen signifying satisfaction and good times.

Any progress upwards forecasts eventual success in life. However easy or hard it is relates to how smooth or difficult it will be to achieve your **ambitions.**

Win or give any kind of **award** and prosperity is just around the corner.

See yourself as a **champion** at sports and your current enthusiasm for something will soon fizzle out. If someone else becomes a champion you can expect some small successes.

Pass an **exam** and all your hopes will be fulfilled.

Dream of being **famous** and you are trying for something that is really out of your reach. Try and cut your cloth to suit you more. Dream of a famous person and it's a sign to keep trying. Help is at hand from a surprise source.

Any kind of success that provides **gain** – be it financial or otherwise—and the greater the gain the bigger the warning to look after your money. But if you make gains dishonestly business will boom or you can expect to recover a loss.

Hit the **jackpot** and you are in for some hard work with precious little reward. See someone else win a jackpot and you can gain something with a lot less effort than you thought.

See yourself as a **millionaire** and you are about to profit from a past favour. Meet one and it is a warning to seek advice before making any commitment.

SUFFOCATION A medical check-up would be well advised.

SUICIDE You need a change of scene or to relax more. Things are clearly getting on top of you.

SUMMER *See also*: Heat; Time. See this in any other season and you are about to hear some surprising news.

SUN *See also*: Darkness/Light; Weather. Bright and clear and success will soon be yours. A red sun forecasts a struggle but you will win in the end. Sunrise predicts new doors about to open for you and if you see the sun set exciting changes are around the corner.

SUNDAY *See also*: Time. Seen on any other day this is an omen of change at home and at work.

SUNDIAL Tell the time with it and your most cherished wish is about to come true. Otherwise it predicts some pleasant social events.

SUNSTROKE *See also*: Heat. Some unexpected family responsibilities are looming. Don't panic. You'll cope.

SUPERNATURAL See an **apparition** and good news is coming. Unless it frightened you—then it's a warning to have a medical check-up. Seeing the apparition of a dead relative signifies prosperity. Good health is forecast if the apparition wears white, but if it's black your lover is about to behave totally out of character and it could cause bitter recriminations.

A walking **ghost** indicates set-backs and money worries. A talking ghost is a sign you are deluding yourself about things. Face facts. If you don't run away from the ghost, both business and love will go well.

Any form of **magic** spells unexpected changes. They may be hard to understand at first but all will make sense in the end.

The **occult** says some secret info is about to come your way. You can use it to your advantage.

A **seance** is a sign you shouldn't be too proud to ask for help.

Your social life is about to perk up if you see a **witch**, but it's not a good sign for your love life. You could soon find yourself disenchanted.

SWAMP Put away those credit cards. You can't afford to keep spending so much. Walking in one is a warning your current relationship is no good for you.

SWEEPING A lucky omen. Your troubles will be swept away and you'll soon be in the money.

SWEET *See also*: Food. A dream of contrary. Sweets symbolise bitterness. Give them away and you could be in for a break with your partner. Eat them and it's a warning not to make any rash decisions. They could cost you dear.

SWIMMING *See also*: Sea/Water/Travel. If you are naked this is a lucky omen. In a suit and you will soon be blushing socially. Teach someone to swim and money luck is coming. Swim towards the shore and you will have to work hard to get what you want. Things are bound to go well at work if you see a swimming pool but if it is empty don't make snap judgements of people you have only just met. You could be unfair to them.

SWING Something is hanging in the balance. It will work in your favour if you are patient.

SWORD Small setbacks are on the horizon. See it drawn from its scabbard and it is a warning to sort out your money problems. If you don't they will only get worse.

TABASCO This is hot stuff and so are you at the moment! An exciting new romance is on the cards.

TABLECLOTH A clean one and it will be smooth sailing both at work and at home. But if it's dirty family squabbles are round the corner.

TABLET It's a sign you are irritable if it is the medical kind. Take them and it suggests you are being indecisive. See them in a bottle and you are worrying too much. A tablet of stone is a warning not to be so inflexible.

TACK Hammer them in and you will soon come to the aid of a friend. Pull them out and it is a warning not to speak out of turn. It will only cause upset.

TAILOR See him at work and an unexpected journey is on the cards. See yourself as a tailor and it would be better to keep your secrets to yourself.

TANGLE If it's string or thread then that secret affair you are contemplating will complicate your life in a way you will find too hot to handle. If it's undergrowth it's a sign you are living on your nerves.

TAPESTRY Some wonderful surprises are predicted. And even better, you will enjoy yourself without having to spend a penny!

TAR This is a sign you are bogged down in your love life. Perhaps a change of partner might be a good idea? See it on your clothes and it is a warning not to repeat gossip.

TAX *See also*: Money. You are going to have to pay out in some way if taxes worry you. If not you can expect to prosper.

TEA Cold tea predicts a break in an emotional relationship. Hot and your sharp wit will attract someone of the opposite sex. Drink tea and it's time to go it alone at work.

TEACHER *See also*: School. See yourself as one and it's a warning you can't ride every horse in the race. Decide what to do and stick to it.

TEETH Not a good omen. Toothache suggests you are not happy about a certain situation. Lose a tooth and you are afraid of losing a loved one. Lose all of them and you are full of anxieties about the future. Having a filling predicts pleasures. An extraction shows you are suffering at present. False teeth forecast unhappiness in love and a major crisis on the way. Bad or broken teeth show that a relationship that is important to you is breaking down.

TELEGRAM Sending one is a sign you are brimming with confidence. It will stand you in good stead at work. Receive one and it shows just how bored you are. Don't let apathy take over—get out there and fight.

TELEPHONE Use it and a minor tiff with your partner is going to explode into a major row. Answer it and the next few days will be beset with problems.

TELESCOPE You simply aren't seeing things clearly at the moment. Try taking a different view.

TELEVISION Buy a set and your financial future is shaky. Give one away and you are lacking in self-confidence at the moment. Repairing one is a sign you are making good decisions. Turn the telly on and it suggests you are feeling a bit sensitive. Turn it off and a new relationship could prove dangerous.

TENNIS A court shows you are feeling a sense of responsibility. See someone playing and promotion at work is just around the corner. Play yourself and it suggests you crave more independence.

TENT Money worries will disappear sooner than you think if you pitch this. But if it falls down you will have to rethink your plans especially where finances are concerned.

THEATRE *See also*: Performing. Empty, this is a sign of boredom. But see a performance and your social life is about to be busy.

THERMOMETER Changes are on the horizon. Buy one and a work project will go well.

THIMBLE Not a good sign. Use one and you will be in for some criticism. A silver one indicates too much pride on your part. And you know what that comes before…!

THORN *See also*: Brambles. Catch yourself on one and your poor choice of friends is doing nothing for your reputation. Pick it off and it's a warning not to gossip.

THUNDER *See also*: Sounds; Weather. Whatever is troubling you most will soon be cleared up if you hear a clap of thunder. Rumbling and that disloyalty you suspected from a friend…well, you're absolutely right. Don't trust them.

TICKET Some long-awaited news is about to arrive and will help you see things much more clearly.

TIDINESS **Arrange** books on a shelf and a project you thought had been abandoned will be renewed. Arranging things in a drawer means you are worried about your problems. Arranging a meal table means good health and strength and is a sign that you are being decisive and confident and deserve praise from the boss. Arranging tea or coffee cups is a warning to try not to be so enthusiastic about something in life.

Dream of **filing** anything and you'd better spell things out clearly to others or it could be the cause of vicious gossip. They are bound to get the wrong end of the stick.

See a **maid** and if you actually have one this is a good omen. If not it predicts a loss of status. For a woman dreaming of being a maid is a sign she is about to step up the social scale.

Some unexpected expenses are on the way if you tidy up your **nails** and have a manicure. Budget for them now or you will be caught short of cash.

See yourself as as a **servant** clearing up after other people and long-awaited happiness will be yours. Having servants predicts money loss.

Tidy up with a **vacuum cleaner** and you are about to wow the opposite sex. But if it breaks down, don't mix business with pleasure. Save those romances for out of the office.

TIME Worrying about the march of time and your **age** is a warning to see a doctor as illness could be approaching. If you worry about your partner's age then you are being deceived. Fretting over a relative's age indicates a death in the family. But see old people in your dream and it is an omen of great good luck.

See events that occur in the **afternoon** and it's generally good for your personal life. A beautiful afternoon means good times are just around the corner. A cloudy one spells small profits and a rainy one good business profits.

If you are a woman an **almanac** is a warning not to sacrifice your personal obligations for a bit of social climbing. For a man it is a sign of a good business deal.

Dream of making or keeping an **appointment** and you must give up some secret scheme you have been harbouring. It simply isn't going to work.

April signifies a trip abroad.

Dream of **August** in summer and you will be successful in what you are doing. Dream of August in winter and you will go on an unexpected trip.

See **Autumn** during another season and you will find friends and friendly gestures where you least expect them.

Write an appointment on a **calendar** and you are about to meet Mr or Ms Right. Tear off a calendar sheet and a surprise present is on its way.

You must stop wasting so much time if you see a **clock**. See yourself winding a clock and you are on the brink of a new love affair.

Any **delays** spell an unsettling period. But if the delay is of a bus, plane, or train your problems will all be connected with money.

The **end** of anything is a symbol of new beginnings for you.

Dream of **January** when it isn't the first month of the year and some perplexing problem will soon be solved. If it is January then money is coming to you.

See **July** at any other time of the year and you must be cautious of all new offers. Delve into them deeply before deciding.

Dream of **June** when it isn't and an exciting new romance is predicted.

Dream of **March** when it isn't and you are in for a disappointment. Something you expected simply won't happen.

You are in for some money troubles if you see **May** at any other time. November and the latter years of your life will be happy and content.

And if you see **October** in any other month someone is trying to persuade you to make a change you don't much like. Be firm. Don't listen to them.

See the **pendulum** of a clock and changes are about to upset your routine. Accept them gracefully and all will be well.

Reach **retirement** age and, sorry, but a lot of hard work is on the way.

See **September** when it isn't and changes for the better are on the way.

Spring is a sign you are at your inspirational best.

Sunday seen on any other day is an omen of change at home and at work.

Money is on the way if you dream of **winter**.

TINSEL This is a reminder that all that glistens isn't gold—don't be taken in by posh appearances. Try scratching the surface a little and see what's really underneath.

TOADSTOOL You will have to fight to get what you want. But persevere and you can do it.

TOILET Legal troubles, probably concerning property, are on the cards.

TOMB *See also*: Death. A dream of contrary. Everything will work in your favour. But if you see yourself locked in it's time to get a medical check-up.

TORCH Flaming or electric, if it's alight your respect for those around you will help at work. But if it's out a disappointment with the opposite sex will lead to a period of apathy. Come on, try and pull yourself together!

TOWEL It's a sign you're fighting fit if it's a clean one. But wet or dirty and you will have to cope with a few frustrations. Money may be tight if you see paper towels.

TOYS *See also*: Childhood/Children. New developments are on the horizon. But if they are broken it suggests you are being a bit childish about something. Try and grow up a bit.

TRAFFIC Ask for help with a problem if you see this go by. Drive in it and family problems will soon be solved. See a traffic jam and you will need a lot of patience over something.

TRAIL Follow one and you can achieve your ambition if you work hard. Lose it and it's a warning not to waste so much time.

TRAIN *See also*: Arriving/Leaving. Board the train and you are rightly optimistic about the future. Get off and a shortlived emotional crisis is on the cards.

TRAMP See yourself as one and your circumstances are about to improve. Give him food and you will soon rise up the social scale. Turn him down and you are in for some hard work.

TRAP For a man setting one is a good luck sign. For a woman it is a warning not to trust a friend. See yourself caught in a trap and it's a bad time to listen to gossip. Simply ignore it, however intrigued you are.

TRAPDOOR *See also*: Doors. Some shock news is about to arrive. Don't let it panic you into any hasty decisions.

TRAY If it's full, good luck is around the corner. Drop it and you will soon regret something you said.

TREASURE Dig for it and your health will improve. Find it and you will prosper.

TREES/PLANTS Healthy blooming **plants** are a sign of good luck in present projects. Wilted, they are a warning of careless planning. Repot or water them and home life will be comfortable. A **tree** is a good omen. Plant one and your love life couldn't be better. Chop one down and your problems will all be of your own making, I'm afraid. Climb a tree and it will be lots of work for little reward for a while. **Tree bark** is a warning to take it steady with the opposite sex. Coming on too strong is a real turn-off, you know. **Tree stumps** are a sign of new beginnings.

Acorns are a sign of immense good luck. Problems will be solved successfully and the sun will shine on all your future plans. Collect them and you will receive a legacy. A sick person holding acorns predicts an immediate recovery.

See an **almond** tree in bloom and happy celebrations are on the cards on the home front.

Apricots growing on a tree signify pleasure and contentment to come.

Trees in **bloom** spell happiness and joy; a line of them unexpected promotion.

Get pricked by a **bramble** and you must expect some reverses. If the brambles don't scratch you then happy days will soon be here again.

Bushes are a signal for action. You will have an offer that means moving house. Hide under bushes and don't do anything that's going to make you feel guilty afterwards. Cut one down, and one of your embarrassing secrets is about to go public. Take cover for a while.

A **cherry tree** predicts trouble is brewing in business. Go more slowly with new projects.

Dream of being alone or frightened in a **forest** and someone you trust is going to let you down. If you are lost in a forest one of your pet projects will be a success. Hide in a forest and something that is difficult now will pay dividends in the end.

Holly is attractive but prickly and that's just how life is going to be for you for a while.

Outdoors **ivy** is a sign of faithful friends. Indoors it predicts personal happiness. Money is coming in the future if you see it growing on a house. Twining round a tree it is a symbol of good health.

A green healthy **leaf** and everything is going your way both at home and at work. Fallen or dried-up leaves are a sign of difficulties and illness.

Patience is the key word especially at work if you see **mistletoe**. But at least you can bet your love life will go well.

Dry **moss** means you are in for a disappointment. But if it is soft and green your love life will simply sizzle.

Be brave and you will be successful if you see **nettles**. But you will have to work hard as well. Get stung and it is a warning you must protect yourself from a disloyal friend or deceitful lover.

Dream of poisonous **nightshade** and it's time to take chances. New ventures, new relationships, all will work out well.

An **oak** tree is a sign of money. See it cut down and you are being deceived.

Olive trees predict prosperity. Pick the olives and success at work will follow.

An **orchard** in bloom is a sign of good luck. Your deepest wish is about to be granted if it's full of fruit. See it bare and you will have a small success.

A loyal friend is about to let you down if you see a **palm tree**. You are bound to be bitterly disappointed.

See the **roots** of plants or trees and it's a sign you should assert yourself more or someone else will benefit from your hard work.

Catch yourself on a **thorn** and your poor choice of friends is doing nothing for your reputation. Pick it off and it's a warning not to gossip.

A **vine** is a lucky omen if it's in bloom. Things beyond your wildest dreams are about to happen. But if it's withered you need to slow down and relax a bit more.

Weeds in a garden are a sign you are keeping bad company and it's ruining your reputation. Dig them out and every cloud on your horizon will have a silver lining.

A **yucca** plant says that both mentally and spiritually life will be full of contentment.

TRIAL *See also*: Legal matters. If you are on trial it is a warning to stick to the tried and tested for a while. Don't attempt anything new.

TRIANGLE Whether it's the shape or the instrument a new opportunity should be grabbed with both hands.

TUB *See also*: Washing. If it's full you could be in for a few family rows. Empty and it's a sign you are being indecisive. Fill it up and things will go wonderfully well at work. Empty it out and some bad news is on the way.

TUNNEL An obstacle dream, if you see yourself struggling through it. Otherwise it's a sign of change. Get through successfully and happiness waits for you.

TWINS Double trouble will soon be followed by twice the pleasure.

TYPING See someone use the slow two-finger

Plate 23 · The Passage of Time

method and money worries are creeping up. But a fast accurate typist is a sign work will go well and you will profit. See yourself typing and you will be financially secure.

TYRE Change one and you are about to get an unexpected demand on your resources. A blow-out is a warning someone is jealous of you. Buy a new tyre and your worries will soon disappear.

UMBRELLA This is a symbol of security. But if it is torn or inside out, your aims will be hit by minor delays and difficulties. Buy one and money matters are going your way. Lose one and a row at work is going to make life difficult.

UNCONSCIOUSNESS See someone in this state and news of an illness is on the way. See yourself thus and a medical check-up would be wise.

UNDRESSING *See also*: Clothes; Nakedness. If it's a child it's time to stand up for your rights. A man is a sign of an unfaithful relationship. A woman shows you are being unscrupulous. You have misplaced your affections if you see yourself undress. If you do it in public it's a sign you need a rest.

UNICORN Not a good sign. You are facing problems caused by people who aren't as trustworthy as you first thought.

UNIFORM For a man wearing a uniform in a dream is a sign his status will improve in some way. For a woman it is a good sign for her love life.

See an **admiral** and it spells success in your social life and career. See yourself as an admiral and dangerous liaisons in your love life are predicted.

Aldermen are a warning not to gamble. See yourself as one and insurmountable difficulties are on the horizon. If you see others with aldermen you must guard against jealous friends.

Any type of **badge**, whether you are wearing it or see it pinned on someone, relates to your security. Whatever kind concerns you most, be it job, family, or money will be yours.

See **cadets** in uniform and you have a lot of hard work to do. If they are drilling it is a warning that someone is deceiving you. You will be cheated by a woman if you see them graduating.

A **captain** means promotion at work for a man. For a woman it is a warning to watch out for jealous friends.

For a woman **epaulets** mean a sizzling new love affair. For a man promotion or a pay rise.

See a **flag** flying and you can expect a few party invites. Raising a flag means money on the way. Lowering one means money luck as well. A display flag means someone out there fancies you. I wonder who it is?

Try and be a bit more organised or you'll get in a muddle if you see people wearing **helmets**. Wear one yourself and it's a warning not to be extravagant.

See **insignia** and despite hostile competition you'll make progress. Wear insignia and an exciting new love affair is round the corner.

Carry a **mace** and it spells danger in love affairs. See someone else bear it and you will receive some kind of distinction.

An **officer** in the services is a sign of security and protection. A police officer is a warning that a friend is going to be careless with money and you will be caught up in their predicament.

See a **soldier** if you are a woman and it's a warning against a casual affair. For a man it predicts changes at work.

UNIVERSITY *See also*: School. Apply to get in and it's a sign you are feeling particularly strong-willed. If you actually go then it's time to stop being so moody. Work there and a happy period is just around the corner. Graduate and a new challenge is about to present itself at work.

URINATING Do it on the ground and you are facing some difficult problems. In the street and you are feeling guilty over something you did in the past. See yourself wetting the bed and money is coming your way. And you and your partner are in for a major row if you see a child wetting itself.

URN *See also*: Death. Made of wood this is a sign of prosperity. China and you are chattering too much lately. You are not very enthusiastic about a current project if you see it full of ashes. Broken, it means you are struggling to overcome shyness about something.

VACUUM CLEANER *See also*: Tidiness. You are about to wow the opposite sex. But if it breaks down don't mix business with pleasure. Save those romances for out of the office.

VALENTINE Receive one and a friend is bound to disappoint you. Send one and a new door is about to open.

VALLEY If it's dark life will be calm and content. Deep and a profitable venture is about to come your way. Green and lush and you are going to have to work hard to get what you want.

VAMPIRE *See also*: Blood. You are full of fears for the future. If he bites you then expect an unpleasant encounter of some kind. Kill a vampire and better times are ahead.

VAN A bringer of good news. If it was carrying household goods things are about to change for the better. Ride in it and the chance to make a fat profit is just round the corner.

VARNISH A sign you are being over-sensitive and it's making you difficult to get on with at the moment. Dark varnish is a sign a misunderstanding should be cleared up. Clear indicates an interesting new relationship. Varnish a door and it's time to show some self-control. Varnish floorboards and unexpected pleasures are on their way.

VASE *See also*: Flowers. If it's glass you are being indecisive. China is a sign of good luck. Full of flowers, it suggests your finances are about to improve dramatically.

VAULT Don't put on any kind of front. People prefer you as you are.

VEGETABLES Not a good sign. Dried or cooked they are a sign of family arguments. Eat them and you are about to lose money. See vegetables growing and you are worrying about something. Pick them and you are the butt of a lot of criticism. Rotten veg spells disappointment.

Artichokes are a warning to be careful in your love life, or it could be acutely embarrassing.

Asparagus spells success. Cooking it means your own plans will go well. Eating it's a good omen for a healthy life.

Eat **beans** and it suggests you will catch some kind of contagious illness. Growing them signifies worries ahead. Buy beans and beware—you're about to be criticised, or even slandered. If you see yourself cooking them, you could be in for a pay rise.

See yourself eating **cabbage** and your job isn't as safe as you thought. Buying it is a sign of good health. See cabbages growing and it's a sign to take care in business.

Carrots predict a surprise windfall. Eat them and you will be very happy—even though you haven't got much money.

Cauliflower is a sign of good health and a more exciting love life. Eat it and things couldn't be better in the future.

Eat **celery** and domestic bliss is just round the corner. See or buy it, and you will be healthy and happy in love.

Eat or cook **leeks** and you could be in for promotion. See them growing, and progress will be slow.

Buy a **marrow** and you will lose money thanks to a relative. Cook or eat one and money luck is on the way.

You will make money by a bit of clever speculation if you dream of **mushrooms**. A few stocks and shares, perhaps? Picking them predicts prosperity. Eat them and you will be promoted thanks to some influential contacts.

Life will be full of ups and downs if you see **onions**. Eat them and money luck is predicted, either through gambling or a legacy. Peeling them is a sign of family troubles. Cook them and you will break with a friend.

If it's **peas** in a tin, then life is going to be complicated for a while. Fresh ones are a sign you're going to be involved in other people's problems. For a man, shelling peas predicts success through a wealthy woman. For a woman it proves her mate is all mouth.

Peel a vegetable and some disappointing news is coming.

Potatoes on your plate and the future is secure. Plant or cook them and a stroke of business luck is on the horizon.

A healthy and happy life is predicted if you eat **spinach**.

VENETIAN BLIND Look before you leap into that new love affair. It could provoke some vicious gossip!

VENTRILOQUIST Listen to one and it's a warning to be careful who you talk to. Not everyone can be trusted. See yourself as one and it's a sure sign a friend is disloyal.

VERANDAH Sit on one and the troubles in your love life will soon vanish. Sleep on one and it's time to keep your back to the wall. Someone is trying to stab you in it! See flowers on a verandah and you are in for a nice surprise.

VET See yourself as a vet and you will be successful at work and earn more money. Visit one and you are about to make a lasting friend. See him treating pets and you will soon have to make a big career decision.

VILLAGE If it's at the seaside you will have to face a few difficulties. A mountain village predicts unexpected gains. In the country you are about to make a big achievement. See a village in the distance and be careful of that 'golden opportunity'. It may not be as good as you think.

VINE *See also*: Fruit. A lucky omen if it is in blossom. Things beyond your wildest dreams are about to happen. But if it's withered you need to slow down and relax a bit more. Black grapes show what an enterprising soul you are. White are a sign of strong friendships.

VINEGAR Drink it and over-indulgence could well make you ill. Simply see it or pour it and you could be faced with an unpleasant duty.

VIRGIN *See also*: Sexuality. She is a symbol of happiness. Though if she is dead you must expect complications at work. Start a relationship with a virgin and fortune is about to smile on everything you do. See yourself as one and you are being a bit naive about something. The Virgin Mary is a warning to be careful with your confidences.

VISITOR You are in danger of letting flattery go to your head if you see yourself visiting. Receiving visitors suggests you are being unjust somewhere along the line.

VOLCANO *See also*: Heat. Erupting, this is a sign you are trying to ignore a potentially dangerous situation. Smoking and a passionate love affair you are about to embark on won't be all it seems. An active volcano is a warning not to make any changes for a while.

VOTE Do this and you are lacking in self-confidence. Try to assert yourself a bit more. Remember you are just as good as the rest.

VOW A happy solution to your problems is on the way.

WADING *See also*: Water. This relates to love and friendship. If the water is clear things will go well. But muddy or murky and you are in for a few disappointments.

WAFER *See also*: Food; Religion. You are feeling like a fish out of water for some reason if you see a wafer biscuit. A communion wafer is a warning you are taking on too much. Something will suffer if you try and do too many things at once.

WAGES *See also*: Money. Pay them and a good opportunity for change is round the corner. Receive them and you could be the victim of theft. Make sure things are secure.

WAGON Pulled by a horse this predicts news from far away. Driving it is a warning not to make any hasty purchases. If the wagon is loaded you are about to get a surprise windfall.

WAITER/WAITRESS *See also*: Food. Seen in a hotel this is a good luck sign. If they serve you at home family problems are looming. Dressed in a black and white uniform they suggest danger is round the corner. Watch out for it.

WALKING An obstacle dream. Do it with ease and you will win an easy victory. Stumble or struggle and only hard work will help you overcome your difficulties.

WALL If it blocks your path this suggests obstacles either romantically or financially. See your partner on the other side and you're in for some long pointless arguments. Walk along the top of a wall and an agreement you are thinking of making could be harmful. Climb over it and you can expect business successes.

WALLET *See also*: Money. A leather one is a sign you are having second thoughts about something. Full of money and you have serious problems to overcome. Find a wallet and an unexpected meeting is on the cards. Lose one and it's time to stop being so indecisive. It's a good time for a little flutter if you see an empty wallet.

WALLPAPER Your social status is about to improve if you see a room being decorated with this.

WALTZ A minor misunderstanding could cause damage to a long-standing relationship. Work things out and it won't cause any permanent harm.

WAREHOUSE This indicates good luck and prosperity. Hard work and a few sacrifices will soon lead to major successes. If you are single your future partner is just around the corner.

Plate 24 · The Weather

WARTS On your hands these are a sign of money to come. The more the merrier. But your generosity could land you in a tight spot if you see them on any other part of the body. Warts on others are a sign of hidden hostility.

WASHING Don't get involved in other people's affairs if you do this by hand. Wash by machine and you could be in for a house move. Wash your hands and face and a nice new friendship is on the horizon.

See an empty **bath** and it's a sign not to make decisions in anger. If it's too hot or cold a pet plan will have to be revised. See yourself getting into a bath fully clothed and you are going to have a fight with your lover. And if you simply see yourself running a bath you are about to have a row with someone.

Bathe in the sea and a fortune beyond your wildest dreams is on the way. Bathe in a lake and your difficulties will pass. In a river and there is a happy surprise coming. Bathing with others is a sign a friend needs your help.

Any kind of **lather** predicts news from a distance.

Do the **laundry** by hand and you are in good shape physically at the moment. Hang it out to dry and you are on the boil mentally. Clean laundry is a mark of good fortune. If it's dirty problems are in store.

Take a **shower** and money is coming your way.

Soap is a good sign for your love life. Soap flakes mean you will have to fight to get what you want. Medicated soap suggests a mystery is about to be solved.

Wash with a **sponge** and you'll be thanked for a good job well done. **Squeeze** water out and a pay rise is on the cards. A dry sponge is a warning not to gamble.

WATCH *See also*: Time. An influential friend is about to come to your aid. See a pocket watch and it's a warning to stop drifting. Do something positive to get your life in order.

WATER Clear and calm this is a good omen. But rough or murky and problems are ahead. Drink water and you are in for some good luck, but spill or throw it and you are going to have to control that temper. Hot water predicts social setbacks, but running it's a sign of lasting happiness. You are in for a pay rise if you see a waterfall. Anything being watered forecasts exciting events.

A full **basin** of water means you will soon find happiness. If it is empty your success is also assured. Drinking from a basin means a love affair is just round the corner. But tread carefully, the first person you meet is not necessarily the right one.

A full **canal** is a good sign for your future security. An empty or near-empty one is a sign to stop spending so much money. See **canal locks** and it's a warning to look for a cuckoo in your nest of friends.

Water in a **dam** warns not to do anything impulsive, especially where money is concerned.

A flowing **fountain** says happiness will be yours. A dry one predicts a period of frustration.

Squirt water from a **hose** and you are in for a little adventure. Use it for a fire and an explosive new love affair is just round the corner. Hose a garden and you are about to make some new friends.

A clear calm **lake** is a symbol of future happiness and success. But if the water is rough or dirty, a difficult period in life is just ahead. Cross a lake in a boat and you will rise in others' estimation. Jump into it and it is a sign of unhappiness. You're worrying too much if you wade or walk into a lake. Try to take things easily.

You are wasting your time if you spot a **leak**. A leaky pipe is a sign to try and find a wider scope for your activities. A roof and misfortune is ahead. See a leaking radiator and you will soon hear news of a birth.

New **plumbing** spells an unexpected opportunity that will help you achieve a long-held ambition. Old or leaky plumbing spells a misunderstanding at work.

Get splashed by a **puddle** and you will be blushing at some social event soon. Keep dry or step round it and someone will help you out of a sticky situation.

See yourself out in the **rain** and an ailing love affair is about to draw to a close. Get drenched in a heavy storm and you are going to come into some money.

A full **reservoir** says you'll soon be in the money. Empty, and times will be hard through no fault of your own. If the reservoir was filling up, the wind of change is blowing new opportunities in your direction.

See a slow-flowing, clean **river** and it's a sign of good fortune. If it is rushing or muddy then trouble is brewing. Fall in and danger is round the corner. Bathe in one and money is coming to you. Swim across it and your hopes will soon be realised.

Take a **shower** and money is coming your way.

A dried-up **spring** predicts bitterness. Drink from a spring and affection for someone is about to be reciprocated.

A **stream** represents life forces. A smooth-flowing clear stream predicts your life will run the same way. Cloudy or rough and that's just how things will be for a while.

Do the **washing** by hand and it's a warning not to get involved in other people's affairs. Do it by machine and you could be in for a house move. Wash your hands and face and a nice new friendship is on the horizon.

See yourself **wade** and it relates to love and friendship. If the water is clear things will go well. But muddy or murky and you are in for a few disappointments.

WEAPONS If the weapon is an **airgun** you should postpone decisions for a while. Buy an airgun and you are being deceived, and if you receive one watch out, you are being double-crossed in love.

If you are hit by an **arrow** it's a prediction of bad luck caused by a surprising person. Loose an arrow and you are in for some unhappiness. A poisoned arrow forecasts major worries and unhappiness.

Artillery is a sign to stop showing off. No one can be loved by everyone. Just try to be yourself.

Dream you are hit by a **bullet** and you'd better have a medical check-up. If you simply see or hear one you could be exposing yourself to a real scandal. Try and be a bit more discreet.

A **cannon** is a sure sign you are worried and may be thinking of doing something risky. If you are a man and see a cannon going off, your professional life is heading for a dodgy patch. For a woman it means a meeting with someone in uniform.

If it's a **dagger** you can expect some surprise news. Dream of carrying one and you should be a bit more tactful or you could land in a sticky

situation. Seeing others with daggers is a sign you will win despite stiff opposition.

Throw a **hand grenade** and you will soon be humiliated thanks to your own hasty behaviour. Simply see one and it is a warning to rely on your own judgement.

Some small set-backs are on the horizon if you see a **sword.** Drawn from its scabbard it's a warning to sort your money problems out. If not, they will only get worse.

WEATHER Good weather registering on a **barometer** says happiness is coming. If it is bad or rainy then sadness and disappointment will follow. See a broken barometer and it is a sign to get a grip on your spending.

A light **breeze** suggests you are in the black money-wise.

A **cyclone** is a warning not to take any risks for at least six months. If you see property damaged by a cyclone, then at least your social life will be happy for a while.

Frost on a wall or window and you are in for an unusual but exciting experience. Lucky you! Dream of frostbite and it is a warning to be extra cautious in everything you do in order to avoid problems, especially in business.

A violent **gale** is a sign you are facing a very tricky situation. Think carefully before you do anything. See something blown away by a **gust** of wind and you are being too possessive with your partner. They are getting fed up with it.

Ice is not a good omen. A vast expanse of ice and snow invariably signals dangers and difficulties. If you break through the ice your fears are groundless. An icy road or path shows you are restless and waiting for something more exciting to happen. Hidden obstacles lie in your path if you see an **iceberg**, but you can get round them if you go carefully.

Icicles say your deepest anxieties will soon disappear. If they are dripping hang on to your money at least for a couple of months.

See **lightning** flash and it predicts long-lasting good fortune. If something is struck by lightning your future plans will meet with success.

If you are out in the **rain** an ailing love affair is about to draw to a close. Get drenched in a heavy storm and you are going to come into some money. A **rainbow** is a sign of good luck—even if you don't find a pot of gold at the end. Pleasant changes are on the way.

Light, powdery **snow** shows what a mischievous mood you're in. If it's turned to ice you have doubts about a lover. Slush is a sign you are being discreet. See snow falling and there will be some interesting changes in your life. And a snowdrift is an omen of unexpected pleasures and money luck.

A **storm** is a sign that only you can change things. You will pull yourself out of the doldrums when you accept that.

Tell the time with a **sundial** and your most cherished wish is about to come true. Otherwise it predicts some pleasant social event.

Bright, clear **sunshine** and success will be yours. A red sun forecasts a struggle but you will win in the end. Sunrise predicts new doors about to open for you and if you see the sunset exciting changes are round the corner.

Hear a clap of **thunder** and whatever is troubling you will soon be cleared up. Rumbling thunder says that the disloyalty you suspect from a friend, well, you're absolutely right. Don't trust them.

Walk into the **wind** and family problems are looming but shelter from it and you will soon get some reassuring news.

WEAVING Peace and contentment will follow if you see yourself doing this. See someone else and you are about to achieve something to your credit.

WEDDINGS A wedding spells happiness—albeit only briefly. But all the other aspects of the dream must also be taken into account.

If you are a man and see yourself as **best man** at a wedding you will find happiness in love. If a woman sees a best man she will have security in the future.

See a **bride** at the altar and it's good news in almost every aspect of your life. If she is on her own, however, your health is slightly risky. If you are with a bride at an altar a secret desire could soon be yours. Kiss a bride and you'll be making a lot of new friends.

One of your pet projects will face delays if you see a **bridegroom**. But don't give up. A new approach will win the day. If his bride is very young it's a warning of sickness in the family.

See yourself as a **bridesmaid** and you are in for a big disappointment. See several of them and happiness is coming.

You'll be the apple of everyone's eye if you see **confetti**. Fantastic social success is on the way.

Elope in your dream and you could soon be splitting with your partner. See others eloping and someone will try and tempt you to make a sentimental journey. Don't. It will only upset you. Dream you are jilted and your love affairs will be constant.

See a **pageboy** holding a bride's train and your love life is going your way. Things are swimming in your direction at work too. Take advantage of it.

Throw **rice** at a wedding and good news is on the way.

An **usher** is an omen of useful new contacts who will help you in the future.

If a bride is wearing a **veil** it spells changes for the better. If it's torn, a mystery will soon be solved.

WEEDS Seen in a garden these are a sign you're keeping bad company and it's ruining your reputation. Dig them out and every cloud on your horizon will have a silver lining.

WEIGHING Whatever is being weighed, including yourself, is telling you someone has their beady eye on you. It's probably at work so be careful not to make any mistakes.

WELL *See also*: Water. Dried-up suggests a new project you are involved with is too risky. Full, a well is a sign a certain situation is about to turn sour. Draw water from it and your love life couldn't be better. Fall down and a vital decision will soon have to be made.

WEST This direction featured in any way predicts a long journey.

WHEAT *See also*: Food. Ripe is an omen of prosperity. Harvested and your current plans will go well. But see it in poor condition and you will soon be faced with a few problems.

WHEEL On a car suggests you will soon get some important news regarding your job. A cartwheel predicts petty tiffs with your partner. See a big wheel at a funfair and you are in for some unexpected changes.

WHEELBARROW Load or push it and you are about to make an exciting new friend. Pulling it is a sign of sad news. Tip it over and you will be asked to take on new responsibilities.

WHIP You have something on your conscience. Either confess it or forget it.

WHISPER *See also*: Speaking. Mind your tongue. A hasty outburst could get you into trouble.

WHISTLE You are in for some criticism if you see yourself doing this. Hear others and one of your current plans will face a set-back.

WIDOW/WIDOWER Seen in mourning this is a sign you are missing someone. If they are crying you are feeling weighed down by current responsibilities. See yourself widowed and you are worrying too much about something that will soon be cleared up.

WIG *See also*: Hair. An omen of change. New faces, new places…all are just around the corner.

WILL Making your own is a sign you are worrying unnecessarily about your health. Someone else's will predict family problems.

WIND *See also*: Weather. A light breeze suggests you are in the black money-wise. A violent gale is a sign you are facing a very tricky situation. Think carefully before you do anything. Walk into the wind and family problems are looming but shelter from it and you will soon get some reassuring news. See something blown away by a gust and you are being too possessive with your partner. They are getting fed up with it.

WINDMILL A working one is a sign of contentment. But if it's damaged it is a warning you are wasting your time on something. Cut your losses and try a new approach.

WINDOW Look outside and travel is predicted. If it's open money matters will improve. Close it and you are about to assume a new responsibility. See a light in a window and changes are on their way. Climb out of one and you will soon solve your problems in an unexpected way. Climb in and you are about to get a new opportunity.

WING *See also*: Birds. See yourself with wings and you'll soon be flying high. A bird with a broken wing is a warning you won't be able to reach your goal. Lower your sights. Don't gamble if you see wings flapping.

WINTER *See also*: Time. Money is on the way if you see this season.

WISHBONE It's a good time for taking chances. Luck is on its way and so is an unexpected gift.

WITCH *See also*: Supernatural. Your social life is about to perk up but it's not a good sign for your love life. You could soon find yourself disenchanted.

WOMEN Sorry, but women spell insincerity, bitterness and resentment. But see a woman with a man and you will feel more confident about things.

WOOD Chop or saw it and you will find the answers to your problems. Buy timber and it's a sign someone feels the same about you as you do about them. Go on. Ask them for a date.

WORK See yourself out of a job and you will shortly have a choice of opportunities. Offer jobs to others and you're getting a bit over-confident about something. It could prove expensive.

A **boss** you get on well with says some surprise news will soon embarrass you. See your direct boss and it's a sign you are far too impressionable. Try and make your own decisions. An angry employer means you have misplaced your trust in someone. But any kind of boss is really a sign that you are feeling insecure. If he is nice to you you've been over-sensitive and feel let down by something a friend has done. If he (or she) is unreasonable, your career could get sticky. Stay calm and decisive.

Dream of a battered **briefcase** and business will be successful. A new one means don't make changes without finding out the facts first. A briefcase full of papers is a warning to pay more attention to your personal life. An empty one means current plans will go well. Lose your briefcase and you can expect a small profit. Find one and you must watch your step in business otherwise there'll be trouble.

See any kind of **business** and you're in for a rough ride. You'll find yourself fighting hostile or even dishonest competition. But if business documents feature, all will be resolved in your favour.

Get a place on the **board** and there will be good news in business or legal matters.

Resign or lose your **directorship** and you are going to lose some status thanks to your own foolishness. Don't do anything you'd be ashamed of if others found out about it.

See a **factory** and you will have a struggle on your hands but success in the end. See yourself working in a factory and some good changes are on the way.

See **files** and you'd better spell things out clearly to others or it could be the cause of vicious gossip. They'll get the wrong end of the stick.

Look for a **job** or get the sack and you are about to be promoted. If you're offered a job it's time to pay more attention to detail at work.

See a man doing any kind of **labouring** work and a lucky coincidence is round the corner. It will bring both money and respect. If he is having a rest it shows your enthusiasm is lacking at work. Try and shape up.

If the boss turns you down for that **pay rise**, money is coming from a surprise direction. If he gives it to you it is a warning to pay more attention at work or you could be demoted. Pay someone a salary and money matters will go well.

Resign from a job and major changes are on the horizon.

Retire from work and, sorry, but a lot of hard graft is on the way.

See yourself with a **secretary** and it's a sign old habits are holding you back. Employ one and your status is about to improve.

WORLD *See also*: Foreign Places/People. All sorts of journeys are predicted. See the end of the world and it's a dream of contrary. It signifies new beginnings.

WRAPPING If it's a present it's time to reveal your true feelings for someone. Wrapping goods in a shop shows it's a good time to consolidate your position at work.

WRESTLING See these fighters and you are in for a stroke of luck. Engage in it yourself and it is a warning not to gamble.

WRINKLES Your popularity is about to soar sky high. Enjoy it!

WRITING *See also*: Reading/Writing. Handwriting is a warning not to trust one of your friends. See yourself writing and you must try not to be so impulsive. Think first and act last. See others writing and you should trust your own judgement. Listen to advice but make up your own mind.

-RAY *See also*: Doctors/Hospitals. See a doctor examine the result and you are confident about your future. See yourself X-rayed and good news is coming from a distance. A chest X-ray predicts a new friendship with someone of the opposite sex.

ACHT *See also*: Sea/Water/Travel. The tide of money luck will soon be flowing your way. And your highest hopes will be realised if you see yourself entertained on a yacht.

YARN Wind it into a ball and you will soon make new friends. Black and someone might not be doing things your way but you must allow them to be an individual. Tangled yarn is a warning not to be so obstinate. White predicts a short journey.

YAWNING Negative thinking is holding you back. Thinking positively will make things happen to you.

YEAST A large sum of money is about to come to you. It could be an inheritance or even a pools win!

YODELLING A lucky omen. All will go well—especially affairs of the heart.

YOLK *See also*: Food. Egg yolk is a sign your ambitions are pitched too high. Beat one and an attractive business proposal is about to come your way.

ERO A sign you are wasting your energy. Try and change direction.

ZINC *See also*: Metals. You can make solid progress in every direction.

ZIPPER *See also*: Clothes. If it is broken or stuck you will soon be blushing socially. Zip it up and all those little minor irritations will soon be cleared up.

ZODIAC See or study this and you will have fame as well as fortune.

ZOO *See also*: Animals. Lots of travel is on the cards if you visit this. Take a child and life will be profitable.

INDEX OF RELATED DREAM SUBJECTS

For an interpretation of these other dream subjects, look up the cross-reference in the main part of the book

ABBEY *See:* Religion.

ABBOT *See:* Religion.

ABORIGINE *See:* Foreign Places/People

ABSCESS *See:* Ill-health.

ABUSE (verbal) *See:* Anger/Confrontation

ACADEMY *See:* Childhood; School.

ACCELERATING *See:* Driving.

ACCENT *See:* Speaking.

ACCORDION *See:* Music.

ACCUSING *See:* Anger/Confrontation.

ACE *See:* Cards.

ACHE *See:* Pain.

ACORN *See:* Trees/Plants.

ACQUITTAL *See:* Legal matters.

ACTING *See:* Performing.

ACTOR OR ACTRESS *See:* Performing.

ADAPTING *See:* Change/Transformation.

ADENOIDS *See:* Ill-health.

ADMIRAL *See:* Uniform.

ADMIRATION *See:* Relationships.

ADRIFT *See:* Sea/Water/Travel.

ADVANCEMENT *See:* Success.

ADVOCATE *See:* Legal matters.

AFFECTION *See:* Relationships.

AFFILIATION *See:* Government.

AFRICA *See:* Foreign Places/People.

AFTERNOON *See:* Time.

AGNOSTIC *See:* Religion.

AGONY *See:* Pain.

AIR GUN *See:* Weapons.

ALARM *See:* Sounds.

ALBATROSS *See:* Birds.

ALCOHOL *See:* Drink.

ALDERMAN *See:* Uniforms.

ALIBI *See:* Legal matters.

ALLIGATOR *See:* Animals.

ALMOND *See:* Food; Trees/Plants.

ALTAR *See:* Religion.

ALTERATIONS S*ee:* Change/Transformation; Home.

AMBER *See*: Colours/Gems

AMERICA *See*: Foreign Places/People.

AMETHYST *See*: Colours/Gems.

ANAEMIA *See*: Ill-health.

ANCHOR *See*: Sea/Water/Travel.

ANCHOVY *See*: Fish/Fishing.

ANGEL *See*: Religion.

ANGLING *See*: Fish/Fishing.

ANKLE See: Human body.

ANNOUNCEMENT *See*: Communicating.

ANNULMENT *See*: Relationships.

ANT *See*: Insects.

ANTEATER *See*: Animals.

ANTELOPE *See*: Animals, Hunting.

ANTIDOTE *See*: Ill-health.

ANXIETY *See*: Fear.

APES *See*: Animals.

APPAREL *See*: Clothes; Nakedness.

APPENDICITIS *See*: Ill-health.

APPLE *See*: Fruit.

APPOINTMENT *See*: Time.

APPREHENSION *See*: Fear.

APPROVAL *See*: Appreciation.

APRICOT *See*: Fruit; Trees/Plants.

APRON *See*: Clothes.

AQUAMARINE *See*: Colours/Gems.

ARABS *See*: Foreign Places/People.

ARBITRATION *See*: Legal matters.

ARCADE *See*: Places/Settings.

ARCTIC *See*: Foreign Places/People.

ARENA *See*: Places/Settings.

ARGUING *See*: Anger/Confrontation.

ARM *See*: Human body.

ARTERY *See*: Blood.

ARTHRITIS *See*: Ill-health.

ARTICHOKE *See*: Vegetables.

ASIA *See*: Foreign Places/People

ASPARAGUS *See*: Vegetables.

ASPIC *See*: Food.

ASTHMA *See*: Ill-health.

ASTONISHMENT *See*: Confusion.

ATTIC *See*: Places/Settings.

AUCTION *See*: Buying/Selling.

AUGUST *See:* Time.

AUNT *See*: Family.

AUSTRALIA *See*: Foreign Places/People.

AUTHOR *See*: Reading/Writing.

AUTOGRAPH *See*: Reading/Writing.

AVOCADO *See*: Food.

AWARD *See*: Success.

BABOON *See*: Animals.

BACHELOR S*ee*: Relationships.

BACK *See*: Human body.

BACKGAMMON *See*: Games.

BACON *See*: Food.

BADGER *See*: Animals.

BAGPIPES *See*: Music.

BALCONY *See*: Places/Settings.

BALLAST *See*: Sea/Water/Travel.

BANANA *See*: Fruit.

BANISHMENT *See*: Arriving/Leaving.

BANJO *See*: Music.

BAPTISM *See*: Religion.

BARN *See*: Places/Settings.

BAROMETER *See*: Weather.

BARGE *See*: Sea/Water/Travel.

BAT *See*: Animals.

BATH *See*: Washing.

BATHROBE *See*: Clothes.

BATTLE *See*: Anger/Confrontation.

BAY *See*: Sea/Water/Travel.

BEACH *See*: Sea/Water/Travel.

BEANS *See*: Vegetables.

BEAR *See*: Animals.

BEATING *See*: Anger/Confrontation.

BEAVER *See*: Animals.

BED/BEDCLOTHES *See*: Furniture; Sexuality.

BEDBUGS *See*: Insects.

BEDROOM *See*: Places/Settings; Sexuality.

BEEF *See*: Food.

BEER *See*: Drink.

BEES *See*: Insects

BEETLES *See*: Insects.

BEETS *See*: Vegetables.

BELFRY *See*: Places/Settings.

BELT *See*: Clothes.

BENEFITS *See*: Money.

BERRIES *See*: Fruit.

BEST MAN *See*: Weddings.

BET *See*: Gambling.

BIGAMY *See*: Relationships.

BILIOUSNESS *See*: Ill-health.

BILLIARDS *See*: Games.

BISCUIT *See*: Food.

BISHOP *See*: Religion.

BLACK *See*: Colours/Gems.

BLACKBOARD *See*: School.

BLADDER *See*: Human body

BLASPHEMY *See*: Religion.

BLEATING *See*: Sounds.

BLEEDING *See*: Blood.

BLOSSOM *See*: Flowers; Trees/Plants.

BLOWS *See*: Anger/Confrontation.

BOAR *See*: Animals.

BOATS *See*: Sea/Water/Travel.

BONUS *See*: Money.

BOOKS *See*: Reading/Writing.

BOOTS *See*: Clothes.

BORROW *See*: Bank; Money.

BOSS *See*: Work.

BOUQUET *See*: Flowers.

BRA *See*: Clothes.

BRAKES *See*: Driving.

BRANDY *See*: Drink.

BRASS *See*: Metals.

BREAD *See*: Food.

BREAST *See*: Human body.

BRONCHITIS *See*: Ill-health.

BROOCH *See*: Jewellery.

BROTHER *See*: Family.

BUCKLE *See*: Clothes.

BUFFALO *See*: Animals.

BUGLE *See*: Music.

BURIAL *See*: Death.

BURNING/BURNS *See*: Fire.

BUSHES *See*: Trees/Plants.

BUTTER *See*: Food.

BUTTERCUPS *See*: Flowers.

BUTTERFLY *See*: Insects.

BUTTOCKS *See*: Human body.

BULLFROG *See*: Animals.

BURGLAR *See*: Crime; Police/Prisons.

BUTTONS *See*: Clothes.

BUZZARD *See*: Birds.

BUZZER *See*: Sounds.

CABBAGE *See*: Vegetables.

CABINET *See*: Furniture.

CADET *See*: Uniform.

CAKE *See*: Food.

CALF *See*: Animals.

CAMEL *See*: Animals.

CANADA *See*: Foreign Places/People.

CANCER *See*: Ill-health.

CANNON *See*: Weapons.

CANYON *See*: Places/Settings.

CAP *See*: Clothes.

CAPTAIN *See*: Uniform.

CARDINAL *See*: Religion.

CARGO *See*: Sea/Water/Travel.

CARROTS *See*: Vegetables.

CATS *See*: Animals.

CATERPILLARS *See*: Insects.

CATHEDRAL *See*: Religion.

CAULIFLOWER *See*: Vegetables.

CELERY *See*: Vegetables.

CELLO *See*: Music.

CEMETERY *See*: Death.

CHAIR *See*: Furniture.

CHAMELEON *See*: Animals.

CHAMPAGNE *See*: Drink.

CHANT *See*: Music; Sounds.

CHAPEL *See*: Religion.

CHATTER *See*: Sounds.

CHEEKS *See*: Human body.

CHEESE *See*: Food.

CHERRIES *See*: Fruit; Trees/Plants.

CHESTNUTS *See*: Food.

CHICKENS *See*: Birds.

CHILBLAINS *See*: Ill-health.

CHIMES *See*: Sounds.

CHOCOLATE *See*: Food.

CHOIR *See*: Music.

CHURCH See: Religion.

CIDER *See*: Drink.

CITY *See*: Places/Settings.

CLIFFS *See*: Sea/Water/Travel.

CLOAK *See*: Clothes.

CLOCKS *See*: Sounds; Time.

CLOGS *See*: Clothes.

CLOVES *See*: Food.

COAT *See*: Clothes.

COCK *See*: Birds; Sounds.

COCKATOO *See*: Birds.

COCONUT *See*: Food.

COFFIN *See*: Death.

COLLAR *See*: Clothes.

COMMANDMENT *See*: Religion.

CONCERT *See*: Music.

CONFETTI *See*: Weddings.

CONTRACT *See*: Legal matters.

CONVENT *See*: Religion.

CORAL *See*: Colours/Gems.

COTTAGE *See*: Places/Settings.

COURT *See*: Legal matters.

COUSIN *See*: Family.

COW *See*: Animals; Cattle.

CRAB *See*: Fish/Fishing.

CREMATION *See*: Death.

CROCODILE *See*: Animals.

CROSS *See*: Religion.

CUCUMBERS *See*: Food.

CURLS *See*: Hair.

CUSTARD *See*: Food.

CYMBALS *See*: Sounds.

DATES *See*: Fruit.

DAUGHTER *See*: Family.

DEBT *See*: Money.

DEER *See*: Animals.

DELAY *See*: Time.

DESERT *See*: Places/Settings.

DESK *See*: Furniture.

DETECTIVE *See*: Police/Prisons.

DIAMONDS *See*: Colours/Gems.

DICE *See*: Gambling.

DISGUISE *See*: Deception.

DITCH *See*: Places/Settings.

DOGS *See*: Animals.

DOLPHIN *See*: Animals.

DOME *See*: Places/Settings.

DONKEYS *See*: Animals.

DOUGHNUTS *See*: Food.

DOVE *See*: Birds.

DRAGON *See*: Animals.

DRESS *See*: Clothes.

DUCKS *See*: Birds.

DUEL *See*: Anger/Confrontation.

EAGLE *See*: Birds.

EARS *See*: Human body.

EARWIG *See*: Insects.

ECLIPSE *See*: Darkness/Light.

EELS *See*: Fish/Fishing.

EGGS *See*: Food.

ELBOW *See*: Human body.

ELEPHANT *See*: Animals.

EMERALD *See*: Colours/Gems.

EMU *See*: Birds.

ENGINE *See*: Driving.

ERMINE *See*: Clothes.

ESKIMO *See*: Foreign Places/People.

EVIDENCE *See*: Legal matters.

EXPLOSION *See*: Sounds.

EYELIDS *See*: Human body.

EYES *See*: Human body.

FATHER *See*: Family.

FEATHERS *See*: Birds.

FEET *See*: Human body.

FERRET *See*: Animals.

FIG *See*: Fruit.

FINGERS *See*: Human body.

FIREPLACE *See*: Fire.

FLAME *See*: Fire.

FLAMINGO *See*: Birds.

FLAT *See*: Apartment.

FLEAS *See*: Insects.

FLIES *See*: Insects.

FLUTE *See*: Music.

FOREHEAD *See*: Human body.

FOX *See*: Animals; Hunting.

FROGS *See*: Animals.

FUDGE *See*: Food.

FUNERAL *See*: Death.

GARLAND *See*: Flowers.

GEESE *See*: Birds.

GIN *See*: Drink.

GIRAFFE *See*: Animals.

GLOVES *See*: Clothes.

GNAT *See*: Insects.

GOAT *See*: Animals.

GOD *See*: Religion.

GOLDFISH *See*: Fish/Fishing.

GONG *See*: Sounds.

GOOSEBERRIES *See*: Fruit.

GORILLA *See*: Animals.

GRANDPARENTS *See*: Family.

GRAPEFRUIT *See*: Fruit.

GRAPES *See*: Fruit.

GRAVE/GRAVESTONE *See*: Death.

GUITAR *See*: Music.

GUMS *See*: Human body.

HAEMORRHAGING *See*: Blood.

HAGGIS *See*: Food.

HAM *See*: Food.

HANDS *See*: Human body.

HANGOVER *See*: Drink.

HARE *See*: Animals.

HARMONICA *See*: Music.

HARP *See*: Music.

HAT *See*: Clothes.

HAWK *See*: Birds.

HEAD *See*: Human body.

HEARSE *See*: Death.

HEATHER *See*: Flowers.

HEDGEHOG *See*: Animals.

HEELS *See*: Human body.

HEN *See*: Birds.

HINGE *See*: Doors.

HIPPOPOTAMUS *See*: Animals.

HIPS *See*: Human body.

HOCKEY *See*: Games.

HOG *See*: Animals.

HOLLY *See*: Trees/Plants.

HONEY *See*: Food.

HOOD *See*: Clothes; Deception.

HORSE *See*: Animals.

HUSBAND *See*: Family.

JOB *See*: Work.

JOKER *See*: Cards.

JUDGE *See*: Legal matters.

JUICE *See*: Drink.

JURY *See*: Legal matters.

KANGAROO *See*: Animals.

KETCHUP *See*: Food.

KETTLEDRUM *See*: Music.

KIDNEY *See*: Food.

KILLING *See*: Death.

KILT *See*: Clothes.

KITTENS *See*: Animals.

KNEE *See*: Human body.

KNOB *See*: Doors.

KNOCKING *See*: Sounds.

KNUCKLE *See*: Human body.

ICE CREAM *See*: Food.

IGUANA *See*: Animals.

INDIANS *See*: Foreign Places/People.

INSANITY *See*: Ill-health.

JACKAL *See*: Animals.

JACKET *See*: Clothes.

JADE *See*: Colours/Gems.

JAM *see*: Food.

JAWS *See*: Human body.

JELLY *See*: Food.

JELLYFISH *See*: Fish/Fishing.

JET *See*: Colours/Gems.

LAMB *See*: Animals.

LARD *See*: Food.

LARYNGITIS *See*: Ill-health.

LAVENDER *See*: Flowers; Smells.

LEAD *See*: Metals.

LEEK *See*: Vegetables.

LEG *See*: Human body.

LEMON *See*: Drink; Food.

LEOPARD *See*: Animals.

LETTUCE *See*: Food.

LIE *See*: Deception.

LIGHT *See*: Darkness/Light.

LION *See*: Animals.

LIPS *See*: Human body.

LIVER *See*: Food; Human body.

LIZARD *See*: Animals.

LAMA *See*: Animals.

LOBSTER *See*: Fish/Fishing.

LUNGS *See*: Human body.

LUTE *See*: Music.

LYNX *See*: Animals.

 MAC *See*: Clothes.

MACARONI *See*: Food.

MAGISTRATE *See*: Legal matters.

MAGPIE *See*: Birds.

MARROW *See*: Vegetables.

MARSHMALLOW *See*: Food.

MASK *See*: Deceptions.

MEASLES *See*: Ill-health.

MEAT *See*: Food.

MELON *See*: Fruit.

MERRY-GO-ROUND *See*: Childhood/Children.

MIDWIFE *See*: Doctors/Hospitals.

MINK *See*: Clothes.

MOLE *See*: Animals; Human body.

MONKEY *See*: Animals.

MOSQUITO *See*: Insects.

MOTH *See*: Insects.

MOTHER *See*: Family.

MOUSE *See*: Animals.

MOUTH *See*: Human body.

MUSHROOMS *See*: Vegetables.

MUSSELS *See*: Fish/Fishing.

MUSTARD *See*: Food.

NAVEL *See*: Human body.

NECK *See*: Human body.

NIPPLE *See*: Human body.

NOODLES *See*: Food.

NOSE *See*: Blood; Human body.

NUN *See*: Religion.

NURSE *See*: Doctors/Hospitals.

NUTS *See*: Food.

NUTMEG *See*: Food; Smells.

OAK *See*: Trees/Plants.

OATS *See*: Food.

OBITUARY *See*: Death.

OLIVES *See*: Food; Trees/Plants.

OMELETTE *See*: Food.

ONIONS *See*: Vegetables.

ONYX *See*: Colours/Gems.

OPAL *See*: Colours/Gems.

ORANGE *See*: Fruit.

OSTRICH *See*: Birds.

OTTER See: Animals.

OWL *See*: Birds.

OXEN *See*: Animals.

 PALM *See*: Human body; Trees/Plants.

PANCAKE *See*: Food.

PANDA *See*: Animals.

PANTS *See*: Clothes.

PARAPET *See*: Bridges.

PARCEL *See*: Arriving/Leaving.

PARROT *See*: Birds.

PEACH *See*: Fruit.

PEANUTS *See*: Food.

PEARLS *See*: Colours/Gems; Jewellery.

PEARS *See*: Fruit.

PEAS *See*: Vegetables.

PETTICOAT *See*: Clothes.

PIANO *See*: Music.

PIG *See*: Animals.

PINEAPPLE *See*: Fruit.

PIZZA *See*: Food.

PLUM *See*: Fruit.

PORCUPINE *See*: Animals.

POSTMAN *See*: Post Office.

POTATO *See*: Vegetables.

PRUNES *See*: Fruit.

PUZZLE *See*: Confusion.

PYJAMAS *See*: Clothes.

PYTHON *See*: Animals.

 QUAIL *See*: Birds; Food.

QUARTZ *See*: Colours/Gems.

 RABBIT *See*: Animals.

RACCOON *See*: Animals.

RADISH *See*: Food.

RAID *See*: Police/Prisons.

RAISINS *See*: Food.

RAM *See*: Animals.

RAT *See*: Animals.

RATTLE *See*: Childhood/Children; Sounds.

RATTLESNAKE *See*: Animals.

REINDEER *See*: Animals.

REVOLVING DOOR *See*: Doors.

RHINOCEROS *See*: Animals.

RHUBARB *See*: Fruit.

RICE *See*: Food; Weddings.

RING *See*: Jewellery.

ROCKING HORSE *See*: Childhood/Children.

ROSES *See*: Flowers.

RUBY *See*: Colours/Gems.

RYE *See:* Food.

 SABLE *See*: Clothes.

SAINT *See*: Religion.

SALAD *See*: Food.

SALE *See*: Buying/Selling.

SALMON *See*: Fish/Fishing; Food.

SANDALS *See*: Clothes.

SAPPHIRE *See*: Colours/Gems.

SARDINES *See*: Fish/Fishing; Food.

SATIN *See*: Clothes.

SAUSAGE *See*: Food.

SCALLOPS *See*: Fish/Fishing; Food.

SCARF *See*: Clothes.

SEAL *See*: Animals.

SEAWEED *See*: Sea/Water/Travel.

SEESAW *See*: Childhood/Children.

SERMON *See*: Religion; Speaking.

SHARK *See*: Fish/Fishing.

SHAWL *See*: Clothes.

SHEEP *See*: Animals.

SHIRT *See*: Clothes.

SHOES *See*: Clothes.

SHRIMP *See*: Fish/Fishing.

SHROUD *See*: Death.

SILK *See*: Clothes.

SISTER *See*: Family.

SKIRT *See*: Clothes.

SLIPPER *See*: Clothes.

SNAIL *See*: Animals; Food.

SNAKE *See*: Animals.

SOUP *See*: Food.

SPAGHETTI *See*: Food.

SPHINX *See*: Foreign Places/People.

SPIDER *See*: Insects.

SPINACH *See*: Vegetables.

SQUIRREL *See*: Animals.

STEAK *See*: Food.

STETHOSCOPE *See*: Doctors/Hospitals.

STOCKINGS *See*: Clothes.

STORK *See*: Birds.

SUGAR *See*: Food.

SUNDAE *See*: Food.

SURF *See*: Sea/Water/Travel.

SURGEON *See*: Doctors/Hospitals.

SUSPENDER *See*: Clothes.

SWAN *See*: Birds.

TABLE *See*: Furniture.

TAMBOURINE *See*: Music.

TART *See*: Food.

THROAT *See*: Human body.

TIE *See*: Clothes.

TOAD *See*: Animals.

TOMATO *See:* Food.

TROUSERS *See*: Clothes.

TRUMPET *See*: Music.

TURKEY *See*: Birds; Food.

UNDERTAKER *See*: Death.

UNFAITHFULNESS *See*: Deception; Relationships.

USHER *See*: Weddings.

VEIL *See*: Clothes; Weddings.

VELVET *See*: Clothes.

VENISON *See*: Food.

VEST *See*: Clothes.

VIOLIN *See*: Music.

VULTURE *See*: Birds.

 WAIST *See*: Human body.

WAISTCOAT *See*: Clothes.

WASP *See*: Insects.

WATERCRESS *See*: Food.

WATERMELON *See*: Fruit.

WEASEL *See*: Animals.

WHALE *See*: Animals.

WINE *See*: Drink.

WOLF *See*: Animals.

WOODPECKER *See*: Birds.

WORMS *See*: Insects.

 XYLOPHONE *See*: Music

 YAM *See*: Food.

YUCCA *See*: Trees/Plants.

 ZEBRA *See*: Animals.

ZIRCON *See*: Colours/Gems.

ZITHER *See*: Music.